MW00579873

Becoming Sui Sin Far

Becoming.
Sui Sin Far

Early Fiction, Journalism, and Travel Writing

by Edith Maude Eaton

Edited by Mary Chapman

McGill-Queen's University Press

Montreal & Kingston • London • Chicago

© McGill-Queen's University Press 2016

ISBN 978-0-7735-4721-6 (cloth)
ISBN 978-0-7735-4722-3 (paper)
ISBN 978-0-7735-9912-3 (ePDF)
ISBN 978-0-7735-9913-0 (ePUB)

Legal deposit second quarter 2016
Bibliothèque nationale du Québec

Printed in Canada on acid-free paper that is 100% ancient forest free
(100% post-consumer recycled), processed chlorine free

This book has been published with the help of a grant from the Canadian
Federation for the Humanities and Social Sciences, through the Awards
to Scholarly Publications Program, using funds provided by the Social
Sciences and Humanities Research Council of Canada.

McGill-Queen's University Press acknowledges the support of the Canada
Council for the Arts for our publishing program. We also acknowledge the
financial support of the Government of Canada through the Canada Book
Fund for our publishing activities.

Library and Archives Canada Cataloguing in Publication

Sui Sin Far, 1865–1914
[Works. Selections]
Becoming Sui Sin Far : early fiction, journalism, and travel
writing by Edith Maude Eaton / edited by Mary Chapman.

Includes bibliographical references and index.
Issued in print and electronic formats.
ISBN 978-0-7735-4721-6 (cloth). – ISBN 978-0-7735-4722-3 (paperback).
– ISBN 978-0-7735-9912-3 (ePDF). – ISBN 978-0-7735-9913-0 (ePUB)

1. Sui Sin Far, 1865–1914 – Bibliography. I. Chapman, Mary Megan, 1962–,
editor II. Title.

PS8487.U44A6 2016   C813'.52   C2016-900368-X
                                          C2016-900369-8

Contents

SELECTED LATER FICTION (1896–1906)

CROSS-CONTINENTAL TRAVEL WRITING (1904)

APPENDICES

Acknowledgments

Without a community of scholars, recovery work of this scale is almost impossible. This book would not have come into being without the many remarkable Eaton scholars whose diligence, intuitions, and detective work guided my own recovery project. I would like to thank Diana Birchall, Dominika Ferens, Annette White-Parks, Jean Lee Cole, Martha Cutter, Carol Helfer, June Howard, and Karen Skinazi for generously sharing their discoveries of works by Eaton and her sister with me; Eaton descendants Paul and Elizabeth Rooney, Diana Birchall, Eileen Hathaway, and Celine Laferrière for encouraging my work; and Yu-Fang Cho, Charles Johanningsmeier, and Supaporn Yimwilai for sharing their scholarship on Eaton with me.

For encouraging conversations about tactics and methods, outlooks and frames, I would like to thank Kate Adams, Leslie Bow, P. Gabrielle Forman, Ellen Gruber Garvey, Theresa Strouth Gaul, Teresa Goddu, Barbara Green, Cat Keyser, Laura Laffrado, Victoria Lamont, Jean Lutes, Paul Ohler, Leslie Paris, Jeannie Pfaelzer, Marjorie Pryse, Shirley Samuels, Jennifer Tuttle, Sarah Wilson, and Elizabeth Young.

After studying Edith Eaton in a purely Americanist context, it was a steep learning curve for me to come also to an understanding of her place in Canadian letters and in Asian Canadian Studies. For their Canadianist guidance and much more, I am grateful to Margery Fee, Carole Gerson, Sherrill Grace, Faye Hammill, Karyn Huenemann, Dean Irvine, Laura Moss, and Katja Thieme. For their prompt and thorough responses to queries about Asian Canadian history and Chinese language, I am grateful to Hilary Chung, Wei Li, and Henry Yu, and, most of all, to my generous and inspiring colleague Chris Lee, without whose encouragement and support this book would not have been possible!

Thank you also to the "Editing Modernism in Canada" project, the Social Sciences and Humanities Research Council of Canada Standard Research Grants and ASPP programs, and UBC for their financial support. Without Rose Casey, Gillian Dunks, and Reilly Yeo, crackerjack research assistants who were supported by these grants, I would have lost my way repeatedly: Reilly finessed spreadsheets first established by the inimitable Rose and supervised a raft of other research assistants, including Alayna Becker, Kim Duff, Grant Hurley, Alyssa MacLean, Meaghan McAneeley, Genie McLeod, Marie Morrison, Matt Oakes, Martin Parlett, Kathleen Patchell, Simon Rolston, Judith Scholes, Szu Shen, and Amanda Wan. Gillian Dunks – long after she had stopped working for me – continued to answer my panicky questions about bits and pieces of our research that were very difficult to keep track of and to her I will be eternally grateful.

Special thanks to Kyla Wazana Tompkins, Diana Birchall, and Martha Cutter for help obtaining images at the eleventh hour, to Kirsten MacLeod for sharing her marvelous magazine cover collection with me, and to UBC's Interlibrary Loan staff for their help tracking down rare periodicals.

Finally, I'd like to thank my family – Jeffrey, Jasper, and William – who have lived with Eaton for many years (or, at least, that may be how they sometimes felt)! Thank you for being patient and encouraging, Jeffrey especially: I couldn't do any of this without your support!

Introduction

After all I have no nationality and am not anxious to claim any.
Individuality is more than nationality.
("Leaves from the Mental Portfolio of an Eurasian," 230)

When Edith Maude Eaton (1865–1914) published *Mrs. Spring Fragrance* in 1912 under the pen name Sui Sin Far, her "dainty stories of Chinese life" ("Literary Notes" 388) were praised for having "a subtle, alien charm" ("The New Books" 187). Printed on pages lightly embossed with orientalist illustrations of birds and flowers and bound in elegant red cloth covers stamped with gold lettering and illustrations of dragonflies and flowers, this book established Eaton's reputation as a sympathetic chronicler of North America's Chinese. Eaton was celebrated for "know[ing] Chinese character intimately" and for "appreciat[ing] the romance and tragedy of Chinatown" ("Book Table" 468).

When the recovery of Eaton's work began almost seventy years later, scholars eagerly inserted her into the national literary narratives of both the United States and Canada as an early ethnic American voice. In 1974, the editors of *Aiiieeeee! An Anthology of Asian American Writers* praised her for being "one of the first to speak for an Asian-American sensibility that was neither Asian nor white American" (Chin et al. 3–4). S.E. Solberg called her the "first Chinese-American fictionist" (27). Amy Ling heralded her as a "pioneer Chinamerican writer and feminist" ("Edith Eaton" 287). A diverse chorus of scholars – from Elizabeth Ammons to Patricia P. Chu – saw her as anticipating a later tradition of Asian American women's literature that included the works of authors such as Jade Snow Wong, Maxine Hong Kingston, Amy Tan, Shirley Geok-lin Lim, and Fae Ng.[1] Chu, in particular, has argued that Eaton "anticipates later [Asian American] writers' concerns with identity, racial and gender oppression, the search for ancestry and

The cover of *Mrs. Spring Fragrance*, issued by Chicago's A. C. McClurg & Co. in 1912. Image courtesy of Martha C. Cutter.

filiation, and the problems of Americanization [as] embodied in Asian American versions of the immigrant romance" (100). Since her recovery, Eaton's fiction and non-fiction have been championed by American Studies scholars for inaugurating an ethnic American literary tradition and for examining the dynamics of race "within a U.S. national framework" (Pan, "Transnationalism" 87). A few years after she was incorporated into the Asian American literary canon, Eaton was also taken up as an Asian Canadian writer. In 1990, James Doyle observed that "the example of Edith Eaton points up the need for more research in a specialized but vital area of Canadian literary history" ("Research" 34). In 1994, drawing on a very small selection of Eaton's texts that referenced or had been written in Canada, where she lived for about twenty-six years, Doyle identified Eaton as one of "the earliest creative writers in Canada to deal with Asian people and topics" ("Sui Sin Far and Onoto Watanna" 50) and began filling in the "Canadian background" that scholarship focused on Eaton's fifteen years in the US had effectively ignored. Doyle's work was followed by White-Parks' 1995 biography, which detailed Eaton's Montreal years, as well as by important essays such as Maria Ng's 1998 essay "Chop Suey Writing," Guy Beauregard's 2002 essay "Reclaiming Sui Sin Far," and Bennett Fu's 2004 dissertation on Asian Canadian women's writing, which identified Eaton as "the first Chinese Canadian woman writer to probe the conflation of ethnic hybridity and transgressive sexuality and to challenge conventional nineteenth-century conceptions of gender and culture" (29). Together, these scholars argued that, through her earliest journalism about Montreal's Chinese community, her strident letter to the editor of the Montreal *Star* lambasting legislators who advocated increasing the Head Tax, and her first Chinese-themed short stories set in or inspired by Montreal's Chinese community, Eaton exposed Canadian racism, challenged Canada's policy toward Chinese immigrants, and worked to improve the lot of diasporic Chinese and their families in Canada. On the basis of this scholarship, Eaton's "A Plea for the Chinaman" was included in Laura Moss and Cynthia Sugar's ground-breaking 2008 *Canadian Literature in English*, the first anthology of Canadian literature to include texts by Eaton.

These moves to recover Eaton as an important ethnic American and ethnic Canadian writer were motivated by desires to make literary canons more diverse but have, paradoxically, oversimplified her complex subject position in the process. Yu-Fang Cho observes that critics mapped "[Eaton's] mixed heritage almost directly onto [her work]," assuming that she was sympathetic to the Chinese "due in no small part to her half Chinese heritage" (*Uncoupling* 99). David Shih argues that reading Eaton *only* as a foremother to current Asian American writers and to the field of Asian American literature "requires her interpellation as a discrete racial and national subject to the neglect of [her] alternate subject positions" (49). The same observation can be made about Eaton's reception as a foremother to Asian Canadian writers. Eaton, Shih insists, "resisted identifying herself solely along racial or national lines" (49). Throughout her oeuvre, Eaton demands that individuals be recognized as individuals rather than for their nationality or any other collective identity: "After all I have no nationality and am not anxious to claim any. Individuality is more than nationality ("Leaves" 230).

Eaton's complex biography exposes the limitations of interpreting her oeuvre solely along racial or national lines. She was born in 1865 in a silk-weaving town in Northern England. Her white British-born father, Edward Eaton, spent many years in Asia, first fighting in China's Tai Ping Rebellion alongside British General Charles Gordon and then pursuing business interests in both China and Japan (White-Parks, *Sui Sin Far* 12–13). Her Chinese-born mother, Achuen "Grace" Amoy, had been purchased at a very early age by the leader of a Chinese acrobatic troupe with whom she toured the US, Europe, and the British Isles until she was rescued by London missionaries who believed she was being abused (Salter 168–70). Eaton's parents met and married in China, where Edward was then working in the silk trade and Grace was training to be a missionary. They returned to England after the birth of Eaton's older brother in 1864. A year later, only months after Eaton's birth, the family immigrated to New York, where Eaton's father established a wholesale drug and dye business. The family returned to England in 1868, settling in London briefly, but in 1872 ventured to North America again.[2] They sailed to New York[3] but settled in the predominantly French Canadian city of Montreal, where Eaton's father earned his living as a commissioner merchant, clerk, bookkeeper and, later, artist.[4] After living in Montreal for twenty years, Eaton worked as a journalist and stenographer in Northern Ontario (Fort William/Port Arthur, now Thunder Bay, c. 1892) and Jamaica (1896–97) and then moved to the US to pursue a career as a

Portrait of Edith Eaton. Image courtesy of Diana Birchall.

writer, supplementing her income with journalism and stenographic work. By 1914, Eaton had lived in England, French Canada, Northern Ontario, the Caribbean, and several port cities in the US and had experienced the ethnic, racial, and cultural settings of the contact-zones in these diverse locales.

Like Yen Moy, the Australian-born, Chinese-speaking albino "Britisher" whom Eaton describes in "Born a Britisher" (96, italicized numbers refer to pages in this volume), Eaton defies categorization. As a downwardly mobile child in a family with genteel Victorian pretensions, an unmarried childless woman who published stories about domesticity and child-rearing in women's and children's magazines, a British subject raised in French Canada who spent most of her professional life in the US, a half-Chinese who repeatedly passed as white, and a half-Chinese person who crossed the US-Canada border without difficulty, Eaton occupied multiple subject positions in terms of class, gender, and nationality, as well as race. Critics should follow her lead and recognize her complexity.

Eaton's insertion into the canons of Asian American and Asian Canadian literatures is also based on a small fraction of her oeuvre that is extremely narrow in terms of genre, subject, style, and perspective: the thirty-seven works of sentimental Chinatown fiction published in *Mrs. Spring Fragrance*, most of which first appeared in US magazines between 1908 and 1910, as well as twenty-four additional texts, almost entirely Chinatown fiction and journalism, collected by Annette White-Parks and Amy Ling in *Mrs. Spring Fragrance and Other Writings* (1995). Unfortunately, this small number of predominantly Chinatown-focused texts has encouraged scholars to efface important aspects of Eaton's perspective, particularly her investigation of her non-Chinese racial heritage and experience (Shih 48).

In the twenty-one years since the publication of *Mrs. Spring Fragrance and Other Writings* in 1995, however, a surprisingly large number of previously unknown or never republished periodical works written by Eaton have come to light. Published over the course of her twenty-six-year writing career, in a range of genres, on various subjects, in diverse styles, and from a variety of perspectives, these texts demand that scholars reassess Eaton's place in North American literary history. They make clear that Eaton was not simply a sympathetic chronicler of North American Chinatowns; she was also an early middlebrow author, an early North American woman journalist, and an important transnational, or even post-national, author who questioned the coherence of ideas about ethnic and national identity, on which, ironically, her critical reputation has been based.

EATON'S EXPANDED OEUVRE

When S.E. Solberg published "Sui Sin Far/Edith Eaton" (1981), his "checklist" of Eaton's works identified twenty-two works of fiction, including five stories that had appeared in periodicals before being re-printed in *Mrs. Spring Fragrance*, and several works of ethnographic journalism. White-Parks, in the bibliography to her 1995 book, added forty-two works to this list, including early California Chinatown fiction; some early fiction, Montreal Chinatown journalism, and letters to the editor; later Los Angeles and Seattle Chinatown journalism; and one important autobiographical text, "Sui Sin Far, the Half Chinese Writer, Tells of Her Career" (*Sui Sin Far* 245–7). Many of these texts were collected in White-Parks and Ling's *Mrs. Spring Fragrance and Other Writings*. Since the 1995 publication of that landmark volume, however, numerous other texts by Eaton have been found, many of which have a non-Chinatown focus. In 2002, Dominika Ferens recovered forty-five uncollected works, including thirty-one articles that Eaton wrote for Jamaica's *Gall's Daily News Letter* between December 1896 and May 1897, several of which investigate the racial dynamic in that predominantly black British colony governed primarily by a powerful Anglo-British minority, as well as more unsigned Montreal journalism; the "Selected Writings by Edith Eaton" in Ferens' *Edith and Winnifred Eaton: Chinatown Missions and Japanese Romances* (201–4) listed a total of ninety-eight periodical and newspaper publications by Eaton. In 2004, Martha J. Cutter discovered "Away Down in Jamaica," an unknown story by Eaton about a Caribbean mulatta seeking revenge on her seducer (Cutter, "Sex"). In 2011, June Howard added to this expanding oeuvre when she located "The Son of Chung Wo," a story about a Chinese man passing as Japanese – a theme that Eaton scholars associate more with Edith's sister Winnifred, who published under the Japanese pseudonym Onoto Watanna (Howard, "The Son of Chung Wo"). In 2012, Carol Kim Helfer found the anonymous "A Visit to Chinatown" (see Appendix A), an 1896 *New York Recorder* interview with Sue Seen Far that includes a lengthy section of what Eaton later published as "The Chinese Woman in America." In 2011, Hsuan L. Hsu edited a reprinted version of the original *Mrs. Spring Fragrance*, making several stories by Eaton not included in White-Parks and Ling's collection newly available.

In the past ten years, I have discovered more unknown texts by Eaton. Late one night in 2006, I typed "Edith Eaton" into the search bar of Google Books and was surprised when a link to an unfamiliar story came up. "The Alaska Widow" features a Seattle stenographer who divorces her husband on their wedding day when she discovers that he had abandoned a Native American Alaskan woman and their mixed-race child at the end of the Alaskan Gold Rush. He later dies in the Philippines in the aftermath of the Spanish American War (Chapman, "An Edition"). This story, originally published in the April 1909 issue of *Bohemian Magazine*, is unlike any story collected in *Mrs. Spring Fragrance* in its setting, depiction of a non-Eurasian mixed-race child, and use of the signature Edith Eaton, which scholars had come to believe Eaton had abandoned after her adoption of the pen name Sui Sin Far in 1896. Finding "The Alaska Widow" made me wonder how many other texts by Eaton had not been included in her 1912 story collection and how their themes, styles, and perspectives might challenge our understanding of an author we had come to think of solely in terms of sympathetic accounts of American Chinatowns written under her familiar Chinese pseudonym.[5] Since stumbling across "The Alaska Widow," I have located more than 150 uncollected texts by Eaton, rendering obsolete the bibliographies carefully assembled by Solberg, White-Parks, and Ferens. Eaton's expanded oeuvre, now consisting of over 260 texts, demonstrates that she was far more prolific than previously believed, publishing quite actively throughout her career, including the years 1905–09 when she was once believed to have taken a "hiatus" from writing (White-Parks, *Sui Sin Far* 144).

Contrary to popular depictions of Eaton as a poor woman who worked as a stenographer to subsidize her less profitable activities as an author, the size of her oeuvre and range of her publication venues suggest that for periods of time, particularly in the final years of her career, Eaton earned her living entirely through her writing. They also suggest that she was incredibly popular. As early as 1900, Eaton sent her autograph to a seventeen-year-old

New England fan who had written the editor of *The Land of Sunshine* asking for it (Eaton to Rugg, 18 Jan. 1900). By 1904, her sensational fiction was being syndicated in newspapers from Alabama to Oklahoma through the Daily Story Company and by 1908, her stories for children were being syndicated in newspapers across the US and Canada. When she died in 1914, her obituary appeared in newspapers across North America.

Eaton's expanded oeuvre shows incredible diversity in terms of genre, venue of publication, subject matter, style, and assumed audience. In addition to the short Chinatown fiction for which she is best known, Eaton wrote many other kinds of fiction: didactic tales for children set in foreign lands, middlebrow fiction, and even syndicated sensation fiction. She published in many other genres, including objective journalism, "stunt" journalism, travel writing, ethnography, literary sketches, and poetry, not to mention letters to the editor, interviews, reviews, and advertising copy. Later in her career, she also published autobiography and translations.[6]

Eaton's diverse body of work appeared in a far wider range of publications than has previously been acknowledged. Between 1888 and her death in 1914, Eaton published in almost sixty Canadian, US, and Jamaican magazines and newspapers for diverse readerships. As a young woman living in Montreal, she submitted humorous pieces to the nationally circulating US newspapers *Texas Siftings,*[7] *Peck's Sun,* and the *Detroit Free Press* (Eaton, "Sui Sin Far, the Half Chinese" 292) as well as special-interest magazines such as *The National Stenographer.* While at the start of her career her fiction appeared mostly in small Montreal literary magazines such as *Dominion Illustrated* and *Metropolitan* and fin-de-siècle "little" magazines such as *Fly Leaf* and *Lotus,* at the peak of her career her works were published in widely circulating US magazines such as *Century* and the *New England Magazine.* Her Chinatown fiction, ethnography, and journalistic reportage were featured in regional magazines such as *The Land of Sunshine, Out West, Overland, The Westerner,* and *The Traveler* as well as in travel magazines such as Southern Pacific Railway's *Sunset.* Her risqué sensation fiction – depicting infidelity, divorce, suicide, and miscegenation – appeared in *The Bohemian* and in syndicated columns published in newspapers across the US at the same time that her morality tales for adult and child readers were appearing in missionary magazines such as *Sabbath Recorder, Congregationalist and Christian World,* and

The Christian Evangelist. Many of her tales about children around the world, which appeared first in *Youth's Companion, Little Folks, Everyland* and the "Children's Pages" of *Good Housekeeping* and *American Motherhood*, were later syndicated in newspapers across the US. Her middlebrow fiction, ethnography, and children's fiction appeared in numerous mass-circulating monthly women's magazines, from the radical *New Idea Woman's Magazine* and racially inclusive *Gentlewoman* to the more conservative *Ladies' Home Journal* and *Woman's Home Companion*. Eaton's works also appeared in reform publications like *The Independent,* muck-raking magazines like *Hampton's,* story papers such as *Short Stories,* pulp fiction magazines such as *People's,* and illustrated literary and news magazines such as *Leslie's Weekly.* Over the course of her career, she also published journalism, letters to the editor, and/or original fiction in daily newspapers in seven cities in three countries: in Montreal's *Witness* and *Star,* Kingston [Jamaica]'s *Gall's News Letter,* Los Angeles' *Express,* Seattle's *Post-Intelligencer,* Chicago's *Evening Post,* New York's *Evening Post,* and Boston's *Globe* and *Evening Transcript.*

This expanded oeuvre reveals many startling things about the author we have come to know as Sui Sin Far. First, it challenges the presumed centrality of China and Chinatowns to Eaton's work. Throughout her career, Eaton resisted the advice some people gave her to "'trade' on [her] nationality," to "dress in Chinese costume, carry a fan in [her] hand" ("Leaves" 230) and at various points in her career she expressed frustration that the publishing world tended to understand her only as the writer of tales about the Chinese. While at least one hundred of her known short stories are set in North American Chinatowns and/or China and over eighty works of journalism have a Chinatown focus, many of her other works of fiction and journalism focus on white New Women: stenographers, actresses, journalists, and schoolteachers. Given that, as Cho notes, she wrote in "genres associated with white women writers" (*Uncoupling* 99) and, as Hsuan L. Hsu notes, most of her work is "implicitly addressed to white, middle-class women" (Hsu, *Mrs. Spring Fragrance* 15), texts in Eaton's oeuvre that focus on white protagonists invite us to read her work in the context of popular white middlebrow women writers such as Willa Cather, Mary Austin, and Ella Higginson, as well as realist writers such as Edith Wharton. Eaton published in many of the same magazines in which Cather, Austin, Wharton, and Higginson pub-

lished.[8] Sensation fiction published beginning in 1904 under the name Edith
Eaton, such as "Taken By a Storm," "The Woman's Part," and "Monte Cristo's
Baby," as well as local-colour fiction such as "As a Kitten" and "Who's Game?"
published beginning 1908, provide further evidence that Eaton was making
an effort to write popular works for a mainstream audience from the more
dominant white perspective. She may have been referring to one of her stories in this vein when, writing to the editor of *Century* in 1903, she described
the manuscript she enclosed in vague terms as "not a Chinese story ... This
one is a change" (Eaton to Johnson, 24 Dec. 1903).

Eaton's expanded oeuvre also reveals the previously unrecognized sig-
nificance of her career as an early woman journalist. More than a third of
her works are journalistic, reporting on various "beats" – from fashion to
Chinatown to society to legal disputes – for newspapers in Montreal, Jamaica,
Los Angeles, Seattle, and Boston, not to mention reportage on murders, fires,
and smallpox outbreaks for an unidentified "big paper down East" ("Fire
Fly's Christmas Budget" *106*). Eaton's journalism invites comparison with
that of America's Nellie Bly, Elizabeth Jordan, and Nixola Greeley-Smith, as
well as Canada's Grace Denison, "Kit" Coleman, Sara Jeanette Duncan, and
Elizabeth Banks.[9] Writing for newspapers not only taught Eaton the lean
style of objective reportage but also provided her with an opportunity to ex-
periment with the embodied mode of turn-of-the-century "stunt" journalism. It also gave her access to many communities, most notably North
America's diasporic Chinese community. As Bennett Fu insists, Eaton's Montreal journalism "provided this young writer with rich source materials for
writing and ensured her literary career" (30). Indeed, as Ferens has observed,
many of Eaton's short stories are "extended readings of motifs and images
from her newspaper reports" (59).

Her expanded oeuvre also invites us to recognize Eaton's efforts to
examine racial identities beyond the Chinese. Writing from Jamaica in 1897,
for example, Eaton told the editor of *Land of Sunshine* that she was "scheming
to write some West Indian stories" (Eaton to Lummis, 30 January 1897);
stories such as "Away Down in Jamaica" (*171*) and "The Sugar Cane Baby,"
along with Eaton's Jamaican journalism, encourage us to consider Eaton's
work in terms of what Sean Goudie has called "Caribbean American regionalism." Other stories supply further examples of what critics have

suggested are examples of comparative racialization (Hsu, *Sitting in Darkness*). Eaton's sustained investigation of Métis (in "The Alaska Widow"),
mulatto (in "Away Down in Jamaica" *171* and "They Are Going Back to China"
62), Arabian (in "Asof and His Pony"), East Indian (in "Your Sun and My
Sun"), and Persian (in "The Laughing Fountain") subjects provide more
evidence that she should be read comparatively with turn-of-the-century
authors such as First Nations authors E. Pauline Johnson and Zitkala-Ša,
African American authors Charles Chesnutt, Nella Larsen, Pauline Hopkins,
and Zora Neale Hurston, and Jewish American author Miriam Michelson, all
of whom also negotiate contemporary ideas of racial and ethnic identity in
their works.[10] At the same time, Eaton's Japanese stories for children –
including "The Little Embroidery Girls" (1909), "The Hawk and the Chicken"
(1910), "The Folding Fans" (1911), "The Stuffed Duck" (1911), and "The Story
of To-To-Yo-Yo" (1911) – complicate the critical binary that has tended to
read Edith Eaton as the "good" sister, who wrote from an authentic Chinese
position, in contrast to the "bad" sister, Winnifred, who fraudulently assumed
the Japanese authorial identity of Onoto Watanna.[11]

READING EATON TRANSNATIONALLY

Eaton's expanded oeuvre also invites us to read her in terms of transnationalism – that is, in terms of border-crossing, border-straddling, and
border-challenging. One central image in her later fiction, explored first
in her journalism, is the geopolitical border between Canada and the
US. When Eaton began writing, Montreal was the largest city in the newly
founded Dominion of Canada and its economic and cultural centre. With
its port and railway station only sixty miles from the US border, Montreal
was a significant hub in a nexus of railways, canals, and steamship lines
that linked eastern Canada with the US, as well as with western Canada,
Asia, and Europe. Like other cities in which Eaton lived, Montreal was a
contact-zone where numerous cultures intermingled, including a Catholic
francophone majority, a small ruling class of Protestant immigrants from
Scotland and England, and a small but growing number of immigrants, including some from Asia.

Chinese men began to immigrate to Canada from the Pearl River Delta region of southern China (primarily Guandong Province) to pan for gold in the late 1850s; later, they came to build the Canadian Pacific Railway. Immigration patterns changed in 1882, when the US passed the Chinese Exclusion Act, the first law preventing a specific ethnic group from immigrating to the US. This act made immigration into the US from China possible only for merchants and Chinese immigrants returning from abroad who entered through the same American port from which they had departed and who could present certificates of identity to US customs officials.[12] After 1888, when the Scott Act made Chinese immigration to the US even more difficult by invalidating identity certificates and barring Chinese labourers travelling abroad from returning, many of the between 20,000 and 30,000 Chinese who had emigrated to the US and were now stranded outside its borders attempted to return to the US via Canada (Delgado 77). Canada became a "back door" and Montreal the eastern Canadian "rendezvous" for "all Chinamen coming to the United States, except those who go to Cuba" ("Chinamen Smuggled In" 6), because Canada, although it imposed a $50 head tax at ports of entry on all Chinese immigrants beginning in 1885, did not ban Chinese immigration outright until 1923.[13] Beginning in 1885, Chinese men travelled by steamship from China to Canadian Pacific ports on the west coast, paid the $50 head tax to enter Canada, journeyed to Quebec by rail, and then waited in Montreal boarding houses owned by Chinese merchants until they could arrange to cross the border. Some prepared elaborate emigration applications, including photographs and affidavits that claimed they had immigrated to the US years earlier but had recently gone to China without proper documentation. Others memorized "life stories" that made them out to be merchants who had already established businesses in American cities. Some bribed railway agents, customs officials, or interpreters to facilitate crossing at regular border crossings or attempted more dangerous routes across land or water. By 1894, Chinese were crossing the border illegally from Quebec at a rate of about 100 per week, each man paying about $200 to those who assisted his transit (about $5,000 in today's dollars). The scale of these operations was so large that it prompted a *New York World* reporter to infiltrate a New York smuggling ring whose Montreal agent in 1894 was boarding house owner Wing Sing. The resulting exposé identified boarding house operator Sang Kee as the Montreal agent of a Boston smuggling ring and one of the "smartcat smugglers in Canada"("Chinamen Smuggled In" 6).

Eaton's family was intimately connected with Montreal's transnational community, particularly the "smugglers and the smuggled" whom Eaton mentions in her "Plea for the Chinaman." Her Chinese-born mother, Grace, was one of the few Chinese women in Montreal in the 1890s, and, encouraged by a Montreal missionary who had recently worked in China, had introduced herself to the wives of Wing Sing and Sang Kee (Eaton, "Girl Slave" 44). US immigration and naturalization records and newspaper reportage reveal that Eaton's father, Edward, was a "kingpin" in Montreal's smuggling community, one of the two "most skillful men at the business" and "one of the old school in this line" whose "hairbreadth escapes ... fights with officers and ... struggles ... with the Chinamen in [his] charge would fill a volume" ("Smuggling of Chinese" 6). He was arrested in 1896 for smuggling three Chinese from Montreal into upper New York State in the bottom of a lumber wagon ("Smuggling of Chinese" 6); twenty years later, he was arrested for conspiring to smuggle Chinese into the US. Newspaper accounts also refer to "three ladies residing in Montreal" (*Plattsburgh Press*, 15 August 1896) who helped him escape from jail after his first arrest and describe one of his daughters, a "bright young lady who speaks English and Chinese with equal fluency," as assisting her father at his trial ("In United States Court"). A 1900 newspaper article mentioned "clever women [who] left the [smuggling] business" after 1896, "women who invented, perfected and carried out the plans" for Edward Eaton and his partner's escape from the Plattsburgh jail and "brought them the necessary tools" as well as women who can "still ... be found sharing in the business of smuggling Chinamen, [who] usually do very good work, for as messengers or advance agents in the US they cannot be beaten. Sometimes they accompany the party, and one woman prides herself on the fact that she has made several trips by sleigh with a male smuggler, each time driving two Chinamen disguised as women over the border" ("Smuggling of Chinese" 6).

It is possible, given the intimate knowledge of "smugglers and the smuggled" she claims in her journalism, that Eaton herself was the "bright young lady" who helped her father and/or one of the "women" who "left the business" after 1896. Details about Chinese being smuggled across the US border show up repeatedly in Eaton's Montreal journalism, which describes railway officials, immigration agents, boarding house owners, smugglers, Chinese merchants visiting from New York and Boston, and men who take incredible risks to move undetected "across the line." "Thrilling Experience" (59) provides a near first-person account of smugglers' successful crossing of the St Lawrence River at a particularly treacherous part of the River. As many scholars have noted, the border trope recurs in Eaton's fiction, for example, in "The Smuggling of Tie Co," "Tian Shan's Kindred Spirit," and the newly recovered "Woo-Ma and I." Martha Cutter has interpreted the act of smuggling – "the illicit crossing of a body into a foreign space" (Cutter, "Smuggling" 147) – as a "trope in Sui Sin Far's fiction ... that involves the traversal of the identificatory practices that create a domain of racialized and feminized abject bodies, as well as a crossing, and perhaps a crossing out, of the borders that govern these bodies" (147). Cutter reads the geopolitical border metaphorically, as producing and policing binaries of gender, race, and sexuality that are disrupted by cross-dressed characters, hyphenated identities, and homosexual subtexts.

In addition to presenting smuggling as a metaphorical intervention in categories of race, gender, and sexuality, Eaton's expanded oeuvre makes clear that the trope of smuggling is also used to challenge absolute categories of national identity and citizenship and to promote a transnational or even post-national understanding of identity. Rather than affirming fixed nationality or citizenship through images of settlement, assimilation, and permanence, Eaton finds it more productive to depict her subjects in motion. She frequently describes historical people and fictional characters in transit: riding trains between the west and east coasts, travelling by steamship between China and North America, or journeying by horse, horse car, row boat, war canoe, bicycle, yacht, merchant ship, or junk. Few of her fictional characters are content to stay still: think of the smuggler who enjoys "running backwards and forwards across the border" in "Tian Shan's Kindred Spirit" or Eaton's Chinese merchant persona, Wing Sing, who confesses to an "infirmity": he is "fond of travel" ("Wing Sing on His Travels" 5 July 1904, 227). In "Leaves from the Mental Portfolio of a Eurasian," Eaton confesses: "When I am East, my heart is West. When I am West, my heart is East" (White-Parks and Ling 230). Being in transit functions as a trope for

the state of "in-betweenness" for those with complex post-national identities. The diverse historical and fictional characters whose stories Eaton tells
yearn for flexible subject positions that can encompass their complex racial,
ethnic, legal, gender, sexual, religious, and class identities, whether they are
Chinese immigrants struggling to fit into North American society, North
American-born Chinese juggling inherited cultural traditions and the traditions of the society in which they live, the mixed-race individuals with
whom Eaton most identifies, or multicultural/multinational individuals
whose genealogies and lived experiences complicate their senses of self.

Claudia Sadowski-Smith has read the undocumented border-crossers in
Eaton's known "border fictions" as "tricksters who move across boundaries
of gender and nationality to escape personal or social restrictions or to
resolve complex dilemmas" (54). Eaton's expanded oeuvre offers scholars
further evidence with which to challenge the "nation-centered models of
understanding literary and cultural traditions" (Goudie 294) through which
her work has been approached in the past. In "Writers Without Borders,"
Carole Gerson echoes Sadowski-Smith and Goudie when she encourages us
to read writers such as Eaton as "consistently operat[ing] in a transnational
framework: triangulated with Britain and the U.S." (16). Given Eaton's biography, her publication venues, and the themes of her work, a transnational
approach to her work that considers the triangulated oceanic spaces of both
the Atlantic and the Pacific makes sense.

THIS EDITION

Eaton's career can be divided into three phases: the first phase loosely comprises a period of authorial experimentation between 1888, when Eaton's
earliest known publications began to appear in Montreal newspapers and
magazines, and about 1898, when, after having tried out Sue Seen Far, Sui
Seen Far, and Sui Sin Fah, she committed to spelling her new pen name
Sui Sin Far. During this decade, Eaton published imitative fiction under the
signature Edith Eaton; women's page material and letters to the editor signed
E.E.; and a Jamaican newspaper column as Fire Fly or Canadian Fire Fly. She
also wrote unsigned journalism about Chinatown and, through the process

of getting to know diasporic Chinese in Montreal, gradually began to identify herself as Eurasian. During these years, French Canada, Caribbean Jamaica, and Imperial China – three distinct sites on the edges of an expanding British empire – inspired her complex meditations on nationality, citizenship, and identity.

The middle phase of Eaton's career comprises the decade between 1898 and 1908, years during which she lived on the west coast of the US and published fiction for adult readers about Chinatown or China, ethnographic journalism, and travel writing, mostly under her Chinese pen name. During this phase, she published primarily in west-coast regional publications, such as *Land of Sunshine* and *Westerner*, and earned her living primarily as a stenographer.

The third phase comprises the six years between 1908 and her death in 1914 – her mature phase – when she achieved legitimacy as a national author by publishing primarily in widely circulating national periodicals such as *Good Housekeeping* and earned her living almost entirely through her writing. During this period, her narrative attention shifted from stories about Chinatowns to stories for and about children from around the world as well as autobiographical works, many of which were syndicated in newspapers and magazines across the country.

Becoming Sui Sin Far assembles seventy texts by Eaton, most of which were written during her first phase (1888–98) and inspired the tropes and themes of her more mature work. The one exception, a travel narrative published in 1904, revisits the tropes and themes of her early years in Montreal through a second Chinese persona. Eaton's earliest fictional and journalistic representations of North American Chinese were based on the unique experiences of the small, largely transient, Chinese community she encountered in downtown Montreal in the decade following Canada's implementation of the Head Tax in 1885. Scholars have often noted that Asian Canadian literature is frequently "included and cast as a subset of Asian American literature" (Lo 5), while authors like Eaton have been made to effectively "pass" as Asian American authors by scholarship that ignores the particular demographic, cultural, and historical differences between Canada and the US.[14] Sadowski-Smith, for example, worries that the more globalized tendencies of recent Asian American Studies researchers "leave no room for the distinctive histories and identities of Asian Canadian communities" (52). Marie Lo has, similarly, pointed out that American racial formation is not "transposable or equivalent in a Canadian context" (1). Nor are "the effects of racialization" in Canada and the US "uniform and transparently visible" (Lo 1). Texts collected here will enable scholars to see more clearly "the stress [Eaton] placed on the specificity of her Canadian settings and the treatment of the Chinese in Canada," an emphasis that Sadowski-Smith suggests has been obscured by the institutionalization of Eaton's work within US ethnic and regionalist paradigms (53). Canada exerted a very important influence over Eaton: as her biographer Annette White-Parks acknowledges, "the main road" for Eaton "invariably started from and led back to eastern Canada" (4). She lived and worked mostly in Montreal until she was about thirty-three. It was there that she learned the stenographic skills that supported her throughout much of her adult life and it was there that she published her earliest fiction, poetry, and journalism. At the same time, texts collected here show the surprisingly transnational inspiration, scopes, themes, and settings of Eaton's work – from England to French Canada to the Caribbean to the many regions of the US – in an era of early Canadian nation-building, US imperialism, and North American expansion. Certainly, Eaton's biography as well as the biographies of her parents were significantly transnational and her prismatic oeuvre reflects this transnationalism.

This edition is divided into five sections: the first collects nine of her earliest works of fiction, poetry, and literary sketches signed Edith Eaton and published in Montreal between 1888–91; the second section collects seventeen unsigned works of Montreal journalism as well as four letters to the editor of the *Montreal Star* signed E.E. from the 1890s; the third section brings together fifteen works of Jamaican journalism published under the pseudonyms Fire Fly and Canadian Fire Fly (1896–97). Texts in these three sections were all published before Eaton became known by her orientalist pen name. The fourth section assembles ten of Eaton's uncollected early works of fiction, focusing on those set, written, or published on the border spaces between China and the US, Canada and Jamaica, and Canada and the US, written during the years in which Eaton was experimenting with various spellings of her pen name. Both Canada and Jamaica are depicted as transnational spaces through which people, periodicals, and ideas pass. The fifth section reprints her 1904 serialized cross-continental travel narrative, written under the Chinese male pen name Wing Sing, that reflects on the transnational themes examined in the first decade of Eaton's career.

The appendices provide necessary scholarly tools: an interview from 1896 that contains the first known reference to Eaton's use of her Chinese pen name; a timeline; and an updated bibliography including details about re-printings.

EARLY MONTREAL FICTION, POETRY, AND LITERARY SKETCHES (1888–1891)

In "Sui Sin Far, the Half Chinese Writer, Tells of Her Career," Edith Eaton remembers that her mother was a "fascinating story teller" (White-Parks and Ling 289). Winnifred Eaton's fictional portrayal of her family in her 1916 novel *Marion: The Story of an Artist's Model* describes the Eatons as a household of storytellers: "We would tell each other stories which we invented as we went along" (37). When the first of the stories, poems, and literary sketches signed Edith Eaton appeared in Montreal's *Dominion Illustrated: A Canadian Pictorial Weekly* in October 1888, Eaton was twenty-three years old and working as a stenographer for Archibald and McCormick, a liberal Montreal law firm.[15] "Judge Archibald," Eaton writes "read my little stories and verses as they appeared, and usually commented upon them with amused interest" ("Sui Sin Far, the Half Chinese" 292). *Dominion Illustrated*, a seventeen-page weekly printed on glossy large-format paper, had been launched in the summer of 1888 to promote Canadian culture; it published fiction and poetry as well as current affairs, academic news, and editorials. Opportunities to publish fiction in Canada were limited in the late 1880s when Eaton was emerging as a writer.[16] At the same time, according to Nick Mount, "[b]etween 1880 and 1900, the number of periodicals published in the US rose by 88 percent" (36) and many were desperate for original literary content. As a result, Eaton, like many of her Canadian contemporaries, including poets Charles G.D. Roberts, Bliss Carman, and Ethelwyn Wetherald, Mohawk poet and short story writer E. Pauline Johnson, animal fiction writer Ernest Thompson Seton, playwright and fiction writer Marjorie

Pickthall, and *Anne of Green Gables* author Lucy Maud Montgomery sought publishing opportunities in the US.[17] During this period in her career, Eaton tells us, she published "humorous articles" in the Milwaukee-based weekly *Peck's Sun*, a compendium of political satire and humour;[18] in *Texas Siftings*, a popular illustrated literary and humorous weekly edited in New York City beginning in 1884;[19] and in the *Detroit Free Press* ("Sui Sin Far, the Half Chinese" 292).[20] All of these publications enjoyed a broad Canadian readership because, in the late 1880s, Canada was a very young country and its print culture was in its infancy. However, none of the early texts Eaton published in these American periodicals and newspapers has been located.

Texts collected here represent Eaton's earliest known experiments in popular literary genres. "A Trip in a Horse Car" is a literary sketch. "Lines" is a poem, while "In Fairyland" produces what Eaton elsewhere refers to as a "medley of poetry and prose" (White-Parks and Ling 184). In "A Plea for Sad Songs" Eaton takes up the rhetorical form she later deploys to defend diasporic Chinese in "A Plea for the Chinaman." The other texts are short stories that draw on conventions of popular late-nineteenth-century subgenres, from fairy tales to evangelical tract fiction to melodrama to realist fiction.[21]

As a young writer, Eaton acknowledges, "[s]tories of everyday life [did] not appeal to me ... I love poetry, particularly heroic pieces ... [and] fairy-tales" ("Leaves" 222). Eaton's heroic pieces and fairy tales are characterized by romantic characters, such as the narcissistic male poet-genius in "Albemarle's Secret"; romantic imagery and settings (apparitions, moonlight, flowers, and "sylvan haunts"); stock references to the ideal; and archaic diction ("e'er," "thine"). In these texts, she also cites Romantic and Victorian poetry, for example, Byron's "The Corsair" and "To Thomas Moore" in "Albemarle's Secret," Keats's "Ode on a Grecian Urn" in "In Fairyland," and Tennyson's *In Memoriam* in "Misunderstood."[22] Her romantically inflected texts underscore Eaton's fin-de-siècle longing for a dream world of the imagination that serves as an antidote to "this world's great traffic" ("Spring Impressions," White-Parks and Ling 184), as a holiday from the "worry and the strife / Of a toilsome city life" ("Lines" 31). The realm Eaton calls "Fairyland" permits a person to "return to the duties of real life refreshed and calmed," but she cautions against residing in this fantasy world permanently. "[D]o not, ah!

Do not, yield thine whole soul to its fascinations ... [because one risks] for-feit[ing] the blessings and pleasures of the real world when he returns to it" ("In Fairyland" *33*).

Other early works, for example "A Trip in a Horse Car," "The Origin of a Broken Nose," and "Robin," seem more rooted in place. Taking as their set-ting the more recognizable urban-realist Montreal of policemen, street beg-gars, winter festivals, and summer excursions on the St Lawrence, these texts anticipate Eaton's later realist and regionalist work. These works feature young and old, male and female characters who are business people, hypo-critical philanthropists, and French Canadian workers. In her detailed de-scriptions of Montreal's street life, carnival, transportation networks, and charity, Eaton exercises a realist gaze even as she admits the limitations of that gaze when she acknowledges the "unknown ones who hide their sorrow from the world's curious gaze" ("A Trip in a Horse Car" *3*). These realist texts also represent a range of styles and narrative voices. "A Trip in a Horse Car" and "The Origin of a Broken Nose," for example, anticipate some of Eaton's later journalism by taking on first-person narration.

Clearly, much of this early work is derivative of Eaton's readings of canonical and popular British and American literature, thus demonstrat-ing, as Nick Mount has suggested, that most late-nineteenth-century Cana-dian readers were reading reprints of British and American writers. Writers coming of age in the 1880s and early 1890s had "few domestic literary mod-els" and many were reading dime novels and evangelical tract fiction as well as realist works by American authors such as William Dean Howells and Henry James (Mount 31).[23]

SELECTED EARLY JOURNALISM: MONTREAL (1890–1896)

Whether filing stories about fires and smallpox outbreaks in a small north-ern Ontario town to a "big paper down East," publishing sensational accounts of smuggling in Montreal's daily papers, or writing stories signed Canadian Fire Fly for a Jamaican paper, Eaton has much in common with the late-nineteenth- and early-twentieth-century Canadian women journalists ex-plored in recent studies by Marjory Lang, Linda Kay, and Janice Fiamengo,

as well as the turn-of-the-century American newswomen described by Alice
Fahs and Jean Marie Lutes. Born only a few years after more well-known
women journalists such as "Kit" Coleman (1856–1915), Sara Jeannette Duncan (1861–1922), and Nellie Bly (1864–1922), Eaton contributed anonymous
news stories, pseudonymous columns, and outspoken letters to the editor to
newspapers in Canada before continuing her journalistic career in Jamaica
and then in the US. This section samples some of Eaton's early journalism
published in the *Montreal Witness* and *Montreal Star*.

   Eaton's career began during a period of rapid changes in the North
American newspaper business. As newspapers competed for advertising rev-
enues, they began to cultivate a broader readership that included women,
immigrants, and newly literate people. Women, as print culture scholar
Karen Roggenkamp observes, constituted "an untapped reading and pur-
chasing market" (34). To expand readership, newspapers complemented
their emerging authoritative objective reporting of current events with
"softer" news, particularly stories told in a sensational, embodied style that
resembled the era's popular fiction. These "softer" stories were often written by women who drew on the narrative conventions of sentimental romance, sensation fiction, and travel writing. Modern women journalists,
according to Lutes, "renovated conventions of nineteenth-century senti-
mentality to suit a rapidly evolving mass media and developed controversial new models of self-reflexive authorship" (*Front-Page* 3). Instead of
demonstrating neutrality and authenticity, women reporters such as the
New York World's Elizabeth Jordan and Nellie Bly often celebrated the "bodily particularity and personal bias" of their stories (Lutes, *Front-Page* 3). As
Lutes observes, these women reporters "mediat[ed] tensions between pub-
licity and intimacy, journalism and fiction, the abstraction of literary authorship and the visceral experience of embodiment" (*Front-Page* 16).
Eaton's journalism displays such mediation from the very beginning: she
exploits the privacy made possible by writing anonymously or pseudony-
mously in order to assert strong opinions on controversial subjects, from
Chinese immigration to government policy, while at the same time she takes
advantage of the blurred lines between fiction and news to use sentiment to
move readers to adopt her perspectives by making herself a character in several of her news stories.

Newspaperwomen were rare in Canada in 1890. In *Women Who Made the News*, Lang cites an 1891 census that identifies only 35 women out of a total of 786 journalists in Canada. However, popular journalist Sara Jeannette Duncan (writing as Garth Grafton), in the 25 January 1888 instalment of her *Montreal Star* column *Bric-a-brac*, wrote an encouraging response to a young woman who had asked about the prospects of "women in journalism": "Special articles of a light sort," Duncan replies, "are ... in great demand ... [and] these can be written and are written readily by women. Lately, too, certain novel experiences have been undergone by very enterprising dames, to be used later as material for sensational writing ... The prospects are good now" (qtd. Tausky 50). Referencing both the soft feature articles written by women who came to be known as "sob-sisters" and the stunt journalism inaugurated by Bly in the *New York World*, Duncan's reply may have given Eaton the inspiration she needed to pursue her own career in journalism.

Eaton's association with Grub Street began early. By her eighteenth birthday, in 1883, she was "pick[ing] and set[ting] type" ("Sui Sin Far, the Half Chinese" 291) in the composing room of the *Montreal Star*, the leading evening paper in eastern Canada. Unlike many of her contemporaries, who found an opening in newspapers working on the women's pages, Eaton's journalistic start did not involve writing about fashion, although "Hat and Bonnet Philosophy" and "A Chat on Dress" written by E.E. reveal that she was contributing to the women's pages of Montreal newspapers by 1894.

Eaton's first journalistic forays were three brief unsigned news stories about Chinese in transit written in 1890 for the *Montreal Witness*, a popular Protestant daily that championed evangelical Christianity, temperance, and free trade. The earliest is "Land of the Free," an account of a Chinese man whom Eaton describes as having been "pounced on" by a Canadian Customs officer who demands that he pay the $50 head tax "in the name of the Queen of this marvelously free country." Like "Land of the Free" (White-Parks and Ling 179), two articles published later that year in the *Witness* express the reporter's sympathy for Chinese businessmen who must "travel in bond, like a Saratoga trunk" or spend "a few days in gaol for safety" ("A Chinese Party" 43) because of Canadian laws that regulate Chinese immigration. The first of these, with its detailed description of nineteen Chinese men picnicking at Windsor Station, reads like fiction:

Squatting upon their luggage, of which they had an enormous quantity, they produced the daintiest little tea kettles and tea-pots, and tiny
little cups, about the size of a thimble, hand-painted, so fragile that a
breath would reduce them to nothingness – things of beauty that
would have been the despair of the aesthetic boarder, accustomed to
vessels as thick as boilerplate. ("A Chinese Party" 43)

Rather than reporting neutrally, Eaton's early journalistic articles about Chinese in Canada express sympathy for their cruel treatment in a country
whose laws marginalize and alienate them.

For about a year after these brief articles appeared in the *Montreal
Witness*, Eaton worked as a stenographer for a railway executive in a northern
Ontario town that she described as "away off on the north shore of a big
lake" ("Leaves" 224). While there, she filed unsigned news stories by telegraph
about "fire[s]" and small-pox scare[s]" to "one of the big papers down East"
("Fire Fly's Christmas Budget" 108). Fires and smallpox scares could be
described in newspapers in neutral, objective terms, but Eaton's account
suggests that she was more interested in writing "sensational" stories. In an
autobiographical piece about her experience published five years after she
worked there, Eaton describes herself in the third person as a "Special
Correspondent" with whom she is "on intimate terms":

Was she not "Special Correspondent" in the District of Thunder Bay
for one of the big papers down East? Was it not a fact that every accident – fire and small-pox scare – that excited that excitable district
was faithfully recorded by her and sent across the wires through her
special agency? ("Fire Fly's Christmas Budget" 108)

When a murder suspect was arrested in the district, Eaton writes that she
volunteered to visit him in jail "with the idea of … giving a graphic account
of the interview … to the paper for which she worked." However, due to a
failure of nerves, the "Special Correspondent" who insists that "a woman reporter is not afraid of anything" panics before getting the interview. In mock-
heroic hyperbole, Eaton describes her sudden failure of nerves:

The key was turned in the lock; the door [to the jail cell] opened slowly
and cautiously, but strange to say, the "Special Correspondent" did
not start forward eagerly to enter. No, it seemed to those who watched
her that she drew back, hesitated, and her face turned pale. ... The
"Special Correspondent" instead of advancing calmly to the man
whom she had come purposely to see, sitting down by his side, observing his actions and words and taking notes of the same, turned
her back on him and frantically pulled at the door, shrieking "Let me
out! Let me out!" ("Fire Fly's Christmas Budget" *110*)

This sensational meta-fictional account seems inspired in part by popular
female investigative journalism written at the time. For example, in the same
year in which Eaton tried to get this jail-cell interview, popular US journalist Elizabeth Jordan had written a sensational journalistic account of her visit
to the cell of axe-murderer suspect Lizzie Borden for the *New York World*.
Soon after Borden was acquitted, Jordan also published a short story about
a female journalist whose sympathy successfully draws out a murder suspect's jail-cell confession (Roggenkamp, "Sympathy"). Here, however, Eaton
takes the opposite tack, emphasizing her embodied experience while also
insisting on a kind of womanliness that precludes her full participation in the
New Woman journalism exemplified by writers such as Jordan.

The murder that Eaton mentions in "Fire Fly's Christmas Budget" probably refers to a shooting that occurred in Thunder Bay in December 1892;
the smallpox "scare" she mentions is probably the one that occurred there in
April 1893. If Eaton was in Thunder Bay for "about a year," these details give
us a rough idea of when she worked there: from as early as April 1892 until
as late as December 1893. However, neither the "big paper down East" to
which she contributed nor the articles she wrote have been identified.[24]

By May 1894, Eaton had returned to Montreal and opened her own stenography office at 157 James St in the city's financial district, located near
Montreal's Windsor Station through which many Chinese passed. That
month, Eaton and her mother responded to a request from a local clergyman (probably Presbyterian minister Rev. D.C. Thompson) that they visit a
recently arrived Chinese bride. Eaton gained further access to Montreal's

growing Chinese community by volunteering at a local Sunday school and
continued to write Chinatown news for the *Witness* and, beginning in April
1895, for the Montreal *Star*. As a "lady reporter," she was by "special favour"
("A Chinese Child Born" 69) granted access to the intimate lives of Chinese
merchants and their families: their babies' births and "petty rites and ceremonies" ("A Chinese Child Born" 69), their visitors, their living quarters, and
so on. Because of her unique access to Chinese families, local papers gave
Eaton "a number of assignments, including most of the local Chinese reporting" ("Leaves," White-Parks and Ling 223). "From that time I began to go
among my mother's people, and it did me a world of good to discover how
akin I was to them" ("Sui Sin Far, the Half Chinese Writer," White-Parks and
Ling 292).

Most of the unsigned articles that Eaton published in the *Witness* and the
Star speak against contemporary anti-Chinese sentiment by portraying the
Chinese proprietors of boarding houses, laundries, and grocery stores sympathetically: as upstanding middle-class members of Montreal society. Eaton
also documents mixed-race families ("Half-Chinese Children," "They Are
Going Back to China") and the tensions between Christianity and traditional
religious beliefs among diasporic Chinese ("Girl Slave," "Chinese Religion"),
while countering prevailing stereotypes by describing Chinese women with
"feet ... of natural size" who have mastered modern skills such as machine-
sewing ("Girl Slave" 45), Chinese merchants who speak English fluently ("A
Chinese Party"), and half-Chinese children who are clever, handsome, and
intelligent ("Half-Chinese Children" 54).

Eaton also provides detailed documentary information about smugglers
who ferried Chinese men across the border into the US ("Thrilling Experience," "Chinese Visitors"). Her journalism often expresses great sympathy
for smugglers and their "freight" even as she aims for objectivity. In "Seventeen Arrests," for example, she mentions that boarding house operator Wing
Sing, when denying the smuggling charges made in the *New York World* exposé, asked her if she could "write in the paper for me and make it all right
and true? I not know how to write for myself." In "Authors and Their Books,"
a *New York Evening Post* reporter may be alluding to Eaton's having assisted
Chinese men in this way when he notes that "whenever Chinamen got into

trouble in [Montreal] or felt that they had just grievances, they used to come to [Eaton] and she would write out statements of their cases for the newspapers" (6). In "Chinese Visitors," Eaton tropes Montreal's smuggling network sympathetically as a kind of reverse "underground railway" for fugitive Chinese (58).

In all her journalism about Montreal's Chinatown, Eaton explores how performative racial identity can be, thereby anticipating her later fictional explorations of this theme. For example, in "Half-Chinese Children," she describes Eurasian children with "blue eyes, fair hair, and Mongolian features" (54) while in "They Are Going Back" she mentions a boy whose features combine those of a Chinese father and a mother with "a complexion like that of the ace of spades" (63). In "Chinese with German Wives," she describes a German woman married to a Chinese man who wears Chinese clothing so that she can subvert a steamship's rules and stay in the area designated for Chinese women. Two of Eaton's unsigned journalistic pieces also describe individuals who probe the performativity of gender: Chinese men who assume falsetto voices to play female roles in Chinese opera ("Chinese Entertainment") and a laundryman who may be a woman in drag ("Our Local Chinatown").

During this period, Eaton also wrote four letters to the editor of the *Star* defending the Chinese. Rather than sign her full name, she attached her gender- and ethnically neutral initials to the first three letters she sent: "Wong Hor Ching," which praises the lack of rancour of a British Columbian Chinese man wrongly convicted and jailed for murder; "The Chinese Question," which defends Chinese laundrymen's rights in Montreal; and "A Plea for the Chinaman," which advocates the elimination of the Head Tax and defends Chinese from unfounded charges made against them by British Columbian Members of Parliament. "E.E." may have chosen to partially veil her identity because her defence of the Chinese would have been unpopular with many members of the closely knit Anglophone community who read the *Star*. At the same time, in "A Plea for the Chinaman," E.E. identifies herself as a "just person" and a "woman" who "speaks from experience," because she "know[s] the Chinamen in all characters, merchants, laundrymen, laborers, servants, smugglers and smuggled, also as Sunday School scholars and gamblers" (84).

She also mentions a two-week visit to New York that enabled her to "dwel[l] amongst them" (88), a transformative event that initiated the process of her identification with the Chinese. E.E.'s pronouns shift throughout "A Plea for the Chinaman": she occasionally aligns herself with Canadians ("We should be broader-minded" 89), but generally she refers to the Canadian people as "they" or "them" ("Canadians do not employ Chinaman for love; they take them for the use they can make of them ... If they really want to keep the Chinese out ..." 85, 89). When Eaton does refer to Canadians as "we," it is to call upon readers to rise above defining people by nationality: "We should be broader-minded" (89). After several *Star* readers criticized her "Plea for the Chinaman," Eaton signed her fourth letter, "The Chinese Defended," with her full name (which the *Star* linked to "E.E." in a byline), suggesting that by 21 September 1896, she was willing to be publically aligned with her pro-Chinese politics while at the same time insisting that this alignment is based on imagination and empathy rather than on an essentialist understanding of identity. In "The Chinese Defended," she expresses her empathetic identification with the Chinese by appointing herself their spokesperson: "I wish to answer ... [to] giv[e] the Chinese an opportunity to have a fair fight with those who will persist in slandering them" and to be the party to "howl back" (91–2); here she discursively puts herself in the place of the Chinese – "if I were a Chinaman" (93) – and imagines her role to be that of countering stereotypical representations of the Chinese in "dime novels in which Six Companies of Assassins play a conspicuous part" (96). Even though she does not acknowledge her own Chinese background here, all four of Eaton's letters subtly deconstruct the opposition between "John Chinaman" and "our own Canadians" ("The Chinese Question" 76) by arguing that he merely "follows the example which we westerners set" ("The Chinese Question" 76) and by depicting recent Chinese immigrants as "true British Columbians" and Canada's first "pioneers" ("The Chinese Defended" 94).

In several articles from the mid-1890s, Eaton experiments with a more embodied authorial mode that permits increased identification with her Chinese subjects. For example, "Girl Slave" and "Chinese Religion" are both authored from the first-person perspective of a "Lady Reporter"; Eaton's "Thrilling Experience of a Band of Smugglers in the Lachine Rapids" is putatively objective front-page news, but it is written from the embodied viewpoints of fourteen Chinese men and their smugglers who are caught in rapids as they attempt to cross the St Lawrence river en route to the US border. Other news on the *Star's* front page that day displays the objectivity associated with the "invisible reporter" tradition that had become the journalistic standard by the late nineteenth century. Eaton's "Thrilling Experience," however, is the antithesis of objective "hard-boiled" news. Rather than criticize the men's illegal activities, Eaton describes in sympathetic physical detail the great risks the men take en route to the border:

> Out into the current glided the canoe, and in several minutes the party was in the centre of the swift current of the St. Lawrence. Down, down, they sped, the paddlers working like Trojans, but making little headway to the opposite shore. Back in the wake towered the [Canadian Pacific Railway] bridge, and in the distance could be seen the white caps and spray from the turbulent waters of the Lachine Rapids. The canoe now and anon would rise on the heavy swells that were rapidly drawing it towards the cataract of rushing waters. (60)

Assuming a more feminine mode that draws on the tradition of sensation fiction, a mode that enables her to treat some aspects of the story the way a fiction writer would, the article is written with so much close-up detail that the journalist herself appears to have been in the canoe.

Eaton's journalistic experience inspired new subjects for her fiction and encouraged her move away from the ornamental, imitative fiction of her youth. The spare language and objective and embodied styles that Eaton experimented with during this period informed the later sensational and realist fiction she published under the pseudonym Sui Sin Far.

SELECTED EARLY JOURNALISM: JAMAICA (1896–1897)

Soon after writing the sensational account of smuggling that appeared on
the front page of the *Montreal Star*, Eaton was hired as a court stenographer
and reporter for *Gall's Daily News Letter*, the second largest of four Kingston,
Jamaica, newspapers, whose readers were fairly liberal white elites and successful mixed-race planters and manufacturers. Kingston in the 1890s was a
thriving port town of 48,000 people and a destination for tourists coming by
steamship from Boston and elsewhere. "I gave up my office in Montreal,"
Eaton writes, "and accepted a position as reporter on one of the Jamaican
papers because of hard times, dullness in business, and [et]c." (Eaton to
Lummis, 30 January 1897). Eaton replaced her younger sister Winnifred, who
had worked at *Gall's News Letter* until April 1896.[25] As Winnifred recalls in *Me:
A Book of Remembrance* (1915), "the editor could not afford to pay a man's
salary, and being very loyal to Canada, he has been accustomed to send there
for bright and expert young women reporters to do virtually all the work
of running his newspaper" (25). Edith Eaton, in addition to transcribing
proceedings at the Legislature, the Courthouse, and City Hall, built on her
"Women's Pages" experience at *The Witness* to pen articles about local social
events, fashion, and shopping opportunities.

The embodied journalistic mode Eaton experimented with in "Thrilling
Experience" reappears in many of her Jamaican columns. Columns, some of
which are titled "As Others See Us," describe Eaton's first-person experiences as an outsider at Jamaican horse races, exhibitions, celebrity visits,
and church services. She narrates many of these pieces through a "pleasantly chatty persona" (Ferens 69) whom she names Fire Fly or Canadian
Fire Fly – a persona associated with inspiration, energy, and unpredictabil-
ity. Like Eaton as she describes herself in "Leaves from the Mental Portfolio
of an Eurasian," this journalistic firefly is "small but [her] feelings are big"
("Leaves" 222). Through her empathetic "flit[ting]" and "flutter[ing]" ("Fire
Fly and Rum" 105), Fire Fly gains access to sights and people who might otherwise have been difficult to access. In this way, Fire Fly anticipates the later
authorial figure of Mrs Spring Fragrance, who eavesdrops in a non-threat-
ening way in "The Inferior Woman." If, in some of these journalistic pieces,
Eaton is a [fire]fly-on-the wall voyeur, "watching the faces and listening to

the exclamations" ("Christmas Eve") of those she encounters, in others, she also mediates stories through her own body in a manner reminiscent of the stunt-girl journalism of Bly and Duncan. For example, in "The Firefly and Rum," Fire Fly investigates the virtues of a local rum factory by sampling its wares.

> So feeling wicked and wise – wicked, just because – and wise, well, only a wise Fire Fly would think of discovering the merits and demerits of rum from those who make it, the Fire Fly boldly flitted into Geo. Eustace Burke & Bro's. place. (*105*)

Insisting on her body as a source of knowledge in this column and others like it, Eaton "forg[es] a sensational authenticity that [takes] advantage of [her] femaleness rather than apologizing for it" (Lutes 16). Other columns called "Girl of the Period" or "Woman About Town" reflect on clothing's power to either conceal or reveal the individual character of its wearer ("The Girl of the Period: The Theatre") or the power of theatrical impersonation or ventriloquism to assume alternative identities. For example, a short description of a visiting ventriloquist in "The Projectographe" leads the Girl of the Period to recognize that stenographers ventriloquize when they type multiple marriage proposals by their "dictator" bosses.

Texts sampled here demonstrate how Eaton gradually moved away from writing lighter journalism about fashions, beverages, and entertainments in Jamaican society to providing more critical investigative reports of the Jamaican institutions designed to assist the island's poor and disadvantaged, i.e., prisons, poor houses, orphanages, and schools. Ferens notes that Eaton's journey to the Caribbean from Montreal "reenacted the classic journey of the ethnographer from the Western metropolis" to "a South Sea island" (68). Ferens argues that, over her six months in Jamaica, Eaton became more aware of the structural racism and classism of the British colony and her allegiance shifted from the dominant white minority to the oppressed black majority (78). At first, Ferens suggests, Eaton "emphasized the cultural distance that divided her [as a Canadian] from all Jamaicans, white and black" (70). Then she acknowledged her affinity with the predominantly [British colonial] *News Letter* readership. However, in her final columns,

Eaton explored the oppressed racialized positions shared by Chinese and blacks, anticipating the commonality she explores further in her auto-biographical pieces, "The Persecution and Oppression of Me" and "Leaves from the Mental Portfolio of an Eurasian." In Girl of the Period's "A Veracious Chronicle of Opinion," for example, Eaton voices sympathy for a black worker tried for refusing to obey and for striking his white superior who had assaulted him with "racist slurs." "Who would not refuse to obey an order delivered in the manner in which Nunes delivered his to Moulton? Who possessing the spirit of a man would not have resisted being pushed out of the place like a dog?" she asks (126).

Living in Jamaica gave Eaton a greater sense of how she was also "of the 'brown people' of the earth" ("Leaves" 225), an acknowledgment of her own mixed-race identity that encouraged her to explore race further in her fiction. Her months in Jamaica also made clear to her how impossible it was to gen-eralize about individuals on the basis of nationality, as well as other cate-gories of identity such as gender and class. "Jamaica ... is a country where individuality must ever rank higher than nationality," she observed in her 1896 "Kingston Races. First Day" (102). This phrase appears in slightly dif-ferent forms numerous times in her oeuvre – in her 1896 "A Plea for the Chinaman," her 1906 short story "Woo-Ma and I," and her often-cited 1909 autobiography "Leaves from the Mental Portfolio of an Eurasian." In each of these contexts, the phrase is invoked in the context of questioning nation and ethnicity as exhaustive rubrics for understanding identity. As Viet Thanh Nguyen suggests, Eaton uses the term "individuality" to mark an "antiracist form of identity that is resistant to a capitalism that exploits racial differ-ence" (41). In each of these examples, Eaton expresses impatience with dis-courses of nationhood that, by her accounts, reduce complex individuals to general categories and rationalize racism and ethnocentrism. In lieu of national identity, Eaton repeatedly asserts the value of the individual.

Reading Eaton's journalism alongside her fiction exposes significant interplay between them. Many modern women writers, as Lutes observes in Front-Page Girls, launched their fiction-writing careers as reporters, finding the attention to detail required by journalistic reporting and the under-standing of drama and emotion required by sensational journalism, in par-ticular, good training for crafting realist fiction. Like Duncan and Jordan, as well as Willa Cather, Djuna Barnes, and others, Eaton developed new modes of seeing and observing through her newspaper work, modes that inspired her later fiction. Her tendency to write self-referential journalism –stories in which she featured as a character – also informed her critical characterizations of journalists in her later fiction. As Rachel Lee has argued, Eaton uses stories about journalists "to tackle the issue of how to write about Asians without exposing them to a critical white gaze" (268). "'Its Wavering Image'" (1912), for example, features a white newspaperman who cruelly exploits a Eurasian woman's intimacy with him to write an exposé of Chinatown for his paper. Another recently located story, "The Success of a Mistake" (1908), features a young white newspaperwoman whose flawed Chinatown reporting inadvertently breaks up an arranged marriage, a "success[ful] ... mistake" that enables the young Chinese woman to marry the man she loves rather than the groom selected by her parents. Eaton's "Away Down in Jamaica" is unique in depicting a decent journalist figure.

Journalistic observation provided ideal subject matter for the realist and naturalist fiction that Eaton would later pen under her Chinese pseudonym.

SELECTED LATER FICTION (1896–1906)

In his *Bubble and Squeak* column in the October 1896 issue of *The Lotus*, which published one of Eaton's earliest Chinatown stories, Eaton's brother-in-law Walter Blackburn Harte introduces Sui Seen Far to his readers: "Who Sui Seen Far may be in real life no one can guess. But whether a man or a woman, the writer has a real and intimate knowledge of the inner and social life of the Chinese at home and in their exile in this country which has never been shown before in American fiction ... These sketches of Chinese life promise to bring a modest fame to the author in a very little while" (217). Harte had offered Eaton three of her earliest opportunities to appear in US magazines when he published her naturalist story "The Gamblers" in *Fly Leaf*, a "pamphlet periodical of the New – the New Man, New Woman, New Ideas, Whimsies and Things," (*Fly Leaf* title page) in February 1896, and her "The Story of Iso" and more sentimental "A Love Story of the Orient" in the August and October 1896 issues of *Lotus*.[26] Note that Harte's profile of Sui

Seen Far keeps both her gender and her nationality shrouded in mystery. Who was the person behind the pen name and how did he or she become the writer we now know as Sui Sin Far?

Amy Ling ("Creating" 310), Min Song, and Ning Yu have each noted that Eaton's "flowery pen name" may have been inspired by the candid journalism and (anti)sentimental works of nineteenth-century American author Sara Payson Willis, who assumed the hyper-feminine pen name Fanny Fern even as she challenged some of her era's most emphatic gender norms. Eaton may have sought similar latitude, affiliating herself with her Chinese ancestry through a Chinese name even as she sought to unsettle understandings of ethnicity and race. Sui Sin Far is Chinese for "water fragrant flower" or "sacred lily," a type of narcissus exchanged during Chinese New Year. It is clear from Eaton's writings that she had seen the flower in Montreal: she writes in "Chinese and Christmas" that "Lady visitors are often presented with a Chinese lily" (80) during Chinese New Years' celebrations, and in "John Chinaman Entertains" she mentions the "shui-sin-fa" flower as an important aspect of Chinese New Year.

A letter from Eaton to the editor of *The Westerner* in November 1909 offers a richer reflection on the fitness of her pen name when she figures the imagination as a "Chinese lily" rooted in the "slime and mud" of "our unworthy selves":

> [I]magination is itself, to me, the lily of the mind – the Chinese lily – rooted in the slime and mud, yet unfolding a flower so fair that we hold our breaths in wonder; and the greater the wonder, when it springs from our own slime and mud – from our own unworthy selves. ("A Word from Miss Eaton")

Eaton's figuring of the imagination as a "lily" "rooted in … slime" here suggests that the pen name marks her move away from earlier romantic fiction toward literary realism, which Edith Wharton had defined as an effort to "transmute" rather than simply copy real life.[27] Writing as Sui Sin Far, Eaton worked to transmute the realities she had encountered in her journalism, particularly concerning women and children in Montreal's Chinatown, into realist and naturalist stories even as she also transmuted aspects of her own autobiography into her fiction. As Martha Patterson notes, she claimed through her pen name to have "seen far" (105).

After Harte's initial encouragement, Southern California's first literary magazine, *Land of Sunshine: An Illustrated Monthly of Southern California*, was instrumental in furthering Eaton's career under her orientalist pen name. Charles Fletcher Lummis, the magazine's editor and an acquaintance of Harte's, accepted eight short stories by Sui Seen Far that depicted Chinatown life between 1896 and 1900. *Land of Sunshine* regularly featured fiction, non-fiction, and photographs of Native Americans, Spanish Americans, and the American West – promotional regionalist writings that might attract settlers to California. Through his magazine, Lummis encouraged "the best Western literature" (White-Parks, *Sui Sin Far* 86). As Mount observes, Canadian writers knew "about the new regionalist movement led by westerners and southerners" (31) in US periodicals. Eaton's early stories contributed to this movement by providing insights into the rituals and politics of Chinese in North American Chinatowns. Although several stories published in *Land of Sunshine* refer to San Francisco's harbour, parks, mission schools, and Chinese merchants, as well as to recent tensions between the Sam Yups and the See Yups[28] in California, most were signed "Montreal" and written a few years before Eaton had, as far as we know, visited California. Eaton was probably encouraged by Lummis to revise her stories to reference more Californian context so that they would better fulfill *Land of Sunshine*'s mandate. On the basis, perhaps, of her success placing stories in Californian periodicals, Eaton moved to San Francisco in 1898. While living there, she also published Chinatown fiction in regional family journals such as *Traveler: An Illustrated Journal of California and the West* and the *Overland Monthly*, even as she tried to access a wider US readership by submitting manuscripts unsuccessfully to more mainstream national magazines such as *McClure's* and *Ainslee's*.

All the stories collected here explore identity. Eaton's post-1896 fiction demonstrates her efforts to negotiate the complexities of her subject position through characters who struggle with their own complex and often self-contradictory identities. Like her early Montreal fiction, many of Eaton's stories collected in this section depict heterosexual romance. But these tales are inflected with a greater sense of how nation, culture, race, and sexuality can determine or limit one's romantic possibilities. Young Chinese women's marital options are often presented as determined not only by arrangements made by their traditional parents but also by class, clan, sexual experience, and even appearance. The daughters represented in "Ku Yum," "A Love Story of the Orient," "The Story of Iso," "The Daughter of a Slave," "Woo-Ma and I," and "Sweet Sin" all struggle to escape marriages arranged by their parents.[29] Several young women commit suicide in order to avoid their fates whereas others sacrifice themselves to save their fathers' honour.

Several stories have lesbian subtexts, anticipating later potentially queer stories such as "The Story of Tin-A," "Chinese Lily," and "The Success of a Mistake," which Martha Cutter and Jean Lutes have analyzed.[30] Some of these stories feature young women who cross-dress as men, boys who cross-dress as girls, aristocratic young women who pose as slave girls, traditional Chinese daughters who assert themselves as "New Women," and poor men who are mistaken for their wealthier kinsmen. Many of the works of fiction Eaton associates with this pseudonym explore the ways in which identity can be transformed or mistaken. In "A Chinese Boy-Girl" (not included here), a Chinese man dresses his son as a girl to protect him from evil spirits. In "Ku Yum," a homely engaged young woman invites her attractive maid to "take [her] place, dress in [her] clothes, and be Tie Sung's bride" (145). In "The Sing-Song Woman," a Chinese actress exchanges places with a mixed-race girl engaged to marry a Chinese man she does not love. In "The Daughter of a Slave," a poor man is mistaken for his cousin, who is engaged to marry the woman he loves.

They also depict, for the first time in Eaton's fiction, the "troubles and discomforts" ("Half-Chinese Children" 53) experienced by mixed-race women as they struggle to make sense of their divided identities – a topic Eaton first explored in her journalism. In "Woo-Ma and I," the mixed-race protagonist, like the mixed-race protagonist of "Sweet Sin," asks for forgiveness before she kills herself.[31] "Away Down in Jamaica," one of the few works of located fiction that deploys a Caribbean setting and is signed "Edith Eaton," revisits the miscegenation theme through the character of a "brown girl ... adopted by some rich white [Jamaicans]" (174) who goes mad.

Understandably, given Eaton's own itinerancy during this period – "roaming backward and forward across the continent" ("Leaves" 230) – most of the stories included in this section also address the theme of transnational displacement. Young Chinese women must leave their families and travel to the US to fulfill arranged marriages with diasporic merchants; one talkative young Chinese woman is disowned by her family and taken "across the sea" to die "in a strange land" (150); some characters, after living happily in North America for many years, are forced to go "home" to China. The Canada-US border is a central image in several of the stories collected here. In "The Smuggling of Tie Co," for example, a young Chinese woman cross-dresses as a man so that she can be smuggled across the border by the man she loves. The eponymous Woo-Ma, of "Woo-Ma and I," also cross-dresses to work as a smuggler, a device also taken up in "Tian Shan's Kindred Spirit" when a Chinese girl cross-dresses to work as a smuggler so that she will be arrested and reunited with her jailed lover. All three of these "smuggling" stories echo details featured in accounts of Edward Eaton's 1896 arrest: i.e. "a dark, starless sky, a road unlevelled and desolate, a lumbering van, from under the rough covering of which peered the faces of three men with Mongolian features [and] two men, in the uniform of custom house officers, riding at full speed after the van" ("Woo-Ma and I" 196). When Woo-Ma kills herself and her narrator-sister A-Toy preserves the "suit of [boys'] clothes and a peaked cap" (197) worn by Woo-Ma when she worked as a smuggler, it is as if Eaton were writing her own death, disowning a former self and its illicit behaviours, and also claiming a new post-smuggler identity. All these texts use the permeability of national borders as a metaphor for the permeability of other borders, such as race, gender, and sexuality, even as they reflect on the artifice of national belonging or citizenship.

CROSS-CONTINENTAL TRAVEL WRITING (1904)

In early 1904, Eaton informed Robert Underwood Johnson, associate editor of *Century*, that she was "mak[ing] her way [across the country] as a Chinaman" (Eaton to Johnson, 19 March 1904) and tracing the journey in a series of articles for the *Los Angeles Express*, a mass-market newspaper that catered to recent immigrants and prospective migrants to California. It is unclear

whether Eaton literally cross-dressed or simply wrote a travelogue, like Sara
Jeanette Duncan's and Lily Lewis' co-authored *A Social Departure: How
Orthodocia and I Went Round the World by Ourselves* (1890), from the perspective of a man, whom Eaton identified in her first column as Wing Sing,
a "well-known Americanized Chinese merchant" (*201*) with a successful shop
in Los Angeles's Chinatown. White-Parks and Ferens both list six of the
instalments of this travelogue in their bibliographies but the entire travelogue comprises fifteen instalments. At over 15,000 words, "Wing Sing of Los
Angeles on His Travels" is Eaton's longest sustained authorial project,
through which she provides an amazing early twentieth-century account of
transcontinental travel by rail through the US and Canada. It might also be
Eaton's most remarkable act of stunt journalism: posing as a Chinese man
who successfully crosses the US-Canada border several times during an era
of intense border policing.

Like Bly's *Around the World in Seventy-Two Days* (1890), Eaton's travelogue details a long, challenging journey undertaken by a "lady traveller"
(Moss and Sugars 110) at a time when it was not customary for a single
woman to travel without a chaperone. But whereas Bly circumnavigated the
globe, Eaton tracked an elliptical circum-continental route across the US and
Canada during a period in which both nations were consolidating themselves through the completion of railways, conversion of Western territories
into provinces and states,[32] and intense settlement. Wing Sing starts his journey in Los Angeles and goes by rail north to San Francisco; by Pacific Coast
steamer to Aberdeen, Washington; by train to Seattle and Vancouver; by
Canadian Pacific Railway to Montreal; by rail to New York City; and finally
by rail west through both Canada and the US to Seattle. Unlike Bly's journey,
Eaton's is not a race: her trip, which begins on "white man's New Year's" (*202*),
is interrupted by numerous overnight stops in San Francisco and Vancouver,
and by breaks of at least three weeks in Montreal, two weeks in New York, and
another week or more in Chicago and St Paul, before she finally concludes
her journey in Seattle on 18 July 1904.[33]

"Wing Sing of Los Angeles on His Travels" exemplifies the impact on
identity formation of both mass print culture and emigration in Eaton's era.
Eaton, paradoxically, travels across vast distances while remaining stationary

in the railcar, writing as a Chinese man while appearing as a white woman to other passengers. One might expect her travel narrative, like those sponsored by railway companies and/or published in popular periodicals, to trace a process of Canadian or American assimilation; certainly, the railway, built "From Sea to Sea," functioned in both countries as an agent of nationhood (Moss and Sugars 258). But, rather than tracing a process by which one assumes a particular national identity, Eaton's narrative traces a process by which Wing Sing and a transnational North America syncretically influence each other. Significantly, where Wing Sing's journey begins on New Year's Eve in Los Angeles, he reaches Montreal in time to celebrate Chinese New Year. The rail journey functions as a metaphor for the process of becoming a syncretized bicultural subject (both Chinese and North American) and binational subject (both Canadian and American), a process narratively traced through serialized instalments published in a newspaper that encouraged Western settlement.

Wing Sing begins his journey by copying from an Irish passenger who is documenting his trip in a notebook: what he writes down, Wing Sing writes down. When the Irishman says "you must not copy what I write, just put down what you think yourself," Wing Sing responds: "that all right. I think same as you." The Irishman concludes: "Then you must be an Irishman" (204). However, even as Wing Sing mirrors the Irishman's *activity*, his unique racialized *perspective* – signalled in part by Eaton's use of dialect here – challenges preconceptions about the abilities, intellect, and tastes of Chinese men. When a passenger says "See that Chinaman" – and, as Wing Sing tells readers, "his friend look at me and laugh at me," Wing Sing looks back. "I look at him and laugh at him – plenty funny people in America" (202). As a successful entrepreneur who tours the continent looking for business opportunities in his adopted country, Wing Sing provides a new image of the diasporic Chinese man: he travels as a tourist on the railway that Chinese sojourners built for white emigrants. The rail journey permits Wing Sing to move beyond Chinatown, a geopolitical space designed to contain and limit Chinese mobility, and to explore a broader public space in which he may play a role. Instead of foregrounding the westward trajectory of European immigrants to North America and its attendant process of assimilation,

Eaton highlights the reverse trajectory of Asians who arrived at Pacific ports and then travelled east by rail, a trajectory she tropes in terms of class changes distinct from simple assimilation: As Wing Sing observes,

> I now big Mandarin ... I look in mirror ... and see myself look more nice than before I come on car ... I feel much superior man ... I think I gain six pounds since I leave Vancouver. (*205, 210*)

Eaton traces a process of syncretization that exposes the degree to which the continent and its culture are becoming more Chinese. Although most of his fellow passengers are white, the Canadian and American cities Wing Sing visits instantiate the ubiquity of the Chinese in North America: his cousins pan for gold in the Fraser River, own cigar factories in Seattle, run shops in Montreal, and lead the Reform Party in New York City. Wing Sing notes that there are 17,000 Chinese in Canada and 800 in Montreal, thereby decentring both whiteness as the North American standard of the human and the ethnographic description of the other as the implied object of travel narratives.

"Wing Sing of Los Angeles" demonstrates that – like the railways, which fostered an expanding national culture, westward migration, and self-invention enabled by the can-do dynamics of the American frontier – the mass magazines and newspapers in which Eaton published played an important role for both readers and authors in processes of gendered, racialized, and classed self-making. In *Reading Up*, Amy Blair argues, for example, that aspirational readers of mass magazines such as *Ladies' Home Journal* were encouraged to achieve upward mobility and class transformation through articles and stories that permitted them to identify with successful figures and successful social trajectories. *The New Yorker* had a similar effect on its rural readers. Catherine Keyser, in *Playing Smart*, has documented the performativity that enabled authors who contributed to "smart" magazines to both perform and, in many cases, resist gender and class stereotypes promoted by the magazines themselves. This performativity of authorship is characteristic of all modern periodicals, which function as "deliberately and complexly performative authorial environments" (Ardis and Collier 31). For Eaton, the collapse of the spatial gap between the east and west coasts effected by the completion of the transcontinental railroad is accompanied by a cognate collapse of identitarian gaps between subjects produced by reading and writing imaginative literature distributed through mass newspapers and magazines. Eaton's own biographical vehicularity permitted her to imagine points of view not her own which she represented in her writing; she experiences the collapse of identitarian gaps and finds herself productively in the resulting instabilities.

What made Eaton take up the persona of a Chinese man for her story of eastward migration and westward return? Eaton's posturing could be seen as a kind of temporary "passing" akin to the racial, class, and gender masquerades she depicts in her fiction. But to call her adoption of the Wing Sing pseudonym and her narration of cross-continental travel from his perspective "passing" ignores the flexibility of subjectivity that interests Eaton far more than fixed racial and gender identities, a flexibility that the serialized travelogue reveals through its perpetual motion. It is not insignificant that Wing Sing is also the name of the Montreal boarding house owner whom Eaton mentions in several early works of journalism, who was purported to have smuggled thousands of men into the US during the Exclusion Era, possibly by disguising them as Native Americans, women, piles of lumber, or groceries. The historical Wing Sing's actions suggest that identity, like citizenship, is fluid and performative, even as legislation on both sides of the geopolitical border sought to create fixed categories of nationality and citizenship. Moving undeterred across the US-Canadian border and writing periodical fiction and travel journalism about that process helped Eaton see the productive instability of modern subjectivity.

RECOVERING EDITH EATON'S LOST OEUVRE

To recover Eaton's uncollected works, I combined a number of strategies, building on the detective work undertaken by White-Parks and Birchall to recover the biographies of Edith and Winnifred Eaton, as well as on the bibliographic recovery work of Dominika Ferens and Jean Lee Cole. First, I developed a list of Canadian, American, and Jamaican periodicals and newspapers in which had Eaton published or to which she had submitted work, based on information provided in the acknowledgments for *Mrs. Spring Fragrance,* Eaton's autobiographical writings, her letters to and from editors, and other authors' reviews of and introductions to her periodical publications. In her acknowledgments in *Mrs. Spring Fragrance,* Eaton mentions twenty-four periodicals in which her works first appeared:

> I have to thank the Editors of *The Independent, Out West, Hampton's, The Century, Delineator, Ladies' Home Journal, Designer, New Idea, Short Stories, Traveler, Good Housekeeping, Housekeeper, Gentlewoman, New York Evening Post, Holland's, Little Folks, American Motherhood, New England, Youth's Companion, Montreal Witness, Children's, Overland, Sunset,* and *Westerner* magazines, who were kind enough to care for my children when I sent them out into the world, for permitting the dear ones to return to me to be grouped together within this volume. (Hsu 34)

In several of her autobiographical works, Eaton also made general or specific references to periodicals to which she contributed or submitted work. For example, in "Leaves from the Mental Portfolio of an Eurasian," Eaton refers to the "local [Montreal] papers" that patronized her and gave her a "number of assignments, including most of the local Chinese reporting" ("Leaves" 223); she also mentions living in a "little town away off on the north shore of a big lake" (224), a region she identifies in a later piece as the "District of Thunder Bay" ("Fire Fly's Christmas Budget" 108). In "A Word from Miss Eaton" in the *Westerner,* Eaton mentions publishing stories in *Out West* and the *Seattle Post-Intelligencer.* The editor of the *Westerner's* Art and Literature department also notes in his preamble to "A Word from Sui Sin Far" that Eaton's sketches and stories had appeared in *Century, Youth's Companion, Woman's Home Companion,* and the New York *Independent.* In an 1896 article in *Lotus,* Walter Blackburn Harte notes that Sui Seen Far has had stories accepted by *Land of Sunshine* and *Short Stories* (*Bubble and Squeak*). Eaton's correspondence with *Land of Sunshine* editor Charles Lummis and *Century* editor Robert Underwood Johnson, as well as a letter that *Los Ange-*

les Express editor Samuel Clover wrote to Johnson, also mention periodicals to which Eaton submitted stories.[34] To this growing list of US, Jamaican, and Canadian periodicals and newspapers, I added *Fly Leaf, Lotus,* the *Montreal Daily Star, Chautauquan,* and the *Boston Globe* – periodicals and newspapers in which White-Parks had located texts by Eaton – and Montreal's *Metropolitan Magazine, Leslie's Weekly, Gall's News Letter,* and *The New York Recorder* – periodicals in which Cutter, Howard, Ferens, and Helfer had located other texts by Eaton.

I also made a list of Eaton's known pseudonyms. Although most of Eaton's journalism is unsigned, the works that I have located in periodicals and newspapers indicate that Eaton published her signed works under a range of signatures over the course of her career. In addition to her most familiar pseudonym Sui Sin Far, and its variants (Sui Seen Far, Sui Sin Fah, and Sue Seen Far), she continued to sign a variety of texts – mostly middle-brow women's fiction and sensation fiction – Edith Eaton, at least until 1909. She also wrote a regular column under the pen name Fire Fly (or Canadian Fire Fly), and assumed Chinese male personae – Wing Sing and Hip Wo – in two travelogues.[35] Late in the process, I began to realize that in addition to signing letters to the editor E.E., Eaton also published "women's pages" journalism under her gender- and ethnically neutral initials.

Eaton may also have used additional pseudonyms that have yet to be authenticated. For example, "The Colored Glasses," a children's story first published in *Everyland* under the signature Pau Tsu, was attributed to Sui Sin Far when it was referred to in Anita Ferris' *Missionary Program Material* (30); it is possible that the editor of *Everyland* might have confused the author's name with that of one of her characters – there are female characters named "Pau Tsu" in Eaton's "The Americanization of Pau Tsu" (1912), "The Bird of Love" (1910), and "The Fairy of the Rice Fields" (1914) – but it is also possible that Eaton used Pau Tsu as a pseudonym. In addition, a short story – "How White Men Assist in Smuggling Chinamen Across the Border in Puget Sound County" – that appeared under the pen name Mahlon T. Wing in the *Los Angeles Express* in March 1904, between instalments of Wing Sing's travel narrative, may also have been written by Eaton. This story, set on the Washington–British Columbian border, bears a strong formal and thematic resemblance to Eaton's other journalistic and fictional works about smuggling, namely "Thrilling Experience," "Woo-Ma and I," "Tian Shan's Kindred Spirit," and "The Smuggling of Tie-Co."

Once I suspected that Eaton might have published in a given newspaper or magazine, I searched as many issues as possible for the years in which Eaton was most likely to have been associated with that publication, using a combination of digitized and paper copies of these magazines and looking for any of her various pen names. Given the short lives of some modern little magazines and the brevity of Eaton's own career (twenty-six years between 1888 and her death in 1914), the task of looking through bound volumes or tables of contents for key years of monthly magazines was not impossible, although in some cases, I was unable to find complete runs of these titles.

Comprehensive searches of the eleven daily newspapers in which Eaton is known to have published original work, many of which have not yet been digitized, were more challenging. That said, I did strategic searches of select issues of the *Los Angeles Express*, the *Montreal Star*, the *Montreal Gazette*, the *Montreal Witness*, the *Chicago Evening Post*, the *Seattle Post-Intelligencer*, and the *New York Evening Post*, following up biographical clues that suggested particular dates during which Eaton may have published in these papers. Using databases such as *Google News* and *NewspaperArchive.com*, I was also able to locate syndicated works, i.e., sensation stories written expressly for the Daily Story Company and stories for children that originally appeared in magazines such as *Good Housekeeping* and *Ladies' Home Journal*, which had been reprinted in newspapers across the US and Canada. However, further research remains to be done on many of the newspapers in which Eaton published.

Attributing unsigned texts was often quite simple. Following Ferens' lead, I looked for pieces of early journalistic material found in Montreal newspapers and recycled in later signed fiction and autobiographical writing in order to attribute early unsigned journalism. For example, phrases and even paragraphs in later signed fiction and ethnography such as "A Chinese Tom-Boy," "Sweet Sin," "Jessamine Flower," "The Chinese in America," "Chinese Woman in America," and "Leaves from the Mental Portfolio of an Eurasian" first appear in unsigned Montreal journalism, including "Chinese and

Christmas," "Girl Slave in Montreal," "Half Chinese Children," "Chinese Religion," "A Chinese Entertainment," and "Chinese Entertainment." The reverse is also true: while writing a pseudonymous near-daily column for *Gall's News Letter*, Eaton recycled several of her signed early works of fiction – for example, "Robin" (1889) and "The Origin of a Broken Nose" (1889) – and signed literary sketches – for example, "The Typewriter" (1891). She also routinely repurposed unsigned material about Montreal's Chinatown in both unsigned and signed ethnographic writing about other North American Chinatowns. For example, the unsigned "No Tickee, No Washee" (1894) – an article in the *Daily Witness* about Montreal's Chinese laundry businesses – is reproduced in its entirety, with a few strategic revisions, in Eaton's unsigned "Chinese Laundry Checking" (1903) in the *Los Angeles Express* (White-Parks and Ling 210–11) and then again, in part, in her signed "Little Stories of Chinese Life In and Around Seattle." Recycled phrases appear so frequently in Eaton's work that they cannot be explained as occasional borrowing from other authors. Rather, self-plagiarism is one of her defining traits as a self-supporting writer who used journalism as raw material for later fiction or reprinted earlier writing in different publications to fill word-counts and meet deadlines.

Other unsigned texts were more challenging to attribute. However, topics – for example, smuggling, mixed-race children, arranged marriages, and Chinese encounters with white philanthropists – and settings – from Chinese restaurants to laundries to Sunday schools – explored in many pieces of unsigned Chinatown journalism that appeared in Montreal papers during the years Eaton lived there anticipate the topics of her later fiction. For example, themes from "Our Local Chinatown," "Thrilling Experience," and "The Chinese and Christmas" are revisited in "The Smuggling of Tie Co," "Tian Shan's Kindred Spirit," and "The Gamblers." Using biographical clues, proximity to other works by Eaton in the same publication, as well as subject matter and theme enabled me to attribute several unsigned texts to Eaton.

Combined with the journalism, fiction, and ethnography found by Ferens, Cutter, June Howard, and Helfer, the texts I have located bring the number of items in Eaton's oeuvre to over 260 and nearly quadruple the number of works attributed to her in 1995, when White-Parks and Ling's anthology introduced contemporary audiences to her forgotten works.[36] At the same time, there are still chronological gaps in the expanded bibliography – stretches of several months and sometimes years in which no known works by Eaton appear to have been published.[37] These gaps hint at the possibility of an even larger Eaton oeuvre that includes stories and articles buried in the periodicals and newspapers of her day that have not yet come to light.

CONCLUSION

In the second and third phases of Eaton's writing career, the settings of her adult fiction and the concerns she took up in her non-fictional prose expanded far beyond the Canadian settings of her earliest work. In a letter to the associate editor of *Century*, probably written in February or March 1904, Eaton mentioned that she was working on a "little Canadian story ... [about] Hochelaga ... the old fashioned little village in which I spent my childhood days" (Eaton to Johnson, undated) but this Canadian-centred text has never been found. After the 1904 publication of "Wing Sing of Los Angeles on His Travels," Canada does not feature prominently in Eaton's work, with a few exceptions. Although most of her later writings were set in the American states in which she had lived (California, Washington, Massachusetts), as well as New York and Alaska, she increasingly turned her gaze to the broader Pacific Rim, including China, Japan, and the Philippines.

In her fiction for children, her transnational engagement is particularly visible. Although her earliest stories depict children in North American Chinatowns, starting in 1908 when she publishes "The Puppet Show: From Chinese Folklore," Eaton moves her focus almost entirely away from North American Chinatowns to depict children in a range of international settings, beginning with the quickly disappearing society of imperial China: its festivals, rituals, social mores, and class structures.[38] In two Chinese stories for children she published just before her death, "Not Little Too Good" (1913) and "Completion of the Moon" (1914), Eaton depicts the Chinese Revolution of 1911, which transformed China into a republic, in order to demonstrate the degree to which traditional dynastic Chinese society's rituals and traditions had been replaced by new customs and imperatives. Eaton's later children's stories depict numerous other ethnicities, including Hindu, Arabian, East Indian, Persian, and – perhaps most surprisingly – Japanese.

Although the psychological and personal costs incurred by diasporic Chinese because of their legal exclusion from North American citizenship should not be minimized, Eaton's expanded oeuvre complicates the presumed desirability of North American citizenship for diasporic Chinese, suggesting that she thinks that at this period in history Chinese desire mobility – in terms not only of space, but also of class and identity – much more than they desire formal Canadian or US citizenship. The fictional and historical diasporic Chinese characters whom Eaton depicts anticipate what Aihwa Ong has called the "flexible citizenship" (1) of contemporary diasporic Asians in their desire to move between national spaces and to benefit from the opportunities these multiple national spaces represent. In her expanded oeuvre, Eaton frequently defines the most desirable aspect of citizenship less in terms of belonging to some proscribed collective and much more in terms of having the freedom to determine one's own narrative – to chart one's own course and to write one's own story. In her story "Tian Shan's Kindred Spirit," for example, Eaton writes: "Every time he crossed the border, [Tian Shan] was obliged to devise some new scheme by which to accomplish his object, and as he usually succeeded, there was always a new story to tell whenever he returned to Canada" (121). Yet, the narrator notes,

> had he been an American, his daring exploits and thrilling adventures would have furnished inspiration for many a newspaper and magazine article, novel, and short story ... Being, however, a Chinese, he was simply recorded by the American press as "a wily Oriental," who "by ways that are dark and tricks that are vain," is eluding the vigilance of our brave customs officers. (119)

Resisting the objectification that results when one's personal story is dictated by a racist national narrative, Eaton devotes her oeuvre to expressing the multiple facets of her own complex subject position and those of the diasporic Chinese community she chose to represent. Like Tian Shan, Eaton "smuggles" complex characters into "thrilling" transnational narratives through which they can access the rhetoric of self-making without being hampered by the constraining narratives that citizenship might dictate.

NOTES

1 See Ammons 106, Chu 100, Shih 48, and White-Parks 6.

2 See *Passenger Lists of Vessels Arriving at New York, New York, 1820–1897.* Microfilm Publication M237, 675 rolls. Year: *1865;* Arrival: New York, New York; Microfilm Serial: M237, 1820-1897; Microfilm Roll: Roll 250; Line: 17; List Number: 304; Year: 1865; Arrival: New York, New York; Microfilm Serial: M237, 1820-1897; Microfilm Roll: Roll 252; Line: 6; List Number: 495; and 1868 *Passenger Lists of Vessels Sailing to Liverpool,* Steamship Denmark (February).

3 See *Passenger Lists of Vessels Arriving at New York, New York, 1820–1897.* Microfilm Publication M237, 675 rolls. Records of the US Customs Service, Record Group 36. National Archives at Washington, D.C. Year: 1872; Arrival: New York, New York; Microfilm Serial: M237, 1820-1897; Microfilm Roll: Roll 363; Line: 8; List Number: 828.

4 See *Lovell's Montreal Directories* for 1880–81, 1882–83, and 1883–84.

5 See Chapman, "Finding."

6 Eaton had also tried to write plays (Eaton to Lummis, 8 October 1900) and in 1912 had been asked by McClurg to revise another completed manuscript (Eaton to Lummis, 23 March 1912), but this manuscript has never been found.

7 White-Parks incorrectly transcribed this title as *Texas Liftings* (26).

8 Cather published in *New England Magazine, Overland Monthly, Century, Ladies' Home Journal,* and *Woman's Home Companion.* On Cather's periodical output, see the Willa Cather Archive http://cather.unl.edu/index.ss.html. Austin published in *Century, Overland Monthly,* and *Out West* (see Ellis). Washington State author and contemporary Ella Higginson published in many of the same journals in which Eaton's work appeared: for example, *Land of Sunshine/Out West, Short Stories, Overland Monthly, Ladies' Home Journal, Youth's Companion, Century, Westerner: The Truth about the West, Good Housekeeping, People's Magazine, Woman's Home Companion, Seattle Post-Intelligencer, Leslie's Illustrated Weekly, Delineator, Boston Globe, Congregationalist,* and *Detroit Free Press* (see Laffrado). Wharton

published in *Century, Ladies' Home Journal, Woman's Home Companion,* and *Youth's Companion* (see Maureen Howard 920-23).

9 For scholarship on early North American women journalists who were contemporary with Eaton, see Fahs, Fiamengo, Kay, Lang, and Lutes, *Front-Page.*

10 Several scholars have begun this important work. On comparing Eaton to Michelson, see Skinazi and Harrison-Kahan; on comparing Eaton to other racialized New Women writers, see Patterson; on Eaton and Zitkala-Ša, see Diana, Ihara and Cleland, and Pierpont.

11 On the good sister/bad sister critical conversation, see Skinazi and Hattori.

12 The Act also excluded Chinese who had already immigrated to the US from US citizenship. See Daniels, Delgado, Erika Lee, and Mar.

13 Fifty dollars was easily four months' wages at a laundry (Helly 67). The head tax was raised to $100 in 1900 and to $500 three years later. The Chinese were the only immigrant group taxed in this way. By 1923, the Canadian government had collected over $23 million from 81,000 Chinese immigrants.

14 Of course, the study of literature designated "Asian Canadian" is fairly recent. In his overview, "A Long Labour," Donald Goellnicht suggests that the field was only slowly recognized in academic circles (1).

15 In January 1899 John Sprott Archibald was the judge in an important Quebec case on segregation, where he defended the "rights of coloured persons to admission and to seats in any places vacant" in theatres (Johnson v. Sparrow et al). See *Les Recueils* 104–12.

16 Most Canadian publishers published primarily reprints of pirated editions of US and British fiction. Several important Canadian publishers went bankrupt in the fallout from the Panic of 1893 (Mount 22) and Canadian magazines did not pay particularly well.

17 Indeed, Eaton published in many of the same US periodicals as Carman, Pickthall, and Montgomery.

18 Popular stunt journalist, writer and editor Elizabeth Jordan edited the Women's Page of *Peck's Sun* beginning in 1884. It is possible that Eaton submitted work to Jordan, although, as most material on the Women's Page was unsigned, no texts by Eaton have been located.

19 Between 1886–91, *Peck's Sun* had a North American circulation of about 150,000. See http://www.tshaonline.org/handbook/online/articles/edt16.

20 *The Detroit Free Press* occasionally featured Montreal news and features, possibly
     because, beginning in 1890, Detroit was on the Canadian Pacific Railway's route
     from Montreal to Chicago. Eaton's brother-in-law Walter Blackburn Harte notes
     in an 1891 article that the "Detroit, Buffalo, and Boston Sunday papers have quite
     an extensive sale in Montreal" ("Canadian Journalists" 417). Harte had published
     several articles in the *Detroit Free Press* between 1889 and 1890, including "A
     Graphic Picture," a description of Canada's House of Commons (31 March 1889),
     and "A Sphinx in New York" (26 October 1890), and was appointed its New York
     correspondent in December 1890. He may have encouraged Eaton to submit to
     the *Detroit Free Press*; an unsigned 23 July 1892 article covering Rudyard Kipling's
     visit to Montreal may be by her ("Rudyard Kipling's Visit").

21 On the popularity of late-nineteenth-century fairy tales, see Roberts, "Children's
     Fiction" in Brantlinger and Thesing.

22 Her poetry also echoes nineteenth-century British poetry, just as Charles G.D.
     Roberts' verse echoes Wordsworth's and Pauline Johnson's echoes Browning's.

23 On similarities between Eaton and James, see Song, "Height."

24 Although the *Montreal Witness* is one possibility, its coverage of Thunder Bay Dis-
     trict news appeared in a "City of the Plains" column filed from Winnipeg. Simi-
     larly, although the *Montreal Star* featured several "Special[s] to the *Star*" about
     this particular murder and other Thunder Bay news, most of these were reprinted
     from stories that had appeared in the *Port Arthur Herald*. The only other "big"
     Canadian paper that might be described as "down East," the *Toronto Globe*, pro-
     vided detailed coverage of the December 1892 murder but almost no coverage of
     the smallpox scare in April 1893. It is therefore possible the "down East" newspa-
     per is a Boston paper, since Eaton had Boston connections and later published in
     both the *Boston Globe* and the *Boston Transcript*, but I have not consulted these
     papers for these dates.

25 A Miss "Min. E. Eaton" from Montreal mentioned in the passenger list of vessels
     arriving in Boston from Jamaica in April 1896 is almost certainly Winnifred. *Pas-
     senger Lists of Vessels Arriving at Boston, Massachusetts, 1891–1943 Micropublication
     T843. RG085. Roll 18.*

26 Harte may also have encouraged Eaton's move to the US. Certainly he had corre-
     sponded with Ambrose Bierce, who contributed to and/or edited several San
     Francisco publications in the years Eaton lived there (Doyle, "Sui" 40). Harte's
     work also appeared in the *San Francisco Examiner* (Doyle, *Fin de Siècle* 50).

27 In her essay "Tendencies in Modern Fiction," Wharton suggests that "transmutation is the first principle of [realist] art, and copying can never be a substitute for creative vision" and complains that many writers in her period "exchanged [their] creative faculty for a Kodak" (171).

28 Rival groups of Chinese immigrants from different counties in the Pearl River Delta region of China.

29 See Yu-Fang Cho, "Domesticating" and "Yellow Slavery."

30 See Cutter, "Smuggling" and Lutes, "The Queer Newspaperwoman."

31 Although not included here, Eaton's story "The Sing-Song Woman" (1898) also features a Eurasian girl who avoids an arranged marriage to a Chinese man when a jaded Chinese actress wearing a veil stands in for her at a wedding ceremony. Unlike these two more tragic stories, "The Sing-Song Woman," however, ends with romantic happiness for both the Eurasian girl – she is able to marry her white lover – and the Chinese actress, whom the jilted Chinese groom forgives and loves (White-Parks and Ling 125–8).

32 The areas originally known as the Northwest Territories became the Canadian provinces of Saskatchewan and Alberta in 1905. The land designated the Utah Territory became the state of Utah in 1896; land known as Oklahoma Territory and Indian Territory became the state of Oklahoma in 1907.

33 Eaton worked as a journalist at the *Los Angeles Express* for almost a year, beginning in October 1903, contributing articles about local Chinatown missions, betrothals, children, and businesses, as well as a fascinating profile of visiting Chinese reformer Liang Qi Chao (see Chapman, "Revolution"). She says in "Sui Sin Far, the Half Chinese writer, Tells of Her Career" that "the shock of sudden grief [perhaps the death of her brother Hubert in August 1902] so unfitted me for mechanical work" that she gave up her stenography job in Seattle and moved briefly to Los Angeles (White-Parks and Ling 295).

34 In her 30 January 1897 letter to Lummis, Eaton says she is working as a "reporter" for the *News Letter* in Kingston, Jamaica; in her 2 December 1898 letter, she mentions submitting a story to the *San Francisco Examiner*. In her 30 June 1899 letter, she mentions a recent publication in *Overland*; in a 16 September 1900 letter, she mentions publishing in *The Dominion Illustrated*; in an 8 October 1900 letter, she mentions a publication in the *Chicago Evening* Post; in a 23 December 1900 letter, she mentions submitting stories to *McClure's* and *Ainslee's* as well as an acceptance of an article by *Ladies' Home Companion* [actually *Ladies' Home Journal*] and

encouragement from the editors of *Youth's Home Companion*; in a 10 February 1909 letter, she mentions her forthcoming "Chinese in America" series for *The Westerner*. In a 4 December 1903 letter to Johnson, she mentions publications in *Out West*; in her 19 March 1904 letter, she mentions a publication in *Youth's Companion* and her travel series for *The Los Angeles Express*. In a 15 December 1903 letter to Johnson, Clover mentions Eaton's publications in the *Los Angeles Express* and *Chicago Evening Post*.

35 "Hip Wo's Trip as Told by Himself" in *The Westerner* (1909) reproduces almost entirely a section of "Wing Sing of Los Angeles on His Travels."

36 My bibliography lists 264 works, including stories included in *Mrs. Spring Fragrance* (1912) whose original periodical appearances have not yet been determined.

37 Eaton published no known works between May 1897 and March 1898; May 1902 and October 1903; and September 1904 and March 1905.

38 These stories include "Puppet Show" (1908), "Two Little Pairs of Shoes" (1908), "The Crocodile Pagoda" (1908), "The Wild Man and the Gentle Boy: Chinese Folk Lore" (1908), "What About the Cat? transcribed from the Chinese fairy tale" (1908), "The Heart's Desire" (1908), "The Rebel Silkworm" (1908), "Tangled Kites" (1908), "The Little Silk Girl" (1908), "A Tale of the River: A Story for Children" (1909), "Ku Yum and the Butterflies: An Anecdote of Oriental Obedience, Written by a Chinese Woman" (1909), "Whose Father?" (1909), "The Little Wood-Carver" (1909), "The Half Moon Cakes" (1909), "Amoy and Her Dolls: Story of a Little Chinese Girl" (1909), "The Little Duck" (1909), "Ko Ku and the Cat" (1909), "The Sister Flower" (1909), "The Little Fat One" (1909), "Glad Yen" (1909), "The Inferior Man" (1910), "The Kitten-headed Shoes" (1910), "The Orchid's Lesson" (1910), "The Peanut Sifter" (1910), "The Palm Leaf Fan" (1910), "Candy that Was Not Sweet" (1910), "A-Toy's Tea Party" (1910), "The Little Brass Trumpet" (1910), "The Merry Blindman" (1910), "The Dream of Little Yen" (1910), "In the Bamboo Grove" (1910), "The Banishment of Ming and Mai" (1910), "The Dreams That Cooled" (1910), "The Homely Doggy" (1911), "The Silver Leaves" (1912), "The Colored Glasses" (1914), and "The Fairy of the Rice Fields" (1914).

WORKS CITED

Anonymous. "A Visit To Chinatown: Edith Eaton, Known as Sue Seen Far (Chinese Lily), Here from Montreal." *New York Recorder.* 19 April 1896. In Eaton, *Becoming Sui Sin Far,* 239–46.

Ammons, Elizabeth. *Conflicting Stories.* New York: Oxford University Press, 1991.

Ardis, Ann, and Patrick Collier (eds.). *Transatlantic Print Culture, 1880–1940.* Houndmills, UK: Palgrave, 2005.

"Authors and Their Books." *New York Evening Post.* 26 April 1911: 6.

Beauregard, Guy. "Reclaiming Sui Sin Far." In Josephine Lee, Imogene Lim, and Yuko Matsukawa, eds. *Re/Collecting Early Asian America: Essays in Cultural History,* 133–58. Philadelphia: Temple, 2002.

Birchall, Diana. *Onoto Watanna: The Story of Winnifred Eaton.* Urbana: U of Illinois Press, 2006.

Blair, Amy. *Reading Up: Middle-class Readers and the Culture of Success in the Early Twentieth-Century United States.* Philadelphia: Temple University Press, 2011.

Bly, Nellie. *Around the World in 72 Days.* Jean Lutes, ed. New York: Penguin Press, 2014.

"Book Table." Review of *Mrs. Spring Fragrance. Journal of Education* (31 Oct. 1912): 468.

Brantlinger, Patrick and William Thesinger. *A Companion to the Victorian Novel.* Blackwell Publishing Ltd. 2005.

Chapman, Mary. "An Edition of 'The Alaska Widow' by Edith Eaton (Sui Sin Far)." *MELUS* 38.1 (2013): 165–74.

– "Finding 'Sui Sin Far.'" *Legacy* 29.2 (2012): 263–9.

– "A 'Revolution in Ink': Sui Sin Far and Chinese Reform." *American Quarterly* 60.4 (2008): 975–1001.

Chin, Frank et. al. "An Introduction to Chinese and Japanese American Literature." In Frank Chin, Jeffery Paul Chan, Lawson Fusao Inada, and Shawn Hsu Wong, eds. *Aiiieeeee! An Anthology of Asian American Writers.* 1974. New York: Penguin [Mentor], 1991: 3–38.

"Chinamen Smuggled In." *New York World.* 8 July 1894: 1, 6, 7.

Cho, Yu-Fang. "Domesticating the Aliens Within: Sentimental Benevolence in Late-Nineteenth-Century California Magazines." *American Quarterly* 61.1 (2009): 113–36.

– *Uncoupling American Empire: Cultural Politics of Deviance and Unequal Difference, 1890–1910.* New York: SUNY University Press, 2015.

– "'Yellow Slavery,' Narratives of Rescue, and Sui Sin Far/Edith Maude Eaton's 'Lin John' (1899)." *Journal of Asian American Studies* 12.1 (2009): 35–63.

Chu, Patricia P. *Assimilating Asians: Gendered Strategies of Authorship in Asian America.* Durham: Duke University Press, 2000.

Cole, Jean Lee. "Newly Recovered Works by Onoto Watanna (Winnifred Eaton): A Prospectus and Checklist." *Legacy* 21.2 (2004): 229–34.

Cutter, Martha. "Sex, Love, Revenge, and Murder in 'Away Down in Jamaica.'" *MELUS* 21.1 (2004): 85–9.

– "Smuggling across the Borders of Race, Gender, and Sexuality: 'Mrs. Spring Fragrance.'" In Jonathan Brennan, ed. *Mixed Race Literature*, 137–64. Stanford, CA: Stanford University Press, 2002.

Daniels, Roger. *Guarding the Golden Door: American Immigration Policy and Immigrations since 1882.* New York: Hill and Wang, 2005.

Delgado, Grace. *Making the Chinese Mexican: Global Migration, Localism, and Exclusion in the U.S. Mexico Borderlands.* Stanford: Stanford University Press, 2012.

Diana, Vanessa Holford. "Zitkala-Ša and Sui Sin Far's Sketch Collections: Communal Characterization as Resistance Writing Tool." In Ellen Burton Harrington, ed. *Scribbling Women and the Short Story Form: Approaches by American and British Women Writers.* 98–100. New York, NY: Peter Lang, 2008.

Doyle, James. *The Fin De Siècle: Walter Blackburn Harte and the American/Canadian Literary Milieu of the 1890s.* Toronto: ECW Press, 1995.

– "Research – Problems and Solutions: Canadian Women Writers and the American Literary Milieu of the 1890s." In Lorraine McMullen, ed. *Re(dis)covering Our Foremothers: Nineteenth-Century Canadian Women Writers*, 30–6. Ottawa: University of Ottawa Press 1990.

– "Sui Sin Far and Onoto Watanna: Two Early Chinese-Canadian Authors." *Canadian Literature* 140 (Spring 1994): 50–8.

Duncan, Sara Jeannette [Garth Grafton]. "Bric-a-brac." *Montreal Star*, 25 January 1888. In Tausky 50.

– and Lily Lewis. *A Social Departure: How Orthodocia and I Went Round the World by Ourselves.* 1890.

Eaton, Edith. "Away Down in Jamaica." *Legacy* 21.1 (2004): 90–5.

– [Unsigned]. "Born a Britisher." In Eaton, *Becoming Sui Sin Far*, 96–7.

– [Unsigned]. "Chinese Laundry Checking." In White-Parks and Ling 210–11.

– [Unsigned]. "A Chinese Party." In Eaton, *Becoming Sui Sin Far*, 43–4.

– [Unsigned]. "Chinese Religion." In Eaton, *Becoming Sui Sin Far*, 67–9.

– Fire Fly. "Christmas Eve at the Post Office." *Gall's Daily Newsletter*, 28 December 1896: 2.

– [Pau Tsu]. "The Colored Glasses." *Everyland*, March 1914: n. p.

– [Fire Fly]. "Fire Fly's Christmas Budget." In Eaton, *Becoming Sui Sin Far*, 106–11.

– [Unsigned]. "Girl Slave." In Eaton, *Becoming Sui Sin Far*, 44–7.

– [Unsigned]. "Half-Chinese Children." In Eaton, *Becoming Sui Sin Far*, 53–8.

– [Hip Wo]. "Hip Wo's Trip as Told by Himself," *The Westerner* 10.4 (1909): 34–5.

– "In Fairyland." In Eaton, *Becoming Sui Sin Far*, 33–9.

– [Fire Fly]. "The Kingston Races. First Day. Descriptive Sketch." In Eaton, *Becoming Sui Sin Far*, 101–2.

– [Unsigned]. "Land of the Free" *Montreal Witness*. In White-Parks and Ling, 179.

– [Sui Sin Far]. "Leaves from the Mental Portfolio of an Eurasian." In White-Parks and Ling, 218–30.

– "Lines." In Eaton, *Becoming Sui Sin Far*, 31–2.

– [Sui Sin Far]. "Little Stories of Chinese Life in and around Seattle." *Seattle Post-Intelligencer*, 12 September 1909: 1.

– [E.E.]. "A Plea for the Chinaman." In Eaton, *Becoming Sui Sin Far*, 83–91.

– [Unsigned]. "Seventeen Arrests." *Montreal Daily Witness*. 10 July 1894: 1.

– [Sui Seen Far]. "The Sing-Song Woman" (1898). In White-Parks and Ling, 125–8.

– "The Son Of Chung Wo." *Leslie's Weekly* 16 June 1910: 592, 601, 602, 604. *Legacy: A Journal Of American Women Writers* 28.1 (2011): 126–35.

– "The Success of a Mistake" by Edith Eaton (Sui Sin Far)." *Legacy* 29.2 (2012): 270–9.

– [Sui Sin Far]. "Sui Sin Far, the Half Chinese Writer, Tells of Her Career. In White-Parks and Ling, 288–96.

– [Unsigned]. "They Are Going Back to China." In Eaton, *Becoming Sui Sin Far*, 62–3.

– [Unsigned] "Thrilling Experience of a Band of Smugglers in the Lachine Rapids." In Eaton, *Becoming Sui Sin Far*, 59–62.

– [Sui Sin Far]. "Tian Shan's Kindred Spirit." In White-Parks and Ling, 119–25.

– To Charles Lummis. 8 Oct. 1900. Charles Lummis Collection, Southwest Museum and Library, Pasadena, CA.

– To Charles Lummis. 30 Jan. 1897. Charles Lummis Collection, Southwest Museum and Library, Pasadena, CA.

– To Charles Lummis. 2 Dec. 1898. Charles Lummis Collection, Southwest Museum and Library, Pasadena, CA.

– To Charles Lummis. 30 June 1899. Charles Lummis Collection, Southwest Museum and Library, Pasadena, CA.

– To Charles Lummis. 16 Sept. 1900. Charles Lummis Collection, Southwest Museum and Library, Pasadena, CA.

– To Charles Lummis. 8 Oct. 1900. Charles Lummis Collection, Southwest Museum and Library, Pasadena, CA.

– To Charles Lummis. 23 Dec. 1900. Charles Lummis Collection, Southwest Museum and Library, Pasadena, CA.

– To Charles Lummis. 10 Feb. 1909. Charles Lummis Collection, Southwest Museum and Library, Pasadena, CA.

– To Charles Lummis. 23 March 1912. Henry E. Huntington Library and Art Gallery.

– To Harold Rugg. 18 Jan. 1900. Dartmouth College Library Ms. 900118.1.

– To Robert Underwood Johnson. 4 December 1903. *Century* Collection. New York Public Library.

– To Robert Underwood Johnson. 15 Dec. 1903. *Century* Collection. New York Public Library.

– To Robert Underwood Johnson. 24 Dec. 1903. *Century* Collection. New York Public Library.

– To Robert Underwood Johnson. 28 March 1904. *Century* Collection. New York Public Library.

– To Robert Underwood Johnson. 19 March 1904. *Century* Collection. New York Public Library.

– To Robert Underwood Johnson. Undated. *Century* Collection. New York Public Library.

– "A Trip in a Horse Car." In Eaton, *Becoming Sui Sin Far*, 3–7.

– "A Word from Miss Eaton." *Westerner* 11:5 (Nov. 1909): 1.

– [Sui Sin Far]. "A Word from Sui Sin Far." *Westerner* 11:5 (Nov. 1909): 34–5.

Eaton, Winnifred [Watanna, Onoto]. *Marion: The Story of an Artist's Model.* Ed. Karen Skinazi. Montreal: McGill-Queen's University Press, 2013.

– *Me: A Book of Remembrance.* New York: Century Company, 1915.

Ellis, Reuben J. *Beyond Borders: The Selected Essays of Mary Austin.* Carbondale: Southern Illinois University Press, 1996.

Fahs, Alice. *Out on Assignment: Newspaper Women and the Making of Modern Public Space.* Chapel Hill: University of North Carolina Press, 2012.

Ferens, Dominika. *Edith and Winnifred Eaton: Chinatown Missions and Japanese Romances.* Urbana and Chicago: University of Illinois Press, 2002.

Ferris, Anita B., ed. *Missionary Program Material: For Use with Boys and Girls.* New York: Missionary Education Movement of the United States and Canada, 1916.

Fiamengo, Janice. *The Woman's Page: Journalism and Rhetoric in Early Canada.* Toronto: University of Toronto Press, 2008.

Fu, Bennett Yu-Siang. "Differing Bodies, Defying Subjects, Deferring Texts: Gender, Sexuality, and Transgression in Asian Canadian Women's Writing." PhD dissertation, Université de Montréal, 2004.

Gerson, Carole. "Writers without Borders: The Global Framework of Canada's Early Literary History." *Canadian Literature* 201 (Summer 2009): 15–33.

Goellnicht, Donald C. "A Long Labour: The Protracted Birth of Asian Canadian Literature." *Essays on Canadian Writing.* 72.1 (Winter 2000): 1– 41.

Goudie, Sean X. "Toward a Definition of Caribbean American Regionalism: Contesting Anglo-America's Caribbean Designs in Mary Seacole and Sui Sin Far." *American Literature* 80:2 (June 2008): 293–322.

Harte, Walter Blackburn. *Bubble and Squeak. Lotus* (October 1896): 216–17.

– "Canadian Journalists and Journalism" *The New England Magazine 4* (December 1891): 411–41.

– "Graphic Picture." *Detroit Free Press,* 31 March 1889.

– "A Sphinx in New York." *Detroit Free Press,* 26 October 1890.

Hattori, Tomo. "Model Minority Discourse and Asian American Jouis-Sense." *differences: A Journal of Feminist Cultural Studies* 11.2 (1999): 228–47.

Helfer, Carol Kim. "Cultural Imprints: Chinese Elites in Turn-of-the-Century American Print Culture." PhD dissertation, University of California, Irvine, 2012.

Helly, Denise. *Les Chinois à Montréal, 1877–1951.* Montreal: Institut québécois de recherche sur la culture, 1987.

Howard, June. "Introduction to 'The Son of Chung Wo,' by Sui Sin Far [Edith Maude Eaton]." *Legacy* 28.1 (2011): 115–25.

Howard, Maureen, "Notes on the Text," *Edith Wharton: Collected Short Stories,* vol. 1 1891–1910), 920–3. New York: Library of America, 2001.

Hsu, Hsuan L. ed., *Mrs. Spring Fragrance.* [1912]. Peterborough: Broadview Press, 2011.

– *Sitting in Darkness: Mark Twain's Asia and Comparative Racialization.* New York: New York University Press, 2015.

Ihara, Rachel, and Jaime Cleland. "Ethnic Authorship and the Autobiographical Act: Zitkala-Ša, Sui Sin Far, and the Crafting of Authorial Identity." In Begona Simal, ed., *Selves in Dialogue: A Transethnic Approach to American Life Writing*, 63–79. Amsterdam: Rodopi, 2011.

"In United States Court," *Plattsburgh Daily Press*. 6 June 1896.

Kay, Linda. *The Sweet Sixteen: The Journey That Inspired the Canadian Women's Press Club*. Montreal: McGill-Queen's University Press, 2012.

Keyser, Catherine. *Playing Smart: New York Women Writers and Modern Magazine Culture*. New Brunswick, NJ: Rutgers University Press, 2010.

Laffrado, Laura. "Ella Rhoads Higginson, Mary E. Wilkins Freeman, and Pacific Northwest Women's Literary Regionalism." *Legacy* 31:2 (2014): 281–8.

Lang, Marjorie. *Women Who Made the News: Female Journalists in Canada, 1883–1945*. Montreal: McGill-Queen's University Press, 1999.

Lee, Erika. *At America's Gates: Chinese Immigration During the Exclusion Era, 1882–1943*. Chapel Hill: University of North Carolina Press, 2003.

Lee, Rachel. *The Americas of Asian American Literature: Gendered Fictions of Nation and Transnation*. Princeton: Princeton University Press, 1999.

Les Recueils de Jurisprudence du Quebec. 15 (1899): 104–12.

Ling, Amy. "Creating One's Self: The Eaton Sisters." In Shirley Geok-lin Lim and Amy Ling, eds. *Reading the Literatures of Asian America*, 305–18. Philadelphia: Temple University Press, 1992.

– "Edith Eaton: Pioneer Chinamerican Writer and Feminist." *American Literary Realism 1870–1910* 16 (1983): 287–98.

"Literary Notes." *Independent*, 15 August 1912: 388.

Lo, Marie. "Fields of Recognition: Reading Asian Canadian Literature in Asian America." PhD dissertation. University of California, Berkeley, 2001.

Lutes, Jean Marie. *Front-Page Girls: Women Journalists in American Culture and Fiction, 1880–1930*. Ithaca: Cornell University Press, 2006.

– "The Queer Newspaperwoman in Edith Eaton's 'The Success of a Mistake.'" *Legacy* 29.2 (2012): 280–99.

Mar, Lisa Rose. *Brokering Belonging: Chinese in Canada's Exclusion Era*. New York: Oxford University Press, 2010.

"A Montreal Character." *The Detroit Free Press*, 14 November 1886.

Moss, Laura, and Cynthia Sugars, eds. *Canadian Literature in English: Texts and Contexts*. Toronto: Pearson Longman, 2008.

Mount, Nick. *When Canadian Literature Moved to New York.* Toronto: University of Toronto Press, 2006.

"The New Books." *Advance* 97 (1912): 187.

Ng, Maria. "Chop Suey Writing: Sui Sin Far, Wayson Choy, and Judy Fong Bates." *Essays on Canadian Writing* 65 (Fall 1998): 171–87.

Nguyen, Viet Thanh. *Race and Resistance: Literature and Politics in Asian America.* New York and Oxford: Oxford University Press, 2002.

Ong, Aihwa. *Flexible Citizenship: The Cultural Logics of Transnationality.* Durham: Duke University Press, 1999.

Pan, Arnold. "Transnationalism at the Impasse of Race: Sui Sin Far and U.S. Imperialism" *Arizona Quarterly* 66:1 (Spring 2010): 87–115.

Patterson, Martha H. *Beyond the Gibson Girl: Reimagining the American New Woman, 1895–1915.* Urbana: University of Illinois Press, 2005.

Pierpont, Sherri Bell. *Wandering between Worlds: The Effects of Assimilation on Immigrant and Native American Children in the Works of Sui Sin Far, Anzia Yezierska, and Zitkala-Ša.* Brockport: SUNY 1998.

Roberts, Lewis C. "Children's Fiction" in Brantlinger and Thesinger, 353–69.

Roggenkamp, Karen. "Sympathy and Sensation: Elizabeth Jordan, Lizzie Borden, and the Female Reporter in the Late Nineteenth Century. *American Literature Realism* 40.1 (2007): 32–51.

"Rudyard Kipling's Visit to Montreal." *Detroit Free Press,* 23 July 1892.

Sadowski-Smith, Claudia. *Border Fictions: Globalization, Empire and Writing at the Boundaries of the United States.* Charlottesville: University of Virginia Press, 2008.

Salter, Joseph. *The Asiatic in England: Sketches of Sixteen Years' Work Among Orientals.* London: Seeley, Jackson & Halliday, 1873.

Shih, David. "The Seduction of Origins." In Zhou Xioajing and Samina Najmi, eds. *Form and Transformation in Asian American Literature,* 48–76. Seattle: University of Washington Press, 2005.

Skinazi, Karen E.H. "'As to her race, its secret is loudly revealed': Winnifred Eaton's Revision of North American Identity." *MELUS* 32.2 (Summer 2007): 31–53.

– and Lori Harrison-Kahan. "Miriam Michelson's Yellow Journalism and the Multi-Ethnic West." *MELUS* 40.2 (Summer 2015): 182–207.

"Smuggling of Chinese: Unusual Activity Now on the Canadian Border." *Youngstown Vindicator,* 6 March 1900: 6.

Solberg, S.E. "Sui Sin Far/Edith Eaton: The First Chinese-Am Fictionist" *MELUS* 8.1 (1981): 27–39.

Song, Min Hyoung. "The Height of Presumption: Henry James and Sui Sin Far in The Age of Nation-Building." *PhD. Dissertation Abstracts International, Section A: The Humanities and Social Sciences* 58.12 (1998): 4657.

– "Sentimentalism and Sui Sin Far." *Legacy: A Journal of American Women Writers* 20.1–2 (2003): 134–52.

Tausky, T.E. ed. *Sara Jeanette Duncan: Selected Journalism.* Ottawa: Tecumseh Press, 1978.

U.S. Subject Index to Correspondence and Case Files of the Immigration and Naturalization Service, 1903–59. "Record for Edw Eaton."

Wharton, Edith. *The Uncollected Critical Writings of Edith Wharton.* Princeton: Princeton University Press, 1996.

White-Parks, Annette. *Sui Sin Far/Edith Maude Eaton: A Literary Biography.* Urbana: University of Illinois Press, 1995.

– and Amy Ling, ed. *Mrs. Spring Fragrance and Other Writings.* Urbana: University of Illinois Press, 1995.

Willa Cather Archive. http://cather.unl.edu/index.ss.html

Wing, Mahlon T. "How White Men Assist in Smuggling Chinamen Across the Border in Puget Sound County." *Los Angeles Express,* 5 March 1904.

Yu, Ning. "Fanny Fern and Sui Sin Far: The Beginning of an Asian American Voice." *Women and Language* 19: 2 (Fall 1996): 44–7.

FURTHER READING

Abley, Mark. "Profile of Edith Eaton." *Montreal Gazette,* 14 July 1991: D1.

– "Voice from Past Regained." *Montreal Gazette,* 17 February 1996: I1.

Ammons, Elizabeth, and Annette White-Parks. *Tricksterism in Turn-of-the-Century American Literature: A Multicultural Perspective.* Hanover: University Press of New England, 1994.

Bloom, Harold. *American Women Fiction Writers, 1900–1960.* Vol. 3. Philadelphia: Chelsea House Publishers, 1998.

Brown, Julie. *Ethnicity and the American Short Story.* New York: Garland, 1997.

Brown, Linda Joyce. *The Literature of Immigration and Racial Formation: Becoming White, Becoming Other, Becoming American in the Late Progressive Era.* New York, NY: Routledge, 2004.

Brown, Wesley, and Amy Ling. *Imagining America: Stories from the Promised Land*. New York: Persea Books, 2002.

Burrows, Fred. "The Uncommon Club." *New England Magazine* (1912): 193–4.

Callahan, Cynthia. *Kin of Another Kind: Transracial Adoption in American Literature*. Ann Arbor, MI: University of Michigan Press, 2010.

Chartier, Daniel. "Une voix parallèle à la fin du XIXe siècle. Sui Sin Far." In Véronique Pepin and Chantal Ringuet, eds. *Littérature, immigration et imaginaire au Québec et en Amérique du Nord*, 225–46. Paris: L'Harmattan, 2006.

Choi, Yoon-Young. "Contested Space of San Francisco Chinatown in Sui Sin Far's *Mrs. Spring Fragrance and Other Writings*." *Journal of English Language and Literature/ Yŏngŏ Yŏngmunhak* 58.6 (2012): 1023–39.

Chung, June Hee. "Asian Object Lessons: Orientalist Decoration in Realist Aesthetics from William Dean Howells to Sui Sin Far." *Studies in American Fiction* 36.1 (2008): 27–50.

Cutter, Martha J. "Empire and the Mind of the Child: Sui Sin Far' 'Tales of Chinese Children.'" *MELUS* 27.2 (2002): 31–48.

– "Sui Sin Far's Letters to Charles Lummis: Contextualizing Publication Practices for the Asian American Subject at the Turn of the Century." *American Literary Realism* 38.3 (2006): 259–75.

Davis, Rocío G., and Sämi Ludwig. *Asian American Literature in the International Context: Readings on Fiction, Poetry and Performance*. Münster: Lit, 2002.

Degenhardt, Jane Hwang. "Situating the Essential Alien: Sui Sin Far's Depiction of Chinese-White Marriage and the Exclusionary Logic of Citizenship." *MFS: Modern Fiction Studies* 54.4 (2008): 654–88.

Diana, Vanessa Holford. "Biracial/Bicultural Identity in the Writings of Sui Sin Far." *MELUS* 26.2 (2001): 159–86.

DiBiase, Linda Popp. "A Chinese Lily in Seattle." *Seattle Weekly*, 10 September 1986.

Doyle, James. "Law, Legislation, and Literature: The Life of Grace H. Harte." *Biography* 17.4 (Fall 1994): 367–85.

Dupree, Ellen. "Sui Sin Far's Argument for Biculturalism in *Mrs. Spring Fragrance*." In Esther Mikyung Ghymn, ed., *Asian American Studies: Identity, Images, Issues Past and Present*, 77–100. New York, NY: Peter Lang, 2000.

Eng, David L., and Alice Y. Hom. *Q & A: Queer in Asian America*. Philadelphia: Temple University Press, 1998.

Grasso, Linda M. "Inventive Desperation: Anger, Violence, and Belonging in Mary

Wilkins Freeman's and Sui Sin Far's Murderous Mother Stories." *American Literary Realism* 38.1 (2005): 18–31.

Gruber, Laura Katherine. "Unstable Geographies: Context, Representation, and Ideology in American Western Writing, 1885–1927." *PhD. Dissertation Abstracts International, Section A: The Humanities and Social Sciences* 66.7 (2006): 2579.

Hong, Maria. *Growing Up Asian American*. New York: Avon Books, 1993.

Howard, June. "Sui Sin Far's American Words." *Comparative American Studies: An International Journal* 6.2 (2008): 144–60.

Hsu, Hsuan L. *Geography and the Production of Space in Nineteenth-Century American Literature*. Cambridge: Cambridge University Press, 2010.

Huang, Guiyou. *Asian American Short Story Writers: An A-to-Z Guide*. Westport: Greenwood Press, 2003.

Jirousek, Lori. "Spectacle Ethnography and Immigrant Resistance: Sui Sin Far and Anzia Yezierska." *MELUS* 27.1 (2002): 25–52.

Lape, Noreen Groover. *West of the Border: The Multicultural Literature of the Western American Frontiers*. Athens: Ohio University Press, 2000.

Lee, Josephine D., Imogene L. Lim, and Yuko Matsukawa. *Re/Collecting Early Asian America: Essays in Cultural History*. Philadelphia: Temple University Press, 2002.

Lee, Karen An-Hwei. "Prosthetic Texts/Phantom Originals: Translations of Cultural Consciousness in Theresa Cha, Chuang Hua, Sui Sin Far, Kazuo Ishituro, and Virginia Woolf." *PhD. Dissertation Abstracts International, Section A: The Humanities and Social Sciences* 62.7 (2002): 2417.

Lee, Sooyoung. "A Connecting Link: Sui Sin Far's Calling as a Eurasian Writer." *British and American Fiction* 19.2 (2012): 83–104.

Leighton, Joy M. "'A Chinese Ishmael': Sui Sin Far, Writing, and Exile." *MELUS* 26.3 (2001): 3–29.

Li, Wenxin. "Sui Sin Far and the Chinese American Canon: Toward a Post-Gender-Wars Discourse." *MELUS* 29.3–4 (2004): 121–31.

Li, Zhen. "Unsettling Women: Contemporary Diasporic Chinese Women's Writing." *PhD. Dissertation Abstracts International* 73.11 (2013).

Lim, Shirley Geok-lin. "Sibling Hybridities: The Case of Edith Eaton/Sui Sin Far and Winnifred Eaton/Onoto Watanna." *Life Writing* 4.1 (2007): 81–99.

Ling, Mary Ting Yi Lui. *The Chinatown Trunk Mystery: Murder, Miscegenation, and Other Dangerous Encounters in Turn-of-the-century New York City*. Princeton: Princeton University Press, 2007.

Martin, Quentin E. "Sui Sin Far's Railroad Baron: A Chinese of the Future." *American Literary Realism* 29.1 (1996): 54–61.

McCann, Sean. "Connecting Links: The Anti-Progressivism of Sui Sin Far." *Yale Journal of Criticism* 12.1 (1999): 73–88.

"Mrs. Spring Fragrance." *American Antiquarian and Oriental Journal* 35 (July–September 1913): 181–2.

Ouyang, Huining. "Rewriting the Butterfly Story: Tricksterism in Onoto Watanna's A Japanese Nightingale and Sui Sin Far's 'The Smuggling of Tie Co.'" In Laura Gray-Rosendale and Sibylle Gruber, eds. *Alternative Rhetorics: Challenges to the Rhetorical Tradition*, 203–17. Albany: State University of New York Press, 2001.

Peterson, Rachel, and Joel Wendland. "Performing Ethnography and Identity in Sui Sin Far's Short Fiction." In Tanfir Emin Tunc and Elisabetta Marino, eds. *Positioning the New: Chinese American Literature and the Changing Image of the American Literary Canon*, 158–74. Newcastle upon Tyne, England: Cambridge Scholars, 2010.

Pryse, Marjorie. "Linguistic Regionalism and the Emergence of Chinese American Literature in Sui Sin Far's 'Mrs. Spring Fragrance.'" *Legacy: A Journal of American Women Writers* 27.1 (2010): 83–108.

Rich, Charlotte J. *Transcending the New Woman: Multiethnic Narratives in the Progressive Era*. Columbia, MO: University of Missouri Press, 2009.

Roh-Spaulding, Carol. "Beyond Biraciality: 'Race' as Process in the Work of Edith Eaton/Sui Sin Far and Winnifred Eaton/Onoto Watanna." In Sami Ludwig, ed. *Asian American Literature in the International Context: Readings on Fiction, Poetry, and Performance*, 21–35. Hamburg, Germany: Lit, 2002.

– "'Wavering' Images: Mixed-Race Identity in the Stories of Edith Eaton/Sui Sin Far." In Julie Brown, ed. *Ethnicity and the American Short Story*, 155–76. New York, NY: Garland, 1997.

Schlund-Vials, Cathy J. *Modeling Citizenship: Jewish and Asian-American Writing*. Philadelphia, PA: Temple University Press, 2011.

Sibara, Jennifer Barager. "Disease, Disability, and the Alien Body in the Literature of Sui Sin Far." *MELUS* 39.1 (2014): 56–81.

Staples, Joe. "'Discovering' New Talent: Charles F. Lummis's Conflicted Mentorship of Sui Sin Far, Sharlot Hall, and Mary Austin." *Western American Literature* 40.2 (2005): 175–85.

Teng, Jinhua Emma. "Miscegenation and the Critique of Patriarchy in Turn-of-the-Century Fiction." *Race, Gender and Class* 4.3 (1997): 68–87.

Tonkovich, Nicole. "Genealogy, Genre, Gender: Sui Sin Far's 'Leaves From The Mental Portfolio Of An Eurasian.'" In Timothy Powell, ed. *Beyond the Binary: Reconstructing Cultural Identity in a Multicultural Context*, 236–60. New Brunswick, NJ: Rutgers University Press, 1999.

Vogel, Todd. *Rewriting White: Race, Class, and Cultural Capital in Nineteenth-Century America*. New Brunswick, NJ: Rutgers University Press, 2004.

Wang, Bo. "Rereading Sui Sin Far: A Rhetoric of Defiance." In LuMing Mao and Morris Young, eds., *Representations: Doing Asian American Rhetoric*, 244–65. Logan, UT: Utah State University Press, 2008.

Wang, I-chun. "Space and Identity: Hybridization and Boundary Crossing in Sui Sin Far's Poetics of Diaspora." *Canadian Review of Comparative Literature/Revue Canadienne de Littérature Comparée* 36.3 (2009): 274–88.

White-Parks, Annette. "A Reversal of American Concepts of 'Other-Ness' in the Fiction of Sui Sin Far." *MELUS* 20.1 (1995): 17–34.

Yimwilai, Supaporn. "Beyond the Binary: Resistance Strategies in the Writing of Sui Sin Far and Onoto Watanna." *PhD. Dissertation Abstracts International, Section A: The Humanities and Social Sciences* 63.1 (2002): 192.

Yin, Xiao-Huang. "Between the East and West: Sui Sin Far – the First Chinese-American Woman Writer." *Arizona Quarterly* 47.4 (1991): 49–84.

– *Chinese American Literature Since the 1850s*. Urbana-Champaign: University of Illinois Press, 2000.

Zhou, Xiaojing. *Cities of Others: Reimagining Urban Spaces in Asian American Literature*. Seattle: University of Washington Press, 2014.

Early Montreal Fiction, Poetry, and Literary Sketches (1888–1891)

Edith Eaton. "A Trip in a Horse Car."

Dominion Illustrated 1.15 (13 October 1888): 235.

I always had a liking for a ride in a horse car. Other people may enjoy their carriage and sleigh drives, but I, who am of humbler mind, prefer a horse car. There you can be alone, yet not alone. You can lose yourself in a day dream, without any one interfering, or you can interest yourself in the different species of the human family one is apt to meet in this vehicle. Sometimes you meet a friend and enjoy a pleasant chat, and sometimes you have the pleasure of sitting side by side with your worst enemy. You meet all kinds of people in these cars, high and low, rich and poor, the quality and a quantity of the city, and, as "variety is the spice of life," you will understand why I have a weakness for a trip in a horse car.

Many a pleasant half hour, or longer, have I spent riding through the busy streets, engaged in contemplating the faces of my fellow-passengers, catching little glimpses of their lives, and romancing and moralizing, as the case might be. This occupation has afforded me a great deal of pleasure, and, as I do not like to be selfish, and have always wished for some one with whom to share this pleasure, we will journey together in spirit from Mile End to Côte St. Antoine.* Time, about three o'clock in the afternoon.

---

* Mile End is a Montreal neighbourhood that became a working-class streetcar suburb in 1893 with the electrification of tramway service. Côte-St-Antoine is the earlier name of the wealthy anglophone enclave of Montreal that was renamed Westmount in 1895.

Here comes the car. Jump in and make yourself comfortable. It is occupied by two women; one is about forty and the other a girl of eighteen. They are French-Canadians and evidently earn their living by sewing, for each carries a number of coats on her arm, taking them to some shop in the city, probably. Not much pay do these poor women get for their toilsome work – stitch, stitch, stitching, day after day, and yet they seem tolerably happy and contented. It is well for some to be born unambitious.

Some one else is entering the car now – a portly man, with a red face and a merry, comfortable look. He looks around, as if to find somebody to talk to; but, as there is no one who is likely to prove companionable, he at last settles down into an unsettled state until the next passenger appears.

This happens to be a dark little fellow, whom the stout passenger greets with some genial expression in French. Most likely, he is an acquaintance, for they immediately strike up a voluble conversation, and, although I do not understand their language, their gestures and animated expression afford me no little amusement. The car stops again to let in a young lady and a little girl. The young lady has a face which makes one think of something good. Very few people possess a really good face, and it rests tired eyes to gaze upon this one. The little girl is about seven years old, so pretty and winning that I feel quite angry when the form of a young man intervenes between us, and I see that some newcomers have taken their places. These newcomers are a young man and his girl. What strikes me as remarkable about this couple is that the young girl appears to be very proud of her escort and the young man shows plainly that he appreciates himself, if no one else does. He belongs to that class of youths who are sometimes called "mashers"* – that is, they imagine they make a great impression on every girl. It is my opinion that he even thinks he has mashed a couple of typical old maids who are set up just opposite him. One of them, at any rate, does not seem to feel so. I hear her whisper to her companion that she does not know how any girl can be so silly as to be pleased and proud to be seen in the company of such a senseless fellow as the one in front of them. She says this rather spitefully, and I am inclined to say "Sour grapes" (inaudibly, of

* A masher is a man who forces unwanted attention on a woman.

course). But on second thoughts, I refrain from the uncharitable remark, because there does seem some truth in what she says about the young man, and how can we expect one whose heart has lain dormant for years to understand the feelings of a girl in love?

Who is this in dirty rags and a worn-out face, carrying a basket on her arm? Who is this that shrinks into a corner, as if she would willingly shrink out of the world? 'Tis a poor beggar girl, who has perhaps begged money enough to carry her weary limbs home to some miserable den. How wretched, how dull she looks! Life holds nothing bright for such a one. God alone knows what her life is. The sooner 'tis ended the better. Such misery is seen and passed by every day of our lives, and yet, how many think of doing anything to stop it. People preach and preach, but very few obey the old maxim which tells us to practice what we preach. There are some who honestly intend to do good, but when the tale comes for acting they'll let it pass, and chance after chance they miss in this way, until one day they wake up to the fact that their life is over and their dreams have come to naught.

Why is it that so many dream
  Of great deeds to be done?
Why is it that so many dream
  Of honours to be won?
Why is it that men dream and dream
  Till the sands of life are run?*

Why, ah, why is there so much planning and thinking and so little doing? But there is no time to puzzle out conundrums in a horse car, and as a man with his arms full of parcels, presenting a rather funny appearance, is struggling to get a seat near me, I break up the train of thought which is perplexing my brain and thought and interest myself in the fresh arrival. He has tumbled one of the parcels on the floor and a little stream of white sugar is oozing out. A couple of fashionably dressed ladies are just behind him, and I think it would be kindness on their part to let him know that he is losing his sugar, but they take their seats unconcernedly and allow the

* This unidentified poem may be by Eaton.

conductor to notify him of the fact. They choose a seat as far away as possible from the beggar girl, whom they regard with faces of disgust and, after they are comfortably settled, begin a conversation about some mission for which they are collecting contributions. They are rich ladies, good church members, charitable in many ways; but I am afraid they will not have the same position in the next world that they have in this.

The man with the parcels has a great deal of difficulty in preventing them from slipping off his knees, and the efforts he makes from time to time to keep them in place are very amusing. At last he produces a large red cotton handkerchief and ties them up. When this is done he heaves such a sigh of relief that everyone in the car knows he has at last found ease.

The car is pretty well filled now. A young person of the masculine gender, in passing me, has almost pushed me out of my seat – unintentionally, of course. I can see by his face that he is absent-minded, and not only absent-minded, but miserable, though why he should be miserable I don't know. Young, tolerably good-looking, dressed well and healthy, he ought to be happy enough. Perhaps he has been crossed in love. But I cannot tell. Some people would go through life with a gloomy countenance if they had all the blessings of heaven showered on them. It may be that those people who persist in looking miserable desire to be pitied. Well, we do pity them. We pity all those whose lot in life is hard, and we pity them because they require pity; but there is a deeper feeling than pity in our breasts for the unknown ones who hide their sorrow from the world's curious gaze, to whom pity gives positive pain when coming from those who do not understand what they are pitying; for we know that they who sorrow the most give no sign; that the saddest hearts are oft the bravest.

Here comes a man I know. At least, I know him by sight, and I have been told by different people that he is a crank. He is a pleasant looking old fellow, with a queer little way of looking at people, but I do not see anything cranky about him. I think the world is getting rather cranky on the subject of cranks. If a person happens to be a little different from the generality of this world's inhabitants, he or she is sure to be called a crank, or something very like that expressive word.

A fine-looking old lady, with white hair, has a seat between the fashionable ladies and the beggar girl. She does not shrink from coming into contact with a fellow being. Her benevolent face beams upon all around her, and the other ladies, with whom she is evidently acquainted, change their disagreeable looks to amiable ones by the force of her example.

A couple of business men are discussing politics in a corner. It seems to me to be a rather onesided discussion, as one of the men is not at all interested, which can easily be seen by the monosyllabic way in which he replies to his companion. He (the companion) is so enthusiastic that he does not notice the other man's indifference, but goes on discussing and arguing indefatigably.

Now, I have reached my destination and must say good-bye, hoping sometime to have the pleasure of another trip with you.

Edith Eaton. "Misunderstood: The Story of a Young Man."
Dominion Illustrated 1.20 (17 November 1888): 314.

There once lived a very amiable young man. The reason why I call him an amiable young man is because he had a great desire to make every woman he knew happy. How he could accomplish this was his thought night and day.

I

One evening, while deeply meditating upon this subject, an apparition appeared upon him. (Apparitions from the unknown world often appear to spiritual, noble-minded young men, even at the present day.) Well, this mysterious being, divining the thoughts which were puzzling the brain of my hero, addressed him in this wise: "Young man, your great and laudable ambition shall be gratified. A woman's happiness is comprised in one little word, and that word is LOVE. Do not all the great writers of the past and present endorse my opinion? Yea, even though her love be unrequited, she is happier for having felt that noble sentiment. Tennyson says:

'Tis better to have loved and lost

Than never to have loved at all.*

Therefore, young man, if you really wish to make them happy, you must have the power to win their love, which power I am able to give you," saying which the spirit laid its hands upon the young man's head and kept them there while he concluded his speech in the following words: "I do not say that those whose hearts you win will know nought but bliss. No, on the contrary, many will suffer deeply through you and, like the flowers wither and fade away, for love in some cases acts like a disease. You will, therefore, be able to create both happiness and misery, but the happiness will overbalance the misery. Young man, I confer upon you this power on one condition, which is, that you will keep your own heart free. If you do not, the spell will be broken and I will not be answerable for the consequences. Now, promise what I ask and your wish shall be granted."

The young man promised and the spirit vanished.

For some time after the spirit's visit the young man's life was very delightful. Wherever he went, young and old, rich and poor, ugly and pretty, clever and stupid, all kinds and conditions of women followed him with adoring eyes. Those only were not under the spell whose hearts were already given. Wherever [sic] he went to places of amusement, balls and parties, he could pick his partners from among the prettiest and cleverest girls. The daughters of the wealthiest men in the country were willing to become his brides. Servant girls waited on him with the greatest attention. If he happened to go into any store where a young lady served, she was sure to forget to ask for payment for his purchases, and he could have got his board free from any restaurant or place where girls were attendants, if he had so desired.

This was all very nice for a time, but gradually his crowd of devotees (about six hundred) began to show signs of jealousy and resentment toward one another, and some disagreeable scenes were the result, for, having so many, he did not have much time to devote to each one, and being, as stated before, an amiable dispositioned young man, it rather bothered him to think that he could not give each one all the attention she desired. However, he managed to pay his six hundred girls one visit each a week.

* From Tennyson's *In Memoriam A.H.H.*

A hundred visits a day. Sunday he kept as a day of recreation. Truly, he richly deserved it. To work for his living he had no need, for the presents he received from his worshippers, when sold, realized a large income.

Time rolled on, and as it rolled the beings whose happiness this young man was striving for rapidly increased in number. He could not leave his door but a swarm of young ladies would rush after him. Even beggars and crossing sweepers followed in his train. This was all very annoying, but for the good cause in which he was enlisted this heroic young fellow was willing to bear many things. What troubled his tender heart was that some of the girls began to show signs of sickness and fading away, He had to expect this. The spirit had told him as much. Besides, did not these girls experience a kind of melancholy pleasure which they would never have felt if it had not been for him?

II

Well, it came to pass that when about five hundred of the sweetest beings on earth were in a half dying state he fell in love himself, in spite of the promise which he had given the spirit. In spite of the fact that he would lose the power he possessed of casting a spell over the heart of every girl, he fell in love. The spirit had told him that when such a thing happened the consequences would be dreadful – and so it proved, for the young lady, not knowing that her love was returned, and thinking that she only possessed the six hundredth part of his heart, pined away and died. Because he had lost his heart the spell was broken. On her death bed she called her friends around her, many of them her comrades in love, and told them in thrilling tones that she was about to leave them, that there was a fire raging within her which had destroyed all her vital forces. When she had uttered those words her soul departed.

Immediately after her death a great change took place in her friends. They began to revive, and energy and life returned. Yes, fresh life seemed to have been given them, but she who had so lately been their companion lay stiff and cold, and as they looked at her, lying before them, they swore to be revenged on him who had been the cause of her untimely demise. A kind of instinct told them what it was, and who it was, that had made them so miserable, and they forgot that if they had been miserable, they had also been made happy.

The word REVENGE passed from girl to girl, and on the evening of the young lady's burial the churchyard was thronged with deeply aggrieved ones breathing threats and slaughter. Following timidly among the train of mourners, they espied the young man, and one of them, who had a good strong arm, laid hold of him, dragged him before the assembled company, and demanded what was to be done with one who was a destroyer of life, health and peace? The answer was given:

"He who destroys life, health and peace is a murderer. Therefore he must be hanged."

The sentence was no sooner given than it was executed. From a tree, whose branches were strong and elastic, the young man was hung. Hung by the neck by the hands of those for whom he had borne so much, and whose happiness had been his great aim in life. No one felt any pity for him. No one shed a tear. In fact, every one felt that if he could have died a hundred deaths it would not have been more than he deserved.

This was the reward of one who thought not of himself. This was the reward of years spent for the happiness of others. To be put to death by the hands of those very ones for whom he had suffered so many inconveniences, not even allowed to speak a word in his own defence – was not he a true martyr?

This story has in it a lesson for all amiable young men. It is to be hoped they will learn it by heart, for 'tis sad, indeed, to be, like my hero, MISUN-DERSTOOD.

Edith Eaton. "A Fatal Tug of War."
Dominion Illustrated 1.23 (8 December 1888): 362–3.

I

They were two young people with heads hot enough and hearts true enough to think the world well lost for love, and acting on that belief they had given up everything for its sweet sake. It is needless to make a long story of the sacrifices they had made, the troubles they had endured; but suffice it to say that love triumphed over every obstacle, and they were united at last.

Now, this will seem as if I had come to the end of my story; but that is not so. If I could have left them happy after the auspicious day which made them one, my story would then have been finished, but, alas, I did not. They cared not for the loss of friends; poverty had no terrors for them, for their hearts were young and hopeful; but there was something which tinged life with bitterness, which often estranged them, and which, sometimes, made all they had gone through for love's sake seem vain.

This can best be explained by saying plainly that they had both bad tempers, not bad in every way, irritable and vicious, but obstinate, proud and unyielding. Neither would give in, neither would own that they were in the wrong, and so it happened when any of the little inevitable disagreements which must occur in the course of life came about, and which, in most cases, soon blown over, with them, the general result was a period, sometimes short, sometimes long, of utter misery.

Yes, it was this unfortunate similarity of temper which caused nearly all their trouble, for if he thought he was in the right and she thought she was, it was a hard thing for either to speak the first word or yield in the slightest. Of course, love smoothed over many difficulties, but there came a day when even the Power of Love failed to steer them over [sic] the precipice down which they rushed.

II

They had had a slight quarrel over some trifling thing, just enough to cause them to part in the morning without the usual good bye, but their anger cooled as the day wore on; and although neither intended to beg forgiveness, or make up, as they say, yet both felt that there would be a tacit reconciliation when they met again in the evening.

He had promised some days before to take her to a grand concert that night, and as concerts and such pleasures had been few and far between since the day of their marriage, she was looking forward with glad eagerness to the event.

She had got ready his supper, dressed herself in a dress specially made for the occasion, done her hair up in the newest style, and after inspecting her tout ensemble in the glass for half an hour, turned away satisfied. All that was needed was some flowers, and these she was sure her husband would bring as he invariably did on such occasions.

He also was thinking of the concert, or rather he was thinking of the kind of flowers she would like to have, and on his way home he purchased a bunch of red and white carnations, her favorite flowers. The hour being late when he purchased them, and as it would take quite a little time to make up the bouquet, he instructed the girl who waited on him to have them sent to his house as soon as they were ready, as he had no time to wait for them.

He reached home expecting to find his wife in a pleasant humour, the little disagreement of the morning forgotten in anticipation of the prom-ised pleasure; but no pleasant face greeted him. Instead, a gloomy visaged young woman who might have been dumb for all she had to say, opened the door. His wife's quick eyes had seen at the first glance that he had brought her no flowers, and as it was his wont to bring them on occasions like this, she had conceived the idea that he was still angry with her, and if he had a right to be angry, she thought, surely she had too. Therefore it was no wonder that neither her face nor manner were as pleasant as her husband had expected, and he, noticing this, formed the same conclusion about her as she had about him, namely, that she was harbouring bitter feelings on account of the morning's quarrel. Both were in the wrong and both were too proud to speak or make the first advance.

A ring at the bell disturbed the silence which had fallen around them. Charlie (these two people were named respectively Charlie and Helen) went to the door. A thought had struck him. It was this. Since his wife was making herself so unwarrantably disagreeable he would exercise the right of a husband to punish his wife, and not let her have the carnations. Any way, he thought, it would be humbling himself to offer them to her while she was in her present mood. So he deposited the bouquet in the hall and went back to the dining-room. Of course his wife was curious to know who had been or what it was, but as he volunteered no information she did not condescend to ask for any.

Well, they finished their supper, and when the time came started for the concert. Probably they would not have gone at all only their tickets were bought and they were not in a position which would allow of them throwing such things away.

As they passed through the hall, he took the flowers from where he had laid them, and she, seeing what it was he held in his hand, smiled to herself, thinking that after all he had only been teasing her by keeping them back and that he was surely going to give them to her now. In fact, she commenced to feel quite sorry for her own behaviour and would have spoken pleasantly to him had he not worn a very forbidding expression. She waited sometime, but as he did not offer to resign the coveted bouquet, her repentance first turned to surprise, and then silent indignation. So in this state these two silly miserable human creatures walked on side by side until they reached the concert hall.

The concert was very good, and had it not been for their unfortunate quarrel, they might have enjoyed it exceedingly. As it was, they hardly heard anything, but, for all that, when the chief singer's second song was finished, Charlie left no doubt in the minds of the audience that he had some appreciation of music, for he rose from his seat, deliberately, walked to the platform and before his wife's eyes handed the singer his bouquet of flowers.

What evil spirit tempted him to do this I do not know, but he thought he had not been treated fairly and was in a mood to do anything to provoke her who had treated him in that way.

What did Helen think of his act? The loss of the bouquet was really nothing much to her, but she felt that it had been given away on purpose to exasperate her, and as "Revenge is sweet, especially to a woman," the desire to pay him back in some way rose within her breast, so when he returned to her side, with defiant eyes she looked in his face and told him that the seat he had vacated a moment before was engaged. "Nonsense," said he, attempting to move the cloak which she had laid on the chair. "This seat is engaged" she repeated, and there was that in her voice which warned him to desist from trying to regain his seat. He felt uncomfortable, for he was attracting attention standing there, so with slow step and an ashamed sense of looking ridiculous, he was obliged to walk around the room in search of an unengaged seat. He found one after considerable trouble, just a little in front of his wife, and there they sat, almost in view of one another, both unhappier than they had ever been before in their lives.

It was a ridiculously pathetic situation which their tempers had placed them in. The bride and bridegroom of a few months sitting apart at a public concert with hearts full of angry and bitter feelings towards one another. And such a little thing had aroused these feelings. It was so trivial that I almost think they had forgotten how their quarrel commenced. Unbridled passions are sure to bring their own punishment, and these two from childhood up had never been known to yield or to forgive before they were forgiven, and thus it happened "When Greek met Greek then came the tug of war."*

The way they were acting now was disgracefully childish, not befitting a man or woman, and the only excuse that can be given for them is, that they were little more than children in both years and experience. Perhaps, after they had lived together for years, Time might have changed things and they might have grown the most placid old couple that ever lived on the face of the earth. But fate had decided that was not to be.

III

The concert came to an end at last. One of them now would have to make some kind of advance. She waited a moment for him as she could not go home alone at that time of the night. Why did he not hurry and go to her then? If he had all would have been right; but he did not hasten himself, although he intended to go in the end. He kept her waiting, for had she not sent him away from her before the whole audience? This rankled in his mind.

But she was not in a mood to stand any trifling, and just as he was going to come to her she started for the door, and before he could get to her side, was out amidst the throng of people. Blaming himself for his folly, Charlie rushed after, but the crush was so great that there was no chance of him getting near her for some time. He could see his poor little

* Attributed to the Greek poet Homer.

wife struggling on before, and a deep sense of shame for the unmanly way he had acted took possession of him. Love triumphed now over every other feeling, and all his thought was to get near and speak to her.

There was no such sentiment in Helen's mind. She felt more sinned against sinning. If her father and mother and all who had loved and petted her in the days gone by could see her now, she thought, could see the way her husband was treating her. She would never forgive him for this, never forgive him as long as she lived.

IV

They are out in the street, and having past [*sic*] the glare of the lamps which surround the concert hall, are quite in the dark. He strains his eyes to catch a glimpse of his wife's form. They are only about a hundred yards apart and the intervening space is a blank to him. He has reached a crossing. A carriage is returning home at a furious rate. The sound of wheels is muffled for a moment, during which moment an agonizing groan is heard. The crowd turns back, at least part of the crowd, the other part presses forward. Helen turns back, turns back with the ever morbid crowd which must throng around the place where an accident happens. She catches a glimpse of a manly form lying crushed and limp, and with a cry which rings sharp and clear above all the other noises of the night, she rushes forward. It is her husband that is lying there and spattered with blood. Her Charlie, her boy. He is dead, there is not a spark of life in that mutilated young body of his. They try to draw her back, but she heeds them not. She lays her head on his breast.

What is the use of trying further to describe that scene? What is the use of trying to express in words her terrible grief? Imagination may conceive the pitiful spectacle, and all who have hearts and have known what it is to lose a loved one, may perhaps, in a dim kind of way, understand the sorrow of this poor young wife; but only in a dim kind of way double their sorrow or treble it, and it would never reach the depth that hers had. Grief bordering on madness, that was what had taken possession of her. They tried to take her from him, but could not. She wound her arms tight around the neck of her husband and refused to move. But the body had to be taken away, and finding that no kind of persuasion had any effect, force

was used to separate them. Thus, they were torn asunder, never to be
united on this earth.

V

He was dead and they buried him. She, crazy with grief, was taken back to
her girlhood's home, the home which she had left for his sake. Grief, inten-
sified by remorse, preyed on her mind, and after a violent illness she settled
down into a gloomy weak-minded creature whose every hope seemed
blighted, whose life light was quenched. Her morbid mind forever dwelt
on their last day together. She would think over the quarrel, over every
word he had said and blame herself bitterly.

You, who have read this story, will know that she had been no more in
the wrong than he, in fact, the blame lay more on his side; but he was dead
and she was living, and 'tis the living that suffer remorse, not the dead.

This young couple were so childish. The quarrel was so trivial that their
tragic end may seem strange, but "such is life;" we know not what a little
thing may lead to.

If either of these two had had a little less of that stubborn false pride
which causes so much trouble in the world, they would have returned
home from that concert as happy as two birds. His death would have been
averted and she would have been spared long years of anguish.

Edith Eaton. "The Origin of A Broken Nose."
Dominion Illustrated 2.45 (11 May 1889): 302.

So you want to know how I got my nose broken?

Well, it was broken through a woman and a newspaper paragraph.
Seems rather queer, doesn't it? but it is true, nevertheless. Yes; a woman
and a newspaper paragraph caused the disfigurement of my most prominent feature. The woman was the direct and the newspaper paragraph the
indirect cause. A woman's at the bottom of everything, you say? Yes, that
she is. Tell you all about it? All right, I will, as it is not such a long story,
and I like to make myself agreeable to folks.

When I was a young man, and all alone in the world, I lived in M—, one of the chief cities in Canada. There is a peculiarity about the streets of M— which I would like to mention, but am afraid to on account of certain little unpleasantries which might arise. However, I will say this much about them – they are so interesting that the M—ers find them a never-failing topic of conversation. The elders of the city meet within the gates and talk about their streets; fathers, mothers, brothers and sisters have family conclaves about them, and strangers visiting the city make a point of seeing the streets if they see nothing else.

Well, as I said before, I lived in this favoured city. I was a clerk in a dry goods store, worked hard, and had very little time to spend in, and very little money to spend for, recreations.

One dreary evening, in the early part of December, about 8 o'clock, I was sitting in my room bemoaning the hard fate which had left me fatherless, motherless, sisterless, brotherless, and, worse than all, girlless. If you don't understand what this means, let me explain to you that once upon a time I had had a girl – a girl that I used to visit regularly three times a week – a girl with the sweetest blue eyes and softest brown hair – a girl on whom I used to spend all my spare money in candies and ice cream, and for whose sake I wore a battered old hat for three months when I needed a new one badly, thereby making myself a laughing-stock, in order that I might take her to see a play, but who, alas! had ungratefully and heartlessly thrown me over for another fellow who had intentions – at least that is what the girl's father told me. As to me, I did not then, and do not now, know what intentions are.

I was sitting in my room, ruminating on all my troubles, when my eye fell upon an evening paper which lay on the table before me, and the following paragraph attracted my attention:—

"Young men of M—, the time has come for you to distinguish yourselves. We are sure you are all dying to do so, and now is your chance. Do you not live in M—, a city famed far and near for its peculiar streets – streets which are so constructed that they afford the gallant youths of the nineteenth century every opportunity to prove that there are as many true and chivalrous knights now-a-days as there were in the days of King Arthur – and at this season of the year are not these streets covered with ice, upon which many a fair maiden may slip, thereby suffering great and serious loss and damage, and is it not the duty of the stronger sex to protect and help the weaker? Knowing this, do you not think it would be not only a duty but a pleasure for you to sally out in goodly numbers, station yourselves at the corners or wherever the walking may be dangerous, and be on the look-out to help any unfortunate maiden who may chance to come to grief?"

There was a great deal more to the same effect, but I will not inflict it upon you. I pondered over this article long and earnestly and at last came to the philosophic conclusion that it was no earthly use to sit moping over a girl who showed herself to be utterly devoid of sense when she threw over a man like me, and that it would, perhaps, be a good scheme to try and get a little pleasure out of life, while, at the same time, doing what was, obviously, my duty.

Now, I am a man of action, and when an idea enters my mind, I generally carry it out at once. I looked at the clock, and seeing it was only about half past eight, put on my cap and great coat and hurried into the street, bound to do or die.

I soon found a nice, slippery corner, and there I stationed myself. People passed to and fro, and I helped along a couple of old ladles and a lame gentleman, and had the privilege of preserving a drunken man's head from coming in contact with the pavement, but I noticed that all the girls were light and sure of foot. Besides, most of them had escorts, so I had really very little chance to exercise my gallantry.

I was just beginning to think that the man who wrote that paragraph was a humbug, when I espied, advancing timidly, a solitary female. I could see that she was pretty, young and well dressed, and thought I to myself: "Here is a first-rate chance She will be sure to slip when she passes this place, for she has ventured out without rubbers, and I shall have the satisfaction of knowing that this night's weary corner waiting has not been all in vain; that I have saved one pretty girl from an ignominious tumble."

The girl tottered along on the slippery sidewalk, and I waited, expecting every minute to have to go to her assistance. When she was about a foot from where I stood, her body appeared to me to bend slightly forward. I thought she was going – I really did. I sprang towards her. Then – I felt my feet slip from under me, and, with a crash, I fell nose forward, the girl, for all her tottering, getting past the perilous place in safety.

Words cannot express the terrible sensations which ran through every nerve as I lay prostrate on the ground, seeing nothing, hearing nothing, oblivious to all sights and sounds.

"Now, this just serves you right, young man," said the harsh, angry voice of a policeman, as he pulled me roughly to my feet. "What do you mean by molesting peaceable citizens? I have noticed you for nearly an hour standing at the corner, trying your best to annoy the passers-by."

I did not answer, because I could not. I stood motionless where he had planted me, the blood running from my nose.

"Come with me to the station," he said, taking hold of my arm, but, before I had time to move, the girl through whom I had come to grief, and who had turned back, with other passers-by, to view me in my distress, walked fiercely up to the policeman, and says she: "What! take him to the police station? No, you never shall. He is a hero. He –" She could say no more, for, either angry passion at the indignity I had been subjected to, or pitiful compassion for my miserable state, choked her utterance; but she looked like a tigress bereft of her young. (Isn't that the orthodox way of describing a female in a passion?)

Surely I knew that voice. Was it – could it be – my girl, Amelia, who stood there, with flaming cheeks and indignant eyes? Yes, it was – it was.

"No, you shan't take him," she repeated. "He knows me, saw me coming along, thought I would slip, and in trying to save me from falling, fell himself."

The policeman looked from one to the other. "Oh!" said he, "That's it, is it?" He evidently had his own views about the matter, but Amelia's eloquence had some effect, for he released his hold of my arm and allowed me to walk off with her.

So that is how I broke my nose and got back my girl, for Amelia threw over the fellow with intentions, and I again basked in her smiles, under the influence of which I unintentionally married her some months after.

To this day she confidently believes that I knew she was coming down the street, and waited there purposely to help her, and I think it wise not to shake that belief.

Though my nose has made me a man of mark, there are times when, standing before my glass, viewing that appendage, I say naughty things about the writer of that newspaper article and the woman for whose sake I slipped not only on the ice, but into a noose. But those times are few and far between, and if I were to meet that same man, when I am in good humour, I would shake his hand heartily and thank him for giving me the privilege of calling the dearest little woman in the world my wife.

Edith Eaton. "Robin."
Dominion Illustrated 2.51 (22 June 1889): 394–5.

I

Robin was born in Montreal, a beautiful Canadian city on the River St. Lawrence. Robin's parents were poor, hard-working people, respected and liked by all their humble friends. They had a little home which was kept comfortable by dint of hard work and frugality, and in which, protected by a father and mother's care, Robin spent the first five years of his life. He was a bright, interesting child, nervous and delicate, perhaps, but withal showing signs of rare intelligence. A little sister, two years younger than himself, named Alice, was his playmate, and the sister and brother were more than usually attached to one another.

'Twas a happy little household until the father died suddenly of heart disease, leaving his wife and children destitute, for his wages had been small, and though the mother was a careful woman and economized in every way possible, they had just been able to live upon what the father had earned, and not a cent was saved.

It was a sad thing for the poor woman, after the first bitterness of her grief was over, to realize that not only was she bereft of her husband, but that her little ones were homeless and without food unless she herself put her shoulder to the wheel and procured it for them.

In her girlhood days, before her marriage, she had earned her living as a type-setter in a printing office, and she remembered now, with a thankful feeling, that she had that trade to fall back upon.

Before, however, commencing work, the poor woman applied to her husband's late employers for a little aid in order that she might be able to pay the rent of the house they were living in, so that the landlord might perhaps suffer them to remain where they were comfortably settled, instead of driving her with her little boy and girl to seek miserable rooms in a low part of the city, where she would be obliged to go, being unable to pay for better quarters. But the men for whom her husband had toiled for many a year, rich though they were, gave not a thought to the widowed and fatherless, and with stony faces and stonier hearts turned from the supplicant who asked, for the sake of her children, for aid in her distress. They demanded, in icy tones, the reason why she and her husband had been so improvident; why they had not saved. Saved! With the miserable little pittance they had given him? She laughed hysterically at that hardhearted folly. "Oh, well," they at last said, patronizingly, "although we cannot think of giving you money when you are a strong, able-bodied woman, able to keep yourself, and when there are so many charities which we give donations to, and on whose list of subscribers our names are prominently set forth, we will use our influence to help you in putting your children in some institution."

The mother thanked them, but refused the proffered aid, and with sore heart returned to her children. She was poor, but could not part with her only treasures. She found a room in as respectable a part of the city as she could manage to pay for, and then commenced for her the routine of a working woman's life.

Although Robin and Alice were but three and five years of age, she was obliged to leave them alone all day while at her work. And the little things would wait patiently during the long hours until they heard her footstep on the stairs, at six o'clock, when they would both rush pell-mell to the door of the room in which they were confined and greet their mother. Ah! thankful, indeed, was the mother, when she came home tired and worn out, for their kisses and caresses.

But there came a day – a never-to-be-forgotten day – when, on her return from work, a sight met her eyes which broke the brave heart. Her boy lay on the bed, with eyes vacant, from which intelligence had fled forever. It was the result of a fright.

There was a stove in the room and a fire had been lighted in it that day, and Robin, in lifting the top off it to put on more fuel, had somehow caught fire. He was but slightly burnt, as the landlady, a woman of courage and presence of mind, happening to be in the room at the moment, managed to extinguish the flames before they had time to seriously hurt his body; but the delicate, nervous system of the child had received such a shock that he lost consciousness, and when they managed to open his eyes they saw that reason was fled.

The doctor was leaning over Robin when his mother came in, and going up to her he told her, in a few pitying words, what had befallen her boy. Stunned by her great misfortune, she said not a word, shed not a tear, but when they led her to the bed, when she saw her little child's vacant eyes, she turned to those around, the sympathizing but dispensable witnesses of her sorrow, and bade them leave her alone.

Then, when alone, she fell on her knees beside the bed, and for over an hour slow tears fell from her eyes and rolled unheeded down her cheeks.

Her faith and courage were gone; her heart broken. Cheerfully had she toiled for her little ones, for the thought that some day they would reward her had lightened her labour. But now her bright dreams were dashed to the ground, for her boy, upon whom she had rested almost all her hopes, was worse than dead.

She came out of that room a sad-faced, broken-spirited woman. She went back to the dreary routine of her work with every aspiration crushed. Mental depression affected her health, and bad food, sleepless nights, trouble and toil combined caused her to fall an easy victim to a contagious fever which was raging just then in that part of the city where she lived. She left the printing office one afternoon, sick to death, for she had borne up as long as it was possible to do so, and four days after her body was carried to Mount Royal Cemetery, whilst the piteous cry of "Oh! mamma, mamma! I want my mamma!" of her little daughter brought tears to the eyes of all those who heard it.

II

Alone in the world now were Robin and Alice, save for one relative, a brother of their father's, who immediately, on hearing of their mother's death, came and took the children to live with him. Far better if they had been entirely alone, for then they would have had the protection of some charitable institution. This uncle was a bad and dissolute man, whose abode was a den in the lowest part of the city, and who made a livelihood in ways unknown to honest men. What end he had in view when he took the children of a respectable brother, towards whom he had always cherished a bitter animosity, to live with him, will be shown hereafter.

III

A boy and a girl were trudging along one of the dusty thoroughfares of the city of Montreal. Evening is coming on and the children look tired and dejected, as well they may, for they have been out all day, wandering around the streets. A basket, full of odd bits of things, which the little girl carries, proclaims them to be beggars. It must be quite heavy, for the child leans to one side and stops every now and then, but for all that she keeps ahead of her brother, who is lagging along aimlessly a couple of yards behind.

It is Robin and Alice who are thus wearily trudging through the dusty streets. They have learnt a trade; that trade is begging. A very remunerative trade to their uncle when practised by his little nephew and niece.

Their uncle has a family, consisting of his wife and a grown son and daughter. The son was as dissolute and desperate a character as his father, and the mother and daughter were two females of the most depraved type, and for these wretches the children begged day after day, and many a cent did their pitiful young faces draw from the pockets of kind-hearted people, who would not have felt disposed to give to those who were hardened in crime.

Amidst scenes of degradation and vice were these little ones living, and 'twas only their youth and innocence which kept them uncontaminated. Their companions were outcasts from society, at war with the world, and they vented the bitterness of their hearts upon these children, who were too ignorant and helpless to resist them. Hard words and blows did Robin and Alice receive, often without any cause, and the poor little things had got so used to such treatment that they scarcely knew what kindness was. This made them cling to each other with a devotion which was almost pathetic. The boy especially, on account of his misfortune, was knocked around, and often his uncle and that uncle's friends would use him as a butt for their coarse jokes. At such times he would crawl away for protection or sympathy to his little sister, to whom their cruelty caused the greatest distress, lay his head in her lap and weep like a baby, for idiot though he was, he was sensitive in some ways.

If the children had been older and had more sense, they might have escaped from their tormentors, but, as it was, they did not even think of such a thing; so day after day they went out to beg from door to door, and it is on a hot day in June that we see them trudging denwards, and take up their history, which is to be so brief and sad.

The sun shone hot on their heads and the dust rose from the road, and down the street they went until they reached the hovel in which they lived.

They show what they have in the basket, what money they have in a small leather bag which the boy carries. Their uncle and his wife look greedily over everything, and, finding that the children have done unusually well, in an unwonted fit of kindness the woman tells them that they can spend the next day as they like.

The little girl delightedly whispers the news to her brother, and a vacant smile creeps over his face, for, though almost devoid of understanding, he seems to know by intuition she is pleased, and when she is happy or pleased, he is also. He is perfectly harmless, is Robin, and, except for the vacant stare in his eyes and the listlessness of his manner, one would never know of the terrible cloud that darkened his life. He is very childish, and, although ten years old, is treated like a baby by his eight-year-old sister. She looks after him with an almost motherly solicitude.

After a scanty supper the children creep to bed and do not wake till the morning sunbeams, which have made their way into their uncurtained bedroom, dance upon their faces and force them to open their eyes. Then they put on their ragged clothes and leave the house, the other inmates of which are in a state of stupefaction on account of the drunken orgies in which they had indulged the night before.

Robin and Alice wend their way to Jacques Cartier wharf and wait around there till the boat for St. Helen's Island is ready to take on passengers.* They enter the boat and in a very few minutes are on the island. (They had brought home over two dollars the night before, out of which their uncle had allowed them to keep ten cents each, and the children who had often longed to see the island were thus afforded the opportunity.)

It was a perfect day – one of those days wherein every hour is bright and sunny. All clouds seemed to have rolled from the sky. And the river – oh, the river! it sparkled and rippled so; it looked so enchanting that death in its bosom seemed almost to be desired.

And the children who had stepped out of their dark den into the morning's brightness were as happy as it was possible for them to be. The pure air, the sight of the river, and, above all, a sense of freedom put fresh life into them. They scrambled around, enjoying everything in a quiet kind of way, for the children of misery and poverty give not that boisterous freedom to their mirth in which happier and more fortunate ones express their feelings. Living among sights which can better be imagined than described – begging from door to door – had quenched Robin's and little Alice's natural childish exuberance; but this holiday spent on the island and river was like a glimpse of heaven to them. Ah, heaven was very near to one of them that day, though they knew it not.

Tired at last with walking around, they go down to the beach where some boats were lying, for the use of pleasure seekers who might wish to hire one. Ignorant that they who wish to use the boats must pay for them, the children seat themselves in one and Robin takes the oars and paddles out into the river.

There was no one to watch these poor little things. If the boatman had caught them he might, perhaps, have used hard language to them, but there was no one to warn them – no kindly father or mother to tell them that they were in mischief and danger. The novelty of their occupation charmed them; the influence of the air and sunshine exhilarated them; the boat glided on smoothly and floated gradually away from the island with

* Also known as Ile Ste-Hélène, St Helen's Island was made a public park in 1874.

those two little friendless souls, and there were none to miss them. No cry, save the cry of the boatman for his boat, would be raised if they should never return.

Robin scarcely knew how to use the oars, but the current carried them on smoothly and gently, and there is no danger if the children will only keep still. After a while, Robin stops rowing and they sit still, enjoying the unusual peacefulness which surrounds them.

"I am thirsty," says Alice, suddenly leaning over the side of the boat and filling her little hands with water. She leans too much over the side, she loses her balance, the boat rolls over. When it recovers its equilibrium Robin is sitting in a rigid position clutching the sides, but the water has already resumed its ordinary placid ripple over the spot where Alice's golden head has gone down.

The accident has been noticed by a man on the shore, who quickly rows out to Robin and brings him back to the island. He had seen the boat turn over, but he had no idea that there had been two children in it. The people cluster around them, but it is not until Robin, who has been sitting motionless since the accident, stretches out his arms towards the river, calling "Alice, Alice," that they understand that his little companion, who had so lately been rowing around the island with him, is now under the water.

Then they take Robin back to the city, but Alice is not found until the sun, which is now high in the heavens, has risen twice.

IV

We will skip a period of about eight months. It is the month of February and the citizens of Montreal are holding a carnival. It is the night of the storming of the Ice Palace.*

Pushing his way amongst the crowd which has congregated on Dominion Square is a poorly clad boy of about twelve years of age. This boy is Robin. It is a cold night and he wears no overcoat, and his head is scarcely protected by an imitation lambskin cap, from which the lining has been

---

* Beginning in 1883, Montrealers cut giant blocks of ice from the frozen St Lawrence River and constructed ice palaces for their Lenten *carnaval*.

torn. He does not seem to heed the cold nor the people who stare curiously at him. He is looking at the Ice Palace. That is the sight which attracts all eyes. The hands, brains and hearts of the Montrealers have made it something more like a dream of fairyland than the work of man, and under the quiet stars stands a most wondrous palace – a palace which has risen from the River St. Lawrence, for every block of crystal ice was cut from the bosom of that noble river and fashioned by Canadian art into a stately edifice, which strangers from far and near throng to view. St. Lawrence, thy child is worthy to share thy worldwide fame!

But it is not the beauty of the palace that Robin is gazing at. His eyes are fixed on a certain block of ice at the centre and almost at the very top of the Ice Palace.

The storming with fireworks has commenced, and the boy gets as near to it as he possibly can, still watching that huge gleaming crystal with a rapt look in his eyes. What strange fancies fill the boy's head as he stands there? What has caused him to take such a strange interest in the Ice Palace when he was wont to take no interest in anything? It is this: Because he fancies that his little sister is in that glittering, cold, fairy-like habitation; that in one of those blocks of ice which were hewn out of the river in which his sister was drowned she lives. The fireworks glance swiftly around the place where he fancies he sees her. The boy clasps his hands and weeps for fear that they will touch her. "Oh! my little sister. Don't hurt my little sister!" he cries. In his fancy she is beckoning to him, and his spirit is almost transported to her side.

To the idiot boy Alice's death only removed her to another place. He had seen Alice drown; had seen her go down into the waters, and his imagination pictured her living under them; and while the summer had lasted, many an hour had he spent by the river gazing intently into its depths.

Then when winter came, when the Ice Palace was built, when he had seen them building it with ice cut from the river, he conceived the idea that his sister had been taken out in one of the blocks of ice.

Standing amongst the crowd, watching the fireworks play around the Ice Palace, a terrible fear took possession of him that those burning, flying lights would strike her, that they would annihilate her altogether. It was Alice they were firing at he thought. He watched intently. Suddenly a rocket struck the place where it seemed, to his excited fancy, his little sister was confined. Then a whole storm of many-coloured lights was directed to that place.

With a hoarse cry the boy sprang from his crouching position. He could see no more. Away from the crowd he ran. Down the city streets he fled. Whither? No one knew, but he was never again seen alive by any Montrealers.

V

'Twas a pitiful sight. A little lad lying dead on the sandy beach of St Helen's Island. He was lying face downwards when found, yet withal so childishly sad that many a tear rose to the eyes of the onlookers. Ah! few tears had been called forth while he lived and needed love and pity. He had received hard words and blows – been kicked almost as it were into the other world – but none could say a word now, for the majesty of Death was on his brow and nought could again disturb him.

'Tis our poor little friend Robin. Where he had been, how he had lived, since the winter, none knew and none will ever know; but they surmised that he must have known he was dying of a mortal sickness and had managed to crawl to the place where he had seen the one little sister who had been the whole world to him disappear from his sight. There he had lain him down and died silently and unseen, only, perhaps, the loving eyes of those whose home is paradise, watched over his last moments, and their outstretched arms caught his spirit as it escaped from its earthly habitation.

Edith Eaton. "Albemarle's Secret."
Dominion Illustrated 3.68 (19 October 1889): 254.

Albemarle's* eyes were dreamy and his cheek was pale; dark were the locks which waved above his noble brow; tall was his form and slender as a willow and small and shapely were his hands and feet. A fascinating

---

* Albemarle Street in London's Mayfair neighbourhood is linked with Oscar Wilde.

melancholy pervaded his countenance, and his utterances were tinged with the gentle sadness of one who has experienced some strange mysterious sorrow, the memory of which darkens his life and keeps aloof all happiness. When he sang (he was addicted to music) the sweetness of his tones were only rivalled by their sadness. He was a poet – a genius. The world did not acknowledge him as such, but

"Deep in his own heart that tender secret dwelt."*

Being all this, who can blame him if he happened to be rather conscious of the fact that many a fair one viewed him with admiring eyes. Yes, he was well aware of the fact, but he turned from them all, for, thought he, I will not bow down before the shrine of any but a rare and intelligent being, one in whom I shall recognize her who was formed to be my counterpart, one who will comprehend all the undefined longings of my soul, one to whom I can pour out all my ardent love in verse, one who will be able to accompany my spirit in all its ethereal flights. Such a one will I seek out, and when I find her, she, and she only, shall be my bride.

So he wandered around in search of this rare intelligent being, and it happened that strolling through a lonely wood one day, he came across a lady reclining in a sylvan bower. She was in the first bloom of youth and beautiful as a dream. An acquaintance was formed, and our poet discovered that this was she whom his soul had longed for. Ah, thought he, that evening before retiring for slumber, at last I have found the one whose mind is elevated enough to hold converse with mine. In the romantic solitude of the woods did our eyes first behold one another. Fit place for our souls to meet. Kindred sympathies stirred our hearts, and then Albemarle fell to wondering, the while gazing dreamily at the starry, mystic heavens, if those sweet sympathies would ever rivet their hearts together.

So mused he. And she – alas! That I should have to tell this tale!

Three golden weeks have sunk into the ocean of time, golden weeks to our poet, for he has visited the lady of his love every day, haunted her walks and accompanied her when driving. To her he has read volumes of verse; to her he has sung song after song; to her he has dropped many a dark hint of the mysterious sorrow which is eating his heart away.

* A loose quotation of a passage from Lord Byron's *The Corsair: A Tale*.

Well, one halcyon day in the month of June, Albemarle proceeded to
the abode of his divine, carrying with him a roll of verses, the emanations
of his genius which he intended to pour into her ear before leaving.

He found her alone. (Other friends always retreated when Albemarle
put in an appearance.) She greeted him as sweetly as usual, but in her eyes
gleamed a strange light as they fell upon the roll of verses, and her voice
trembled a little (for what reason, we don't know), as she said, " Oh, sir,
I have a favour to ask of you."

Albemarle's romantic soul thrilled with ecstasy at these words. "What
is it?" he said, "only speak the word. I am your true knight, and I will
move heaven and earth to accomplish anything you may desire." "It is
this," she replied, "and as you are fond of poetry, I will put my request
in verse. Listen:

My other friends have left me,
  The false ones and the true;
Won't you follow their example,
  Won't you please to say adieu?"*

Albemarle stood transfixed for a moment. The hair rose upon his head
in horror. His eyes rolled wildly and he clutched at a table for support. At
last issued from his lips in hollow tones, the words, "'Tis what I should
have expected. Alas, my sad fate." Then recovering himself, he added in a
cool, calm tone, "I do your bidding, madam, I go, never to return. This is
but an additional burden to the secret sorrow which is gnawing my heart
away. However, none shall know my grief. Like Byron, I can say:

Here's a sigh for those that love me,
  Here's a smile for those that hate,
And whatever sky's above me,
  Here's a heart for any fate."†

Then came this cruel reply: "Ah, no sir, rather:

Here's a whine for those that love me,
  Here's a scowl for those that hate,

---

* This unidentified verse is probably by Eaton.
† From Byron's "To Thomas Moore."

For whatever food I swallow,
   Indigestion is my fate."
There was a terrible stillness in the room. A door was heard to open, then close. Our poet was gone. He was never heard of more.

She had discovered what the strange mysterious sorrow, the outward signs of which had possessed such a potent charm for many of her sex, was, the discovery had the broken the charm.

This was the secret. Albemarle suffered from Dyspepsia.

Edith Eaton. "Lines."
Dominion Illustrated 4.92 (5 April 1890): 223.

Amidst the worry and the strife
Of a toilsome city life
My tired eyes with gladness view
The wondrous dome of azure hue,
Which hovers o'er me, like a sea
Whose waves are cloudlets, floating free.

Ah! If I could float away
On these fleecy waves, till day
Darkened into night – and then,
With the stars, look down on men,
'Twould be bliss; yes, bliss divine.
But that bliss can ne'er be mine,
For I'm but of mortal birth
And am pinioned to the earth.

Yet, the radiant skies of dawn
Will not let me hopeless mourn.
And in late noon's rosy mist,
Which the sun has gently kissed,

In the aerial forms which rise,
Find I many a sweet surprise.

Is aught below so vast, so grand,
Unspoiled by art, untouched by hand?
Is aught below so fair and free
As yon blue sky which smiles on me?

But, 'tis night – 'tis night I love;
Soft, caressing, like a dove.
Then doth shine the mystic moon,
Then the stars peer through night's noon.
'Tis then I feel in tender mood,
'Tis then I am, if ever, good.
My sad soul seems more pure and free
Under its solemn canopy,
'Tis then my wild and struggling mind
Doth burst the bonds which fain would bind;
'Tis then deep, serious thoughts arise
Thoughts of a world beyond the skies.

Then let them sing of trees and flowers,
Singing birds and leafy bowers;
I – I raise my song more high,
And sing the ever-glorious sky.
Be it dark or be it bright
It is e'er my chief delight,
For its beauty cannot fade
Till Death wraps me in its shade.

Edith Eaton. "In Fairyland."
Dominion Illustrated 5.120 (18 October 1890): 270.

The moon is shining with tranquil splendour and the space between heaven and earth is filled with a soft luminous dimness. There is an influence in the air which will not allow us to slumber, and led by an ever active sympathy with Nature, we wend our way to some well known sylvan haunt where none but invisible people dare intrude, and where we can muse and dream to our hearts' content in the moonlight.

The bewitching, bewildering lovely moonlight. How can we describe it! Let us dip the tip of our pen into its shimmering radiance and perchance we may catch a beam of inspiration. Yet no, such fascinating sprites as moonbeams are not to be caught by aught that is human, for just as we think we have captured one it slips noiselessly away, and so it is the whole time "Catch me if you can!" "Catch me if you can!" until at last we give up our daring attempt.

See how the shadows vary on the green sward as the breeze moves the leaves and transmits the moonbeams from one to the other. Look how the graceful boughs are touched with silver one moment; the next, fade into the night. Those tall trees whose waving tops are bathed in moonbeams remind us of great men whose heads are crowned with glory whilst their lives are hidden in gloom; and there winds a dark forest glade through which the moonlight glimmers, gliding hither and thither like the most ethereal of spirits. In some places where the foliage is not so dense, we can see the forms of maple leaves fantastically outlined on mounds of illumined moss. Let us wander through this glade and think on the eyes that saw too clearly, the lips that spoke too truly, and the hearts that loved too dearly.

There is a fragrance in the air breathed by the herbs and grasses. Complete stillness surrounds us. Even the ordinary noises of the night, the faint murmur of summer insects, the stirring of leaves by the wind, the peevish twitter of some restless young bird. Even these seemed hushed. Our eyes

are heavy. Let us close them and people the solitude in which we are en-
veloped with the fairy folk. Our own dear fairies. They are always welcome,
for they come to us singing:

Wouldst thou have us pensive
  Or wouldst thou have us gay,
Sing a song of gladness
  Or a mournful lay?
Tell us which is sweeter,
  Sad or merry metre,
We will try to please, Sir,
  We thy will obey.

And whether we are merry or sad, their lutes are attuned to the rhythm
of our heart. Here they come, wafted to our view on a sheaf of moonlight.
But to-night they tell no tale, sing no song for us, for they are mourning
the return to earth from fairyland of one who was beloved by them for
many years. List to the sweet notes of their lament:

Inspired by hopeless sorrow,
We waft to thee a strain,
For thou art wandering lonely
Where all our love is vain.
The moon still shines as o'er thy head
It shone so long ago;
But tears bedim its radiance now
For our hearts are full of woe.

Hast thou forgotten fairyland –
The maze of golden light,
The flower-gemmed bowers, the crystal founts,
The skies for ever bright –
Save when the evening shadows crept
Athwart the roseate blue,
And the pale Moon whispered to the Sun:
Say to the world, Adieu?

Hast thou forgotten how the stars
Were thine own "Evening Glories."
Or how their "poetry" taught to thee
The loveliest of love stories?
Ah! then thy spirit leapt beyond
The bounds of human gladness;
But now it soundeth o'er and o'er
The depths of human sadness.

Hast thou forgotten how the peace
Of the eternal sky
Enwrapped thy soul, whilst winds sang low
A soothing lullaby?
Oh! sweet it was to rest secure
With many a fairy friend;
But now thy head unresting lies
And peace is at an end.

Hast thou forgotten how the voice
Of Morning, fresh and clear,
Called thee across the mountains high,
And we, who loved thee dear,
Accompanied thy joyous flight,
And hand in hand we flew
To peaks of beauty and delight,
Known to the free and true.

For thou wert like the summer breeze
That kissed thy happy brow
And sang and wandered where thou wouldst –
Oh! for that freedom now! –
And thou wert true to thine own heart –
For 'twas a trusty guide;

But now, thou knowst not what is truth,
And e'en thy heart's belied.

Hast thou forgot the fairy isles
Where laughing flowers display
Their varied hues, and blush and glow
Beneath the Eye of Day?
So, thoughts like fairest flowers arose
Within thy verdant mind;
But now thy thoughts are naught but weeds,
And shadows round them wind.

Hast thou forgot, canst thou forget,
The moonlit night when we
Would wander o'er all Fairyland
With spirits pure and free;
The soft green turf beneath our feet,
The night blue sky above –
Canst thou forget our care of thee,
Canst thou forget our love?

Oh! fairies of Fairyland, can he whom they mourn ever forget them,
ever forget their country of ever-living beauty, with its boundless skies of
infinite colour, its floods of radiance, its dells and groves of glorious greenness, its floor of verdant harmony, its glittering feathery foliage, its luminous vistas, its green hills undulating far, far away, its transparent sunshot
waters, its lovely odorous flowers? Can he ever forget the time when blithe
and unfettered he wandered wheresoever he would, when no chains cor-
roded his tameless spirit, when, instead of harsh embittering words, the
music of unseen lyres played by unseen minstrels called forth all the ten-
derest emotions and thoughts, sweeter than the sweetest melodies ever interpreted by the eyes? No, never can he forget, and though now immured
in a world which he dare not leave, his heart, that heart which was once so
happy and serene with the peace which comes through trusting, broken,

hardened and unanchored, yet, at times doth the lost music sound in his ears and a fleeting vision of the lost countries pass before his eyes.

Oh! thou who art wearied with a dull, charmless existence, and thou, whose proud intelligence makes thee restless and discontented, this Fairy-land or World of Imagination is a beautiful world, which may be frequented with great pleasure and benefit, and from which thou mayst return to the duties of real life refreshed and calmed. But do not, ah! do not, yield thine whole soul to its fascinations and dwell too long therein, because 'tis a law of Nature that he who thus forgets himself (as was the case with the one whom the fairies lament), forfeits the blessings and pleasures of the real world when he returns to it. Let us think of that most sorrowful one; think how it was possible for him to be all that he had ever aspired to be; think of the happiness he enjoyed; think of the beauty which delighted his eyes; think of the love and sympathy which were his all in the World of Imagination. And then think of him in the real world – a pilgrim and a stranger! Think till the moon charms our sadness away and inspires us to address her. Dear and lovely Moon! As we watch thee pursuing thy solitary course o'er the silent heavens, heart-easing thoughts steal o'er us and calm our passionate soul. Thou art so sweet, so peaceful, so serene, that thou causest us to forget the stormy emotions which crash like jarring discords across the harmony of life and bringest to our memory a voice, scarce ever heard amidst the warring of the world – Love's low voice. Thou art so serious and so pure that it seemeth as if naught that is false or ignoble could live beneath thy gentle radiance, and that earnestness, even the earnestness of genius, must glow within the bosom of him on whose head thy beams fall like blessings. Thou art our teacher and our friend. It seems to us as if sometimes a shade of sadness were cast o'er thee – as if, perchance, thou wert grieving o'er some unrighted wrong; yet, thou continuest thy course as steadily when thy light is dimmed as when it shines the brightest. May our spirits be as invincible. The magic of thy sympathy disburthens us of many sorrows and thoughts, which, like the songs of the sweetest silvan singer, are too dear and sacred for the careless ears of day, gush forth with unconscious eloquence when thou art the only listener. Thou hast the power to make us happy, for thou art truthful and thou art beautiful, and wherever there is truth and beauty there is poetry, and wherever there is poetry there is happiness.

We love thee as all things animate and inanimate must love thee, as the boundless ocean, undulating rivers, still lakes, that carry thine image in their bosoms, love thee. We gaze on thy fair face floating on the clouds above us, and then, looking downwards, behold it, like a mysterious other self, gliding gracefully o'er the waters. Thy witchery is o'er meadow, grove and forest. Thou art, in fact, Nature's fairy godmother. We love thy brother also, the spirit-stirring Sun. Who can resist him? But not as we love thee. The Sun cometh forth with glory, a glory which precedes him. Brilliant banners of light, his messengers, announce his coming and disperse all shadows. The skies blush at his approach. And then when he appeareth, what a rejoicing! The air is astir, the flowers ope, the birds warble, thousands of voices are heard – some loud and clear, some low and soft; but all glad with a gladness which is born of the Sun, and all raised in praise of him. And when he retireth, and when the evening skies which reflect the hues of Paradise have become subdued and dark shades of night are gathering, what a melancholy falleth o'er Nature – flowers close, leaves droop, birds cease singing. All is quiet and still, still and quiet; the Sun is asleep. Yes, we love the gay Sun, the renewer of joyousness, the dispeller of sadness. But not, oh! not, as we love thee, dear Moon. The Sun ariseth in glory, his heralds proclaim his approach and earth awakes and greets him. He departeth also in glory, and in his most brilliant robes waves his adieu. But to thee, sweet Queen of Night, we raise our eyes. Lo! thou art there. No voice, no sign, gave notice of thy coming. Yet, there thou shinest. So, when thou retirest, Nature, who we doubt not loveth thee well in secret, alloweth scarce a flower to ope its eye when bidding thee farewell, and not a voice laments thee, save the voice of one lone bird. Modestly and sweetly dost thou instil the balm of thy presence through the night, and, when thy task is finished, retirest with silent simple courtesy.

Dear and lovely Moon, there are some who say that none but simple folks are fascinated by thy soft light, that love of thee causes melancholy and sentimental fancies, and that thou givest license to the imagination and blindfoldest reason. Wherefore then do we love thee and muse on thee? Give us grace to answer them. Because melancholy is in the human heart, and if the moonlight hath power to bring it to the surface, 'tis only because the defiant gaiety under which melancholy lies buried, cannot exist under the Moon's pure light. Besides "all things are touched with melancholy," and is it not a relief sometimes to be truly melancholy instead of falsely gay? Because, though these are not the days of sentiment, yet, we believe that true sentiment alone makes life worth living. Because, dwelling in the sunlit fields of reason, we fear not to wander at times through the moonlit valleys of imagination. Because we believe that, if the sunlight is beneficent to man, so also must be the moonlight, for the Master of Life created both the Sun and the Moon and made us susceptible to the influence of both. Because, just as the Moon at certain seasons blends with the Sun until the lesser light seems (and only seems) extinguished by the greater, so also ought imagination to blend with reason.

Edith Eaton. "A Plea for Sad Songs."
Dominion Illustrated 7.170 (3 October 1891): 334.

It is the fashion nowadays amongst a large class of people to decry all that is mournful, pathetic, or sad in literature, poetry especially. Now, this is a great mistake. It is not a sin to be sad. What are the natures that cannot suffer and be sad? Are they worth anything? Are they capable of heroism? Can they even know true happiness? And who really cares for them? In our best moments we are sad, not glad. And why? Because life is sad, and it is only when we selfishly hide ourselves, as it were, from trouble and care that we can think otherwise. I am no Pessimist. I believe in the gospel of cheerfulness, but there are times for sadness as well as for gladness, and if there are times for sadness, then, also, there must be songs of sadness. When we are happy and joyous, we like to hear laughter and glad songs. When we are in a melancholy mood, the same merriment pains us, and to try to join in with it often means madness. At such times let that fortunate poet who has the gift and the faculty divine sing sad songs for us poor dumb poets. These songs will give the expression to thoughts which we ourselves have been denied the power of making vocal, and we will be relieved and soothed. This is the poet's vocation. To find proper clothing for the naked thoughts, which struggle and fight like unruly children to leave their home, the mind, but which we dare not let depart unattired. Some of these children trouble us greatly and we would fain put them away. They are the sad thoughts. But the poet takes them, and because they are not so pleasing in themselves as our other children, the happy thoughts, he clothes them in his most eloquent music, and the world, when it hears aright, says: "The sweetest songs are those which tell of saddest thought."

"Oh, give her then her tribute just,
For sighs and tears and musings lowly

There is no music in the life
That sounds with idiot laughter solely;
There's not a string attuned to mirth,
But has its chord in melancholy."
And these are the words of one of our kings of laughter, Tom Hood.*

* Excerpted from popular late-Romantic poet Thomas Hood's "Ode to Melancholy."

Selected Early Journalism:
Montreal
(1890–1896)

Unsigned. "A Chinese Party."
Montreal Daily Witness, 7 November 1890: 7.

A SINGULAR SCENE AT THE WINDSOR STREET DEPOT.

Nineteen Chinamen, having made their "pile" in Boston in the tea and "washee-washee" business, hungered to go back to the land of their fathers and paralyze the natives. It is rather mortifying to have to travel in bond, like a Saratoga trunk, from Boston to Vancouver, but that's what these nineteen successful merchants are doing. The philosophy of the Chinese is – silence, but, no doubt, when they get home they will have a few rather vigorous remarks to make about the beautiful laws of this great country. At the Windsor street depot this morning there was quite an entertainment. The nineteen Chinamen arrived in charge of a Custom's officer, and when they were informed that they could not leave until eight o'clock this evening they proceeded to make themselves comfortable. Squatting upon their luggage, of which they had an enormous quantity, they produced the daintiest little tea kettles and tea-pots, and tiny little cups, about the size of a thimble, hand-painted, so fragile that a breath would reduce them to nothingness – things of beauty that would have been the despair of the aesthetic boarder, accustomed to vessels as thick as boilerplate. Then they dived into their valises and got out hams and canned salmon and bread, and three large turkeys (with the heads still inviolate) whose glossy eyes, as the Chinamen selected toothsome morsels from the breasts, regarded them with mild reproach. So, the tea having been warmed in the refreshment

room and all being in readiness, the Chinamen fell to with such despatch
and evident enjoyment as made the mouths of the C[anadian] P[acific]
R[ailway] pass water. They drank more cups of tea than could well be
counted, and when they had done, Mr. Ching Pah, dressed in irreproach-
able European costume and speaking good English, "and worth," said a
C.P.R. official in an awe-struck whisper, "at least a million dollars," went
over to the Customs officer and said, "Look here, a few of us want to go
down town with some friends. Now, here's a thousand dollars (pulling out
the bills) as a guarantee for our safe return, and you can also come along
with us." Red tape and human nature had a terrible struggle in the breast
of that officer. Human nature knocked red tape out with a right-hander.
The officer remembered that he was a man and that [the] visit was
allowed. He took that $1,000 all the same.

Unsigned. "Girl Slave in Montreal. Our Chinese Colony Cleverly Described. Only Two Women from the Flowery Land in Town."
Montreal Daily Witness, 4 May 1894: 10.*

There is a slave in Montreal – a ten-year-old Chinese girl – the property
of Mrs. Sam Kee.

There are quite a number of Chinese in Montreal. Mr. Chan Tung,
who lives in the hotel on Lagauchetiere street, says there are three hundred.
Most of them are occupied in the Laundry business and the rest are merchants or transient visitors. Messrs. Wing Sing and Sam Kee keep the hotel
on Lagauchetiere street.† Mr. Cheeping is a well-to-do, well dressed individual. The "Witness" recently printed his official declaration that he was

---

* This visit is probably the one to which Eaton refers in "Sui Sin Far, the Half Chinese
Writer, Tells of Her Career" (1912): "One day a clergyman suggested to my mother that she
should call upon a young Chinese woman who had recently arrived from China as the
bride of one of the local Chinese merchants." Many of the phrases in this article also appear
in Eaton's "The Chinese Woman in America" (1897).
† Sam Kee (or Sang Kee) (d. 1908) kept a boarding house on rue de la Gauchetière.

starting a grocery business. He is well informed, talks English quite fluently and has polite manners. He has a cousin, a lad of about sixteen, who goes to school, and whose face is as bright and intelligent as any you could wish to see.

Mr. Wing Sing has a wife – Mrs. Wing Sing.* Not many people can see Mrs. Wing Sing – she is very exclusive, but a lady reporter of the "Witness" saw her recently, and gives this interesting account of her visit.

Mrs. Wing Sing received me very graciously, her round face beaming with smiles. She is considered by her countrymen to be quite a beauty. Her hair is worn drawn tightly back from her forehead, pinned to the back or top of her head and falls in a large spreading loop on her neck. She wore the Chinese costume, pyjamas and blouse of dark blue stuff, a combination of silk and cotton. From out [of] the bell sleeves hung pretty little hands, which were somewhat spoiled, however, by long nails. On her wrists were very handsome greenish-blue jadestone bracelets, in her ears were long silver ear-rings, very delicately enameled. Her feet are of natural size.

With Mrs. Wing Sing was Mrs. Sam Kee, a bride of a few months, and a little Chinese girl of about ten years old, both of whom were in their native dress. Sam Kee's bride "is but a lassie yet" and when I first made my appearance she was demolishing with great gusto some "crisped rice." After shaking hands she disappeared into an adjoining room. All that I can remember of her is that she was very dark, very small, and very much unlike a bride.

As to the child, she is a slave. Well, poor little thing; her face is by no means her fortune. She belongs to Mrs. Sam Kee, and came over with her from China. She is treated more like a sister than a slave, indeed it is the custom in China to look upon slaves as family, and they are treated accordingly.

These three, Mrs. Wing Sing, Mrs. Sam Kee, and the little girl are the only Chinese females in Montreal.

After taking this fact in, and not wishing to appear too curious and personal, I withdrew my eyes from Mrs. Wing Sing and cast them around the

* Mr. Wing Sing (b. Canton, China; d. 1903 Montreal) was a Montreal businessman and boarding house operator suspected of participating in a smuggling ring.

room. It was an ordinarily furnished apartment, very much in appearance like the living room of a European family in moderate circumstances, the only difference being that the walls were hung from top to bottom with long bamboo panels covered with paper, on which were printed Chinese characters, signifying good luck. A sewing machines was visible and in use, a proof that the Chinese do march forward in the van of civilization. Mrs. Wing Sing is quite an expert operator.

That little woman is evidently very amiable, quite jolly, in fact, for she laughed at every sound we uttered, at every movement we made. I couldn't imagine her in a fury. The only words she can say in English are "good, good," "thank you," "nice boy," "nice girl," "come again," "how do you do," "yes," "no."

It's "good, good" with her nearly all the time.

I looked around the four walls within which her life is spent and I wondered how it was she could laugh and be merry. Is it custom or nature that makes her contented with a life that to the daughters of Europe and America seems worse than death? Obedience, never-failing obedience, is the characteristic of the Chinese woman. She loves her parents and those who are put in authority over her because she is taught to do so; she loves her husband because she has been given to him to be his wife; she comes when she's called and does what she's bid. No question of "woman's rights" perplexes her little brains. She takes no responsibilities upon herself, and wishes for none. She has perfect confidence in her man.

So much for what I saw in the hotel on Lagauchetiere street. When coming out I met several Chinese men who spoke to me in English and said that they attended the Chinese Sunday-school of the American Presbyterian Church.* They all spoke in most grateful terms of Mr. [W.] Baikie, the superintendent of the [Chinese] Sunday-school, Mr. George Lighthall, Miss [Alice] Lighthall, Miss Hastings, the superintendents of Emmanuel [Congregational Church] and other Sunday-schools and the many ladies who so kindly interest themselves in teaching them Sunday after Sunday.

* In 1865 the American Presbyterian congregation built a church at the south-east corner of what is now the intersection of René Lévesque Boulevard and Drummond Street in Montreal.

The majority of the Chinese in the hotel, including Mrs. Wing Sing and Mrs. Sam Kee, have nothing whatever to do with the Christian faith, but despite that, the converted and unconverted get on very peaceably and comfortably together.

There are people who say that the Chinese merely go to Sunday-school for the sake of learning the English language. That may be so. The Chinese see that it will benefit them to be able to speak English and they go to learn. The religion that is taught them does not at first strike them as of any importance. They swallow it like a sugar-coated pill, but by and by, when they can understand and read a little English, they become more interested in what is so perseveringly poured into their ears, and in some cases the teachings have gone deep to the heart and been honestly accepted.

The Montreal Chinese mostly hail from Canton, which is situated in the Province of Quang-Tong [Guangdong], south-west China. They are by no means aristocrats, these Chinese. In fact, they belong to the very lowest class of Chinese. Perhaps that is the reason why they are so looked down upon here, but they are very industrious, very persevering, and they have one immeasurable superiority over other foreigners – they are a peaceable people.

Unsigned. "Our Local Chinatown. Little Mystery Of A St. Denis Street Laundry,"
Montreal Daily Witness, 19 July 1894: 10.*

The other day a gentleman happening to enter the Chinese laundry kept by Quing Yuen at the corner of St. Denis and Mignonne streets was surprised to see seated behind the counter a Chinese woman or girl arrayed in Chinese dress. As the costume of the Chinese woman is regulated by law and is not subject to the caprice of fashion or individual taste and is the same to-day as it was many thousands of years ago, except perhaps with a

---

* The surprising presence of a Chinese woman in a Chinese laundry is also explored in the short story "The Smuggling of Tie Co" (1900).

few trifling alterations which do not interfere with the general style, it
might do no harm here to describe a Chinese woman's dress – when she is
REALLY DRESSED UP.

It consists of a short loose robe of dark blue silk, confined at the throat
with a narrow collar; the robe is worn over a full skirt and both are made
of richly embroidered silk; the sleeves are wide and sufficiently long to fall
over the hands, the hair is gathered at the nape of the neck in a sort of mat
and ornamented with flowers made of jewels; the shoes are of light silk,
beautifully worked with gold, silver and colored silks; the under skirt is in
fact so richly embroidered that it
LOOKS ALMOST LIKE BEATEN GOLD.
The Chinese woman wears, not one pair of bracelets, but three or four;
they are generally of solid gold, but the poorer sorts are of jasper or jade
stones.

Mrs. Sam Kee, on Lagauchetiere street, has a pair of gold bracelets
which cost her husband when in San Francisco two hundred and sixty-five
dollars.* The Chinese woman's earrings are more than an inch long and
are composed of gold and three different kinds of stones, pearls being
the favorite.

Of course, an apparition such as this astonished the gentleman exceedingly, especially as he had been told that there were
ONLY TWO CHINESE WOMEN
in the city and they scarcely ever left their homes, which homes were not in
Quing Yuen's laundry. He had just about made up his mind to speak to the
woman when she disappeared behind the counter.

A 'Witness' reporter to-day, after being told the tale, called upon Quing
Yuen to find out who this daughter of the Orient was, and why she happened to be there, when no woman was supposed to be on the premises.
The reporter looked around upon entering the laundry, but all he could
see was five persons working away industriously, and these persons were
decidedly of the masculine gender; not one of them good looking enough
to be a woman.

* Over $6,000 in today's dollars.

AFTER POLITELY ASKING

after the health of the proprietor and his associate, the reporter ventured also to say: –

"And how is your wife?"

"The boss is out," replied one of the men, gruffly, "and he has no wife."

"Oh, excuse me, I thought you were the boss, but it doesn't matter, have you one?"

"Have me what?"

"A wife."

"Oh, no, me no wife."

"I'm sorry for that. Have you? Have you? Have you?'"

The question went round and was answered by each Chinaman in the negative, some of them suppressing a giggle.

"Well, your daughter, then?"

"I have no daughter'" replied the one who had spoken first before.

"None of us have any daughters, there's no kind of women here."

Still the reporter was unabashed. "Perhaps you have some lady friends. Do any Chinese ladies come to see you?"

"No," was the emphatic answer, "no womans ever come to this shop."

The reporter, seeing that he was not wanted at Quing Yen's, departed for

THE LAGAUCHETIERE STREET HOTEL,

thinking that it was likely some information could be obtained there; but on arriving at that place found it absolutely newsless.

The Chinese woman still remains a mystery. One boy who was seen at the hotel suggested that perhaps the woman whom the gentleman had seen was in reality a young man, as a Chinese youth can easily pass for woman. But what would a young man deck himself up in the way that the mysterious person behind the counter was decked for and why should

A YOUNG MAN HIDE HIMSELF

at sight of a stranger. It is customary and natural for Chinese women to be shy, but the men do not suffer in that way. A Chinese woman dresses to please her husband whereas a Chinese man never thinks of dressing himself for the sake of his wife, although he is, as a rule, very kind to her.

The gentleman says that the woman he saw was pretty. It needs a very handsome youth to make a pretty woman, and to European eyes the majority of' Chinese men here are not at all good looking. There are, however, a few exceptions and Mr. Wing Sing has in his store on St. Lawrence Main street, without the slightest exaggeration, an almost beautiful man; but his frame is much too large to pass for a woman's.

Unsigned. "'No Tickee, No Washee.'"
Montreal Daily Witness, 25 July 1894: 10.*

HOW JOHN CHINAMAN KNOWS WHAT BUNDLE TO RETURN
TO EACH PATRON.
THAT SLICE OF BROWN PAPER WITH HENTRACKS ON IT – THE
ARITHMETIC MACHINE.

The Chinese laundrymen have a very peculiar and ingenious method of checking the clothes left with them to be washed. By it they are able to tell exactly to whom the different bundles of washing which come into the laundry belong.

A reporter[,] being curious to find out how this method worked, called on Wing Wah, St. Catherine street, and asked to see one of his checks and also to have the system of their use explained to him. The request was readily complied with. The reporter learnt that making these checks the Chinaman fixes upon some name of a "person, place or thing," as the sign word of a batch of checks for the week, the heavenly bodies, such as the sun, moon or stars, being generally the favorite signs. The word selected is then drawn on the top of the left-hand corner of the check, and after that the checks are numbered, say, from one to a hundred, according to how many the laundryman thinks he will require during the week. The accompanying is an illustration of one of Wing Wah's checks, showing where it is torn in half.[†]

* Much of this article is recycled in Eaton's "Chinese Laundry Checking."

The first figure on the left means "sky," underneath is No. 1, (that is the number of the first check that goes out during the week). These signs are duplicated on the right hand side of the deck and in the centre is Wing Wah's name. When a customer brings in his parcel, the check is torn from the centre; the customer is given one half of the check and the other half is attached to the parcel left in the laundry. In this way both customer and laundryman have each checks, duplicates of one another. When demand is made for the parcel, the given check is matched to the one attached to the washing.

The foregoing is the general system in use, but each laundryman varies it somewhat according to different ideas of convenience and speed. For instance, in place of a name in the centre, the number is repeated.

Should there be any checks left over at the end of the week they are destroyed, and a new batch of checks with a sign word is made. If a customer fails to keep his check or loses it, the laundryman, unless he knows the customer well and is certain that he is the customer to whom the clothes

† This image, like the one reprinted in the *Los Angeles Express* article "Chinese Laundry Checking" is, as White-Parks notes, printed upside down, suggesting that either the printer or Eaton herself could not read Chinese characters accurately.

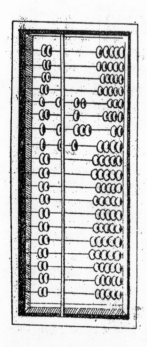

belong, will not give them up, that is, not until
he has made enquiries and satisfied himself
that the person claiming the clothes is actually
the person who ought by right to have them.
It is said, that even according to law, a person
who cannot present a check corresponding
with the one that the laundryman from whom
the clothes are claimed has, cannot recover
anything if the Chinaman refuses to stand and
deliver. There is, however, very little need to
go to law about the matter, as the system
described, in most cases, works admirably.

The arithmetic machine is a device frequently noticed in Chinese laundries. The accompanying is an illustration of the machine
by which the proprietor of the Chinese hotel
on Lagauchetiere street, reckons his gains and
losses, how much each customer pays him, how much change he returns.*
This ingenious contrivance is called the Chinese abacus and answers all
the purposes of numerical figures. It contains a number of little balls of
different colors, strung upon wires fixed in a box and divided into com-
partments, the balls in one division being units, in another fives, and with
these the Chinese add up and multiply with as much facility as the Euro-
peans do with the aid of figures. It is the Chinese system of arithmetic,
and it may be interesting to learn that it has been so long practised that
its invention is attributed to the Emperor who succeeded the "Divine
Husbandman," the same who is said to have found his way through the
forest by means of the compass, and who was the immediate successor
to Fohi, the first mortal or non-fabulous emperor of China.

* The Chinese abacus is said to have been invented by the Yellow Emperor (Huangdi),
father of Chinese civilization, who reigned from about 2697 to 2698 BCE. Fohi, more
commonly known as Fu Xi, was the emperor who reigned prior to Huangdi.

Unsigned. "Half-Chinese Children."
Montreal Daily Star, 20 April 1895:*

THOSE OF AMERICAN MOTHERS AND CHINESE FATHERS.
Some of Their Troubles and Discomforts – They Are Taken Entirely in
Charge by the Fathers and Generally Marry Chinese.

An American lady, the wife of a Chinese merchant, now of this city, but
formerly residing in the United States of America, gives some very interesting information concerning the children of Chinese fathers and white
mothers of whom there are a large number in Boston and New York. She
says that those children, who, for the most part live in the Chinatown of
the Cities, are not by any means to be envied, for the white people with
whom they come in contact that is, the lower class, jibe and jeer at the
poor little things continually, and their pure and unadulterated Chinese
cousins look down upon them as being neither one thing nor the other –
neither Chinese nor white.

The Chinese fathers, however, are, as a rule, very kind and good to their
offspring, and so also are those mothers who are respectable women, having a true affection for their Chinese husbands; but there are a great many
women whose characters would not stand much investigation, and who
have married Chinamen simply for their money and they do not seem to
feel any natural maternal tenderness for their little ones and are only too
glad to give them away or sell them for adoption whenever they have the
chance. To some this unnaturalness might almost seem natural, for the
true cause often lies in the fact that the majority of Chinamen who come
to the States have left behind them wives in their own country, and therefore the children of the American woman can hardly be called legitimate.
They would not be considered so in China were their father to return to

---

* Many passages from this article reappear in Eaton's "Sweet Sin" (1897) and in her
autobiographical writing.

that country, taking them with him. The conditions therefore under which the American Chinese child is "dragged up" are not, to say the least, favorable, to either its mental, physical or moral welfare, and it is not to be expected (although the unexpected sometimes does happen) that we will ever have a celebrated bishop whose father is a Chinaman, whose mother is an American woman. Still, the blighting atmosphere of Chinatown and its vicinity, the sneers and taunting words which are their birthright, the superstitions of their fathers and the careless, indifferent lives (with some exceptions) of the mothers, do not prevent these children from developing and becoming as fine a lot as a globetrotter could wish to see.

There is occasionally to be seen a half Chinese child with bright complexion and fair hair, and these combined with a straight nose, small mouth and wide eyes might easily deceive a stranger, but a person who has been informed of the child's parentage notices at once a peculiar cast about the face. This cast is over the face of every child who has a drop of Chinese blood in its veins. It is indescribable – but it is there. In some families, there are children with blue eyes, fair hair, and Mongolian features, and other children with Chinese hair and complexion and features which are purely Caucasian. Not all of these children are "fair to see" – many are very homely, but some are "pretty as pictures." They are by nature proud and reserved (some say, sullen and hardened). They are quick to understand and appreciate book-lore and the little girls are particularly clever with their needles and can be easily taught the most difficult patterns in embroidery. Numberless

HUMOROUS AND PATHETIC STORIES

are related of these children. One is of a little boy, who after having been persecuted for nearly an hour by a crowd of roughs, turned upon them in a fury, and not being conscious, in his excitement, of what he said, echoed their mocking cry of "Chinese" "Chinese." But almost before the words had died on his lips, a full sense of his terrible mistake overpowered him and he rushed away from his tormentors who were shrieking derisively and hid himself where his father found him and comforted him with a thrashing.

There are a few children, the sons and daughters of wealthy and perhaps Christianized Chinamen who live in more respectable parts of the cities than Chinatown, who attend Sunday schools and day schools and who associate freely with other children. These children certainly appear to be fortunate, for a certain class of people consider them "interesting" and patronize and make much of them. And those of the children who are merry-hearted and light-natured enjoy such treatment and, basking in the sunshine of "patronage," possibly benefit by it. But others who are not susceptible to such petting, feel like a little girl who is recorded to have said to her mother, "Mamma, I'm not going to see Mrs. G.— to-day." "Why not?" said the mother, "she is always so kind to you and gives you more toys than you know what to do with." "Yes!" said the child "but I don't care for the toys. It is just because I'm Chinese that she likes to have me there. When I'm in her parlor she whispers to some people about me, and then they try to make me talk and pick up all that I say and I hear them whisper 'her father's a Chinese' 'Did you know' 'Isn't it curious' – and they examine me from head to toe as if I was a wild animal – and just because father is a Chinese. I'd rather be dead than be a 'show.'"

A Chinese American child cannot really be said to have any religion. The father may have an idol in a private room before which he performs idolatrous rites, the mother may attend some Protestant or Catholic church, but the child has no religion. There are certainly a few boys and girls who are brought up to be Christians – but these are the exception and not the rule. A Chinese father has sole control of his children. He orders their life as he pleases and disposes of them whenever so inclined. That is Chinese law and it has not yet been contested in the United States of America. The boys of a family, however, often drift away from parental influence in American cities and marry American women, but the daughters are usually married to Chinamen, sons of friends of the father. As an instance, there is Lee Fee's daughter. Lee Fee is a New York Chinaman who married a German woman. Lee Fee's daughter was handsome and intelligent. She had been brought up very much like an ordinary American girl in the land of the free, but was married with all the rites and ceremonies of her father's country to a Chinaman. In some families, one daughter is married to a Chinaman, another to an American. It gives food for thought – the fact that a couple of centuries from now, the great-grandchildren of the woman who married an American will be Americans and nothing else, whilst the descendants of her sister, who married a China-

man and probably followed her husband to his own country will be
Chinamen, pure and simple.

CHINESE MARRIAGES.

Even in America the tedious Chinese marriage formalities, as far as possible, are observed by the Chinese. The following will give an idea of what
an immense amount of trouble and anxiety the ceremonies of betrothal
and marriage are to them. The young man's family begins the negotiations.
They engage a go-between to go to some family indicated by them and
tender a proposal of marriage in regard to a daughter on behalf of the
party employing him. If the young man is considered eligible by the parents of the girl, they consult a fortune teller, who decides[,] after consulting some characters, whether the betrothal would be proper. If the fortune
teller decides favorably, the go-between is given a card on which is marked
the hour, day, month and year when the child they wish to betroth was
born, which he delivers to the young man's family, who in their turn consult a fortune teller as to the proposed betrothal. If the second fortune
teller also pronounces favorably, a formal assent by all parties is made to
the betrothment. The betrothal, however, is not considered binding until a
kind of pasteboard card has been interchanged by the families. The family
of the bridegroom provides two of these cards, one having a gilt dragon on
it and the other a gilt phoenix. The phoenix card is retained by the young
man's family as evidence of his engagement whilst the card with the
dragon on is preserved by the girl's family for the same reason. After this,
the betrothal is considered consummated.

At the time when the cards are sent to the family to which the girl belongs, it is also customary to send as a present to her a pair of silver or gold
bracelets and for her family various articles of food, such as pig's feet, a
pair of fowls, fish, etc. When the engagement card is sent back to the family
to which the bridegroom belongs, there is sent as a present a quantity of
artificial flowers, some vermicelli and bread cakes. The flowers are for dis-
tribution amongst the female members and relatives of the family. These
articles are

REGARDED AS OMENS OF GOOD.

From one to five months before the marriage a fortunate day is selected
for its celebration. Generally a relative of the bridegroom or a trustworthy

friend takes the eight honorary characters which denote the birth time of each of the affianced parties to a fortune teller who selects lucky days for the marriage, for the making of the wedding garments, etc. These items are written out on a sheet of red paper, which is sent to the family of the girl through a go-between. If accepted, the time specified is fixed for the performance of the particulars indicated. The next thing is the presentation of wedding cakes and material for the bridal dress to the family of the bride by the other family. Wedding cakes are also presented to the bridegroom's family. The family of the girl on receiving the wedding cakes proceeds to distribute them amongst their relatives and intimate friends. There is also sent with these cakes a sum of money sometimes a large sum, sometimes a small, a quantity of red silk, dried fruits, a cock and a hen, a gander and a goose. Rich families, of course, make more costly presents than the poorer.

At the time mentioned on the betrothal card, the bride's dowry is carried through the streets with as much parade as possible. The wedding day is considered a great day and everything is designed to "show off" *a la* some Westerners. The day before the wedding, the bride tries on the clothes she is to wear for a time after she arrives at her future home. She also has her hair done up for the first time in the style of a married woman.

A Chinese bridegroom is not supposed to behold the face of his wife on the wedding day until the marriage dinner, which takes place in the evening, is set before him, for although the marriage ceremonies may have commenced in the morning early, the bride wears until the evening a thick veil which completely covers her face. When they sit down to dinner, the husband looks at the wife, but says nothing and gives his attention to the good things provided. The bride, however, sits unveiled, quiet and still. According to custom, she must not touch a particle of food. Refreshments are offered to her by friends and attendants, but she is supposed to decline them with thanks. The ordeal of being married, is, in fact, a very trying one to the Chinese girl, or half Chinese girl, for after removing the veil, all the neighbours, guests who were not invited and strangers even, are allowed to enter the house and stare at her. She is obliged to stand and bear with composure all sorts of criticism. She dares not laugh nor give the slightest evidence of anger. Her duty is to be quiet, pleasant looking and calm – even when at her expense jokes and impertinences are indulged in.

The bride's toilet is generally gorgeous and her hair is decked out with
pearls and other jewel ornaments.

Unsigned. "Chinese Visitors"
Montreal Daily Star, 6 July 1895: 4.

The infinite pains taken by the Chinese to get into Canada and the United
States suggest a passion for American life which one would not have expected of them. They lose sleep in devising methods of evading the restrictive laws. The underground railway, by which the slaves used to escape into
Canada, is nothing to the modern inventions of the Chinese for climbing
tariff walls and creeping under the wire fences of Christian civilization.
They are always at it, showing their devotion to America in a hundred
ways, with a pathetic persistence. Still they are not popular. The Chinese
vote is not sought after. No brass band greets them at the station, and
when Ling Lung and Bow Wow get mixed up in a street quarrel even a
Montreal policemen will arrest them with alacrity. But they continue to
come. As long as they are allowed to do the washing of the nation they
seem to care not who makes the laws. But a new feature in their Canadian
life is that they have become unpopular with a portion of Christian
femininity. Not those, of course, who teach them English in the Sunday-
schools, but the more vigorous-minded of the sex who throw stones in the
streets for an evening's amusement, and express opinions of the foreigner
with charming candor.* A plea for police protection has had to be made
in one case. As the Chinese do not know our police system they may be ex-
cused for this lapse from common sense. The situation is serious, because
a woman who can throw a stone is a formidable antagonist. It may be that
the Chinese desire to live in our community is purely mercenary, and
that he is an insincere admirer after all. Even so, the fear that some literary
member of the race may write a book about us some day ought to act as

* An article published in the *Montreal Daily Star* the previous day ("Abusing the Chinee.
How Some White Christians Treat Them, Rotten Eggs and Stones," 5 July 1895) described
young Montreal women who threw rotten eggs and stones at Sang Lung and his brother.

a deterrent to violence.* The picture he could draw of our practical Christianity and our boasted British freedom and protection will go a long way to poison the mind of posterity. And although posterity has never done anything for us, its turn will come some day.

Unsigned. "Thrilling Experience of a Band of Smugglers in the Lachine Rapids."
Montreal Daily Star, 9 July 1895: 1.†

While "Running" Chinese Across the River at Caughnawaga Their War Canoe Is Driven on a Reef at the Mouth of the Cataract.

Fourteen Chinamen, accompanied by three shrewd smugglers from this city, had a narrow escape from going over the Lachine Rapids early on Monday morning, while attempting to cross the St. Lawrence from Lachine to Caughnawaga,†† on their way to Uncle Sam's domains.

The wily Chinese, finding that the new route to the United States via the Sorel Islands‡ was discovered, abandoned that channel in quick order and directed their attention to pastures new. Together with the smugglers, they hit upon an ingenious scheme, a little risky perhaps, but completely safe from the vigilant eye of the United States Customs officers and Treasury officials, as they thought.§

* Anticipates the project Mrs. Spring Fragrance mentions in "The Inferior Woman."
† Many details from this article reappear in "Tian Shan's Kindred Spirit" and other smuggling stories.
†† Also known as Kahnawake; a Mohawk reserve on the south shore of the St Lawrence River, across from Montreal.
‡ These islands in the St Lawrence northeast of Montreal were identified as hiding places for smugglers in 1895.
§ Before the passage of the 1882 Chinese Exclusion Act, the border between the United States and Canada was only loosely monitored. After 1882, border control was tightened. By the mid-1880s, the smuggling of Chinese and drugs across the border had become a popular topic in newspapers and magazines. Bribed customs officials, notaries, Chinese interpreters, and Chinese merchants helped coordinate and pay for the smuggling. Even employees of Canadian railway companies were involved in smuggling.

This time they would run across the river a mile above the Lachine Rapids in a large Indian war canoe, and land in a cove dangerously surrounded by reefs, where pursuit would be impossible. When arranging for this trip, the Chinese miscalculated the danger of the St. Lawrence at this point, and let nothing come into their minds but their one ambition to cross to the land of the free.

On Monday morning, at 3.30, the party left Montreal for Lachine, comfortably ensconced in a large covered express wagon. They arrived at the place designated for their perilous trip near the Canadian Pacific bridge, and after scouting around for some time to see that the coast was clear, embarked in a large Indian war canoe that was in waiting near the rendezvous. It was first arranged to make for a cove above the bridge, but the "guide" misjudged the current at this point, and instead of "striking out" a mile further up the river, let go the ropes from the hiding place. As soon as the big war canoe, with its load of human freight, caught the swiftly running current it swerved quickly round, and in an instant shot between the two shore abutments of the bridge with lightning speed.

Out into the current glided the canoe, and in several minutes the party was in the centre of the swift current of the St. Lawrence. Down, down, they sped, the paddlers working like Trojans, but making little headway to the opposite shore. Back in the wake towered the bridge, and in the distance could be seen the white caps and spray from the turbulent waters of the Lachine Rapids. The canoe now and anon would rise on the heavy swells that were rapidly drawing it towards the cataract of rushing waters.

The occupants now, for the first time, realized their danger, and for a time lost their heads. The paddlers, worn out, quickly changed places with the more robust of the Celestials. Then commenced the race for life. With every plunge of the paddles the canoe rose on the heavy swells and cut its way through the small white caps. It was a case of life or death. On they went; the current getting swifter and the swells heavier. Less than a quarter of a mile off could be seen the raging cataract of the rapids. One hundred yards distant was the shore for which they had risked so much. The work was laborious, but slowly the canoe forged ahead, but as it did so it was carried down stream sideways. Nearer and nearer they approached, until finally the prow of the canoe rounded the reef opposite the rapids and grazed upon the sand of the cove.

All round the spot raged the turbulent waters, and the noise of the rapids two hundred yards distant from shore caused many of the party to utter a word of thanks at their escape from such a narrow call. It is doubtful if another party of Celestials anxious to gain access to Uncle Sam's domains will undertake another such trip.

The whole party went onward with the evident intention of "crossing the line" near Hemmingford and Huntingdon.*

Owing to the energy put forth by the United States Customs officers the smugglers are kept continually on the lookout for pastures new, for no sooner do they get two or three batches of Celestials safely "over the lines" than the officers are after them. The money now paid by the Celestials to get across is so tempting as to cause the smugglers, who are in most cases Americans, to devise schemes of the most hazardous nature to earn the rewards. Probably the shrewdest of this organized band of smugglers between Montreal, Toronto and Boston is a wealthy Chinese resident of the latter city who visits Montreal quite frequently to arrange for consignment of "live stock," and to also give the smugglers "tips" as to the movements of the United States Secret Service men, as, strange to say, this son of the Flowery Kingdom has a keen insight into the workings of the authorities, and in many instances the smugglers' headquarters here are aware that a Secret Service man is on his way to one of their rendezvous before the train is two miles out from Boston.† This is the man that also manipulated the strings for the smugglers of sulfonal and phenacetin,†† and was the first

* Towns in southern Quebec, opposite Clinton County in New York.
† Even though the Chinese Exclusion Act was intended to limit immigration to the US, the Chinese population of Boston grew by 192 per cent between 1885 and 1895, while the Chinese population of New York grew 350 percent between between 1882 and 1900, from 2,000 to 7,000. See J. Thomas Scharf, "The Farce of the Chinese Exclusion Laws," *The North American Review* 166, 494. http://www.digitalhistory.uh.edu/disp_textbook.cfm?smtID= 3&psid=4055 and Jennifer Fronc, *New York Undercover: Private Surveillance in the Progressive Era* (Chicago: University of Chicago Press, 2009, 54).
†† Sulfonal was a popular sedative in the late nineteenth century; phenacetin was a drug used for pain relief and reducing fevers.

to hit upon the hollow cane and umbrella handles for conveying these expensive drugs into the States.

But now that the hot weather is on, there is a falling off in the demand for the [drugs], so the smugglers direct all their time to the Celestials, because there is more money in the latter at this time of the year. With the advent of cold weather commences the "running in" of the drugs and furs again by the "underground route" to Uncle Sam's territory.

In conversation with a *Star* reporter last night, a prominent local Chinaman admitted that the coffin scheme originated with him and that they were manufactured here and shipped to St. John, N[ew] B[runswick] where they were put together and used in smuggling Chinese over the lines into Vanceboro, M[ain]e.* When spoken to regarding the Sorel Island rendezvous, the speaker laughed heartily and said that if it had not been for the United States officers getting on their track considerable money could have been made by this latter route. He boasted openly of the many exploits he had with the customs officials and concluded by stating that there were fully five hundred Chinamen here at present anxiously waiting to "cross the lines."

Unsigned. "They Are Going Back to China: Hundreds of Chinese at the CPR Station"
Montreal Daily Star, 21 August 1895: 2.

They All Have Return United States Passports Good for Six Months – Others Are Returning from China.

The Chinese were in possession of Windsor street station this morning. There were fully two hundred of them, and Messrs. Harry Ibbotson and Arthur Fabian, who have charge of the Chinese branch of the passenger department of the C[anadian] P[acific] R[ailway] had their hands more than full looking after them.† Many of them were dressed in American

* See "In Ventilated Coffins: The Latest Scheme for Smuggling Chinamen into This Country," *Portland Eastern Argus.* 24 April 1895.
† Fabian is also the name of a smuggler in "The Smuggling of Tie Co."

style; a number in the loose blouses which they affect here, and one or two in the odd brightly colored silken Chinese garments which terminate in shapeless trousers tied closely around the ankles, and are not complete without a cap resembling an inverted soup bowl. These latter, however, remained behind with some forty others who had evidently come to see their countrymen off and wish them a merry trip home – for home the remaining hundred and fifty were going.

They all carried certificates or passes from the United States Government, entitling them to admittance within six months from date. Of course, should any of the hundred and fifty remain in China it would be quite possible for the certificates to be handed over to some friends, who resemble the original holders; at any rate the United States custom officials claim that such things are being done occasionally. Mr. Ho Sang Kee, the autocrat of the Chinese hotel business here, was around to shake hands with his friends, and a great number of the travellers seemed to know him. One hundred of the travellers came from New York, the party being in charge of Mr. W. L. Green, who is the C.P.R. passenger agent at New York, and the remainder from Boston. They all left for Vancouver to-day, where they join another contingent which left yesterday.

There was one lady in the party with a complexion like that of the ace of spades. She was the wife of the one of the Chinese, and had a young child, which combined the complexion of its mother with the features of its father. Mother and child seemed to be perfectly at home in their strange surroundings.* This evening and to-morrow two consignments of incoming Chinese are expected. Those who arrive this evening are men who have United States passports, and to-morrow a party of poll-tax men – Chinese who have paid their admission tax to Canada – will come in. These men will have to rely upon the arts of the wily smuggler to get into the States, where Boston is considered the Mecca of the Chinese immigrant. It is said that some of their compatriots have been very successful in this respect of late.

---

* Eaton notes her fascination with the surprising racial mixtures found in Chinatown both here and in the interview she did for the *New York Recorder*. See Appendix A.

E.E. "Letter to the Editor: Wong Hor Ching."
Montreal Daily Star, 31 August 1895: 3.

To the Editor of the Star:

Sir, – Wong Hor Ching lived in British Columbia. Ten years ago when
Wong Hor Ching was about twenty-one years old, a house in the vicinity
of Wong Hor Ching's tent was broken into by some men and the daughter
of the house almost murdered. No one could discover the perpetrator of
the outrage until one day Wong Hor Ching, whilst walking quietly along,
was pointed out by the girl herself as the villain. Wong Hor Ching was arrested and excitement ran so high, and bitter feeling was so intense against
the Chinese that there was talk of lynching him. However, he escaped
death and, upon the girl's statement, was simply sent to the penitentiary
for life. As mentioned before, Wong Hor Ching's age was then twenty-one.
Now, the friends of Wong Hor Ching knew him to be innocent, that it was
a case of mistaken identity, and set to work to prove the fact, but proving
a Chinaman who is accused of a crime innocent, in a place like British
Columbia, is a long and almost hopeless task, and it was not until very
lately that Wong Hor Ching, after ten years' hard labor, was released. And
now I will demonstrate the superiority of a Chinaman's disposition over
a white man's. If Wong Hor Ching had been a white man, he would have
resented very bitterly his unjust incarceration, and become sullen and
hardened thereby; but, being a Chinaman, Wong Hor Ching determined
to make the best of his miserable and undeserved fate, and, whilst in
prison, was so cheerful and contented, so heedful of rules, so industrious
and obedient that he became in time the prison favorite, and every one
from the Governor down to the lowest convict had a good word for Wong
Hor Ching. He is now a free man and has gone back to China, forgetting
to be vindictive to those who imprisoned him, but remembering to be
grateful to those who released him.

E.E.

Unsigned. "A Chinese Baby. Accompanies a Party Now on Their Way to Boston."
Montreal Daily Star, 11 September 1895: 6.

A very interesting company of Chinese ladies and gentlemen were assembled in rooms no. 2 and 4 of the Stanley Hotel. A reporter who had been invited to meet them was much impressed with the kind and courteous manners of the gentlemen and the merry chatter of the ladies, but was somewhat surprised to find that both could not be enjoyed together. The gentlemen received their visitor in room No. 2 and the ladies in room No. 4. So much for Chinese custom. The gentlemen represent a large and prosperous Chinese company called the Moy Company. Their names respectively are Moy Ni Ding, Moy C. Winn, Sun Wah Lung, Moy Dong Fat and Moy Lem. Their places of business in the United States are on Harrison Avenue, Boston; Pell St., New York.

The Ladies are Mrs. Moy Ni Ding, Mrs. Moy C. Winn, Mrs. Sun Wah Lung and Mrs. Moy Dong Fat. Two of these ladies are brides, married but lately by proxy to their husbands, who have been living in the United States for some years. The other two ladies were married a few years ago, just before their husbands left China. Three of the ladies had the pleasure of meeting their husbands at the C[anadian] P[acific] R[ailway] station yesterday, for two it was the first meeting, and, naturally, they were quite excited and a little shy.

Mr. Sun Wah Lung has two wives. The lady who is to go to Boston with him is his second wife; the first one remains in China to look after her children, and is perfectly contented to do so. Mrs. Sun Wah Lung was richly attired, and her small feet bore testimony to her good birth. She is twenty years of age; her husband is about fifty.

Mr. Moy C. Win, who is a singularly intelligent and prepossessing young Chinaman, was born in San Francisco, and is a graduate of an American college. His wife is twenty-six years of age, and is said to belong to a very ancient and honored family. She is tall of figure and very amiable. She also has the "Golden lily" feet of China. Indeed, her pedal extremities pointed with gold and swathed in embroidered scarlet bands, peeping out from beneath her silken skirts, are very much in shape like a calla lily bud and no larger than an ordinary person's big toe.

Mrs. Moy Ni Ding is very pretty in a truly Oriental style. She is nineteen years of age, and her small, oval face, little mouth, vivacious eyes, creamy skin and thick hair might be admired even in America.

Mr. Moy Dong Fat, a good tempered benevolent looking young fellow has a bride of sixteen, a gentle slender girl, who appeared to be somewhat fatigued by her long journey.

—

There is a baby in the company, daughter of Mr. and Mrs. Moy Ni Ding. It is a girl, and seems to receive just as much attention and affection from its father and mother as if it were a boy. Indeed, it is the pet not only of its young mamma, but of her friends as well, who talk enough Chinese baby nonsense to it to turn its head – such a cute little head as it is, shaved all around with a top-knot of thick hair in the centre. Mrs. Moy Ni Ding told the reporter that as soon as a Chinese child is one month old, it is customary to have its head shaved, and the shaving is a very important ceremony. If it is a girl it is done before an image of "Mother"; if a boy before the ancestral family tablets. During the operation incense and candles are lighted in front of the image or the tablets, and a thank offering is presented to the goddess. The day is one of joy and festivity, and is observed with considerable show, especially if it celebrates the shaving of the head of the first-born son. Visitors are invited to bring presents, amongst which are usually twenty painted ducks' eggs.

—

The little girl, Ah So Non, is now fifteen months old. She is probably at the present moment the only pure Chinese baby in Eastern Canada. She was born in China, but will in all probability be brought up in America. There is, however, no likelihood of her adopting American manners and customs, for Chinese parents seem to be more zealous in training their children in the way in which they themselves have been trained, in teaching them to adhere to the long established and stereotyped customs and opinions of their country, and in short, in training them to walk in the way, which according to our ideas, they should not go, than we in

western lands are in educating our children to do what we think is right
and proper.

The ladies are fresh from China, and the whole party are now on their
way to Boston. Mr. and Mrs. Moy Dong Fat, though seen at the Stanley
Hotel, are living with San Kee, on Lagauchetiere street.*

Unsigned. "Chinese Religion. Information Given a Lady by Montreal Chinamen"
Montreal Daily Star, 21 September 1895: 5.

A lady in search of information regarding Chinese beliefs went into the Tye
Loy Company's place of business and made enquiry of the Chinese gentlemen gathered there. She was told that the Chinese religion is, first of all, a
religion of ceremony and its priests are priests of ceremony. The Chinese
child is taught to observe and take part in numerous rites and ceremonies
and grows to adult age surrounded by tablets and representatives of unseen powers, believing in the importance of numberless superstitious
customs. Whether they be Confucianist, Buddhists or Taoists the Chinese
are slaves to ceremony. But it is a mistake they told her to think that the
Chinese bow down in spirit to wood or stone or images made of such
materials. The Chinaman prostrates himself bodily before his ancestral
tablets, his images of male and female divinities, but he worships in spirit,
only the spirit that is supposed to dwell in the image, and not the image itself, which is nothing more to him that what it is – a piece of wood or stone.

Mr. Cheeping declared emphatically that the Chinese worship spirits,
not images. "We worship" said he "in the same way that I have seen people
worship in Notre Dame Church here. We kneel before 'Mother' (Ahmah)
(a Chinese goddess) as the Catholics kneel to the Virgin Mary."

"Have you Churches in China – Chinese Churches?" asked the lady.

"Yes, but we call our Churches, Temples," said a strange Chinese

* 35 The name "Ah So Nan" reappears in "The Three Souls of Ah So Nan."

gentleman. "They are very beautiful and travellers who come to China like to visit them. Then we have Ancestral halls which are not open to the public."

"What are Ancestral halls?"

"Ancestral Halls are places where we worship our Ancestral Tablets. They are private property and if a family is not wealthy enough to possess an Ancestral hall a room in the house is dedicated to the memory of the deceased ancestors."

"What ceremonies do you perform in the Ancestral Halls?"

"At certain times and seasons we burn candles before the tablets and make sacrifices of meat, vegetables and fruits."

The lady knew that the Chinese were very proud of Confucius, and not long since had heard repeated the following stanza, which will give some idea of the regard with which the Chinese cherish the memory of their sage:

"Confucius, Confucius, how great is Confucius.

Before Confucius there never was a Confucius,

Since Confucius, there never has been a Confucius.

Confucius, Confucius, how great is Confucius."*

"Confucius," said one Chinaman, "lived many centuries ago, and most of the Chinese laws and manners have been modelled according to the principles he inculcated. You have no idea how the people in China honor and revere him."

"What did Confucius teach?"

"He taught that the obligations of men consist in doing good to their family, their friends and their country. He taught that obedience to superiors forms the grand basis of society and of government. He taught that filial virtue was above all other virtues. He taught that the five cardinal virtues were politeness, fidelity, benevolence, righteousness and wisdom."

"Are there not three kinds of religion named in China?"

"Yes, Confucianism, Taoism and Buddhism."

"Which is the most popular?"

---

* These lines are also cited in Eaton's "Leaves from the Mental Portfolio of an Eurasian" (1909).

"I think Confucianism; but I think many of the Confucianists are also considered Buddhists and Taoists, because they take part in Buddhist and Taoist ceremonies. Confucianism, pure and simple, is the religion of all the learned men of our country; it is the religion of the Emperor – the State religion."

"What religion do the Chinese who come over to our country mostly follow?"

"The religion of Confucius."

"Where do they worship? They have no churches in Montreal."

"They worship in their own houses – in their laundries – many of them have small places partitioned off from the living room and set apart for worship."

Unsigned. "A Chinese Child Born. At the Hotel on Lagauchetiere Street."
Montreal Daily Star, 30 September 1895: 1.

The First Pure Chinese Child Born in Montreal – San Kee a Happy Man – Some of The Ceremonies Connected with the Event

There is great rejoicing at the Lagauchetiere street Chinese Hotel. San Kee, Montreal's most prominent Chinaman, has a son and heir. It came into the world yesterday, and is the first pure Chinese child ever born in this city. San Kee's face is therefore wreathed with smiles, and his uncles and cousins are congratulating one another and telling tales of "old times" in Chines. "Ah," said one old fellow, "when Yip Kee in Canton had a son born to him we had great feasting and blowing of horns."

A reporter, who by special favor* was permitted to take an all-round look at the interesting baby, found him to be much like other infants of his age and experience – the distinguishing feature, the queue, not having yet

* The "special favour" suggests the reporter is a "lady" who knows the family well.

developed. He cries like other babies and eats like other babies, is healthy, well shaped and, from present indications, will live to be a credit to his father and mother. He wore an embroidered pink robe, made in European fashion, which robe had been selected by San Kee himself for his son's first attiring. It might be here remarked that if babies understood the value of wardrobes, San Kee, Jr., would consider himself fortunate, for he is the possessor of both a Chinese and a European wardrobe.

Immediately after San Kee received the announcement of his son's birth he set censers and sticks of burning incense under pictures and scrolls in different corners of his apartments. In all probability he will give a dinner to his friends within a month's time. It isn't every day that a Montreal Chinaman has a son, and San Kee, like a true Chinaman, believes he has now a substantial reason to make merry.

Mrs. San Kee and her son were skillfully cared for by Dr. Grace Ritchie,* and the baby escaped being subjected to any of the superstitious ceremonies which generally attend the birth of Chinese children. In fact, a Chinese child from the day of its birth is so hedged about with petty rites and ceremonies that it is surprising that so many of them grow to a sensible old age.

——

On the third day after the birth of a Chinese child the nurse washes it before an image of the goddess of children and immediately after being washed the binding of the baby's wrists takes place. In regard to this there is great diversity of practice. Some families simply bind around each wrist one or more [pieces of] ancient cash by means of a red cotton cord; others put around each wrist a loose red string, as though it were a ring. Well-to-do families provide several silver toys and hang them around the wrist. The string used is generally about two feet long, each end being put about the wrists, leaving about one foot of loose string between them. Sometimes a ring of red tape or red cords is worn for several months. When soiled the tape or cord is exchanged for a clean one. The ancient cash is used as a charm in order to keep away evil spirits; the silver toys are designed as omens of good relating to the future life of the child. The wrists are thus

* An early doctor and suffragist in Montreal.

tied together in order to prevent the child from becoming naughty and disobedient. If a child grows up fractious and hard to control, it is said that its mother could not have bound its wrists properly at its birth.

Amongst the many singular observances relating to children the ceremony called "passing through the door" is about the most important. Mr. Cheefung, who was spoken to concerning it, says that some families have it performed regularly every year, others every third year, and others every second year. A day is usually spent in its observances. Several priests come to the residence of the lad's parents and arrange an altar made out of tables placed one upon another. On the top table they place censers, candlesticks and various images of their gods, also hanging up painted pictures of goddesses, the principal one being "Mother." In a convenient part of the room is placed a table, having upon it plates of meats, vegetables and fruit. After everything is properly arranged one of the priests rings a bell while chanting his formulas, another beats a drum, another strikes his cymbals together. The object of all this is to invite certain goddesses to be present to bless the child. A portable door of bamboo wood is built purposely for the occasion in the middle of the room, and after the passing through of the child the priest and the father, which generally takes place at sundown, the door is removed and burnt.

The ceremony called "Going out of childhood" is performed when a child attains to the age of sixteen. It is very similar to the ceremony of "passing through the door."

At the age of sixteen a boy emerges from boyhood into manhood, and a girl from girlhood into womanhood.

San Kee's son should felicitate himself that he is born in Canada and not in China, for Chinese laws, though very good for fathers and mothers, are not at all fair to sons and daughters. It's nice to be a grandfather in China, but one can't help pitying the poor grandsons.

It seems that, although a boy becomes of age when he has reached his sixteenth year, and then becomes amenable to punishment if guilty of a crime, yet he still remains under the control of his parents, and must subject his will to their will and continue to obey them implicitly – and this even when he has passed from sixteen to sixty. Such is the doctrine of the laws of China. No matter how old, how educated, how wealthy – except he has become an officer of the Government and while he is serving the Emperor – he must render prompt and unquestioning obedience to his father and mother. The time never comes when a man, while his parents are living, may engage in the pursuit he chooses, or may keep his earnings for himself, or spend them as he pleases, unless he has their consent and approval. His wages are given to them and they can oblige him to do anything they please without asking his consent, or consulting his preferences. This is law, and were it not that in fact and in practice, despite this law, parents in China show great consideration for their children, every Chinaman with a living father and mother would be intensely miserable.

San Kee has been the recipient of numerous congratulatory messages from friends in Boston and New York. Visitors are not received by Chinese ladies until three weeks after the birth of the child.*

Unsigned. "Another Chinese Baby. The Juvenile Mongolian Colony in Montreal Receives Another Addition – It Is a Girl and There Are Schemes for Her Marriage."
Montreal Daily Star, 12 October 1895: 6.

Another Chinese baby has been born at Sam Kee's Hotel. This time it is a little girl. The father's name is Moy Dong Fat. He and his wife, who is but sixteen years of age, have been visitors at Sam Kee's for the last two months.

To say that Moy Dong Fat is pleased would scarcely be telling the truth. Indeed, he was so disappointed that a daughter instead of a son happened to be his first born that for a time he even refused to look at the child, and it was not until a friend assured him that girls in this country were more highly prized than boys, that he brightened up and became reconciled to the position of being father to a daughter.

Chinese parents have as much affection for their daughters as for their sons and usually treat them as kindly, but in a country like China where women take no part, in fact, never appear in public life, it follows that sons

* Ethnographic details presented here reappear in stories such as "Completion of the Moon."

are more warmly welcomed. The Chinese, however, laugh at the idea entertained by the westerners that they in China put to death girl babies, simply because they are girls. They say that now and then, as in our own country, there are cases of infanticide amongst them, but that it is utterly untrue to say that they kill infants off in a wholesale manner.

When a poor family is unable to rear a girl baby, she is often given away or sold when a few weeks old to some family who take her with the intention of marrying her to one of their sons.

Mr. Moy Dong Fat will remove his family to Boston within a few weeks, but before he goes it is talked of betrothing his little girl to Sam Kee's boy.

Unsigned. "Chinese Food."
Montreal Daily Star, 25 November 1895: 4.

The writer has been through a Chinese kitchen in the city and eaten of many Chinese dishes, all of which, if somewhat insipid to the palate, were very good and nutritious. The chief article of diet of a Chinese laundry-man is rice. It is a very wholesome grain, and the Chinaman cooks its cleanly and beautifully. Watch him eating and you will see that nearly every grain rolls separate as he shovels it into his mouth with his chop-sticks. A bowl of rice flavored with a little soy often forms the dinner of a Chinaman.

Sun-dried comestibles are much used in Chinese cooking, and in their soups and stews one notices floating about various kinds of dried nuts, dried fish and dried vegetables. A favorite dish and a very appetizing one, is meat dumplings, small dumplings filled with minced meat and boiled in a big cauldron. There is nothing on a Chinaman's table to remind us of living animals or birds – no legs, heads, limbs, wings or loins – everything is cut into small pieces, suitable to be handled by chop-sticks. The Chinaman comes to the table to eat – not to work – his carving is done in the kitchen.

At the banquet given by San Kee to his countrymen not long since, there were so many curious and expensive dishes partaken of that only because it is not easy to remember the names of dishes tasted in a state of nervous exhaustion, a full description is not given. There was a stew of shell-fish. It looked suspicious, but the taste was excellent. There were shark fins, boiled to the softest consistency, and something very gelatinous – preserved duck's tongues. There were balls of crab and tripe boiled to a tenderness hard to express. There were slices from the breasts of geese, and boiled eggs of many colors. Added to this were berries and vegetables preserved in vinegar, prawns, ground nuts, preserved ginger, and candied fruits. One peculiarity about the table was that, although it was furnished with sauces of every flavor and strength, salt itself in its pure dinner table state was not to be seen.

A Chinese diet is said to be very good for dyspeptics and men of sedentary habits. It is mucilaginous, nutritious and easily digested.

Unsigned. "Chinamen with German Wives."
Montreal Daily Star, 13 December 1895: 5.

THERE WAS ONE IN MONTREAL RECENTLY.
The Frau Visited China and Was Willing to Become a Woman
of the Celestial Kingdom – Devoted to Her Husband.

There has just left this city for New York a Chinese merchant named Li Sing and his German wife. Mr. Li Sing was married a few years ago whilst living in the States, and last year he took his wife to China with him to pay a visit to his relations. His wife, a pretty young woman of twenty-three, became very much attached to the Chinese, lived in the Chinese quarter of the city, dressed in Chinese clothes, and ate Chinese food. When about to take passage in the vessel which was to bring her to Canada, Mrs. Li Sing asked to be allowed to take up her quarters in that part of the vessel which was allotted to some Chinese women. The Steamship Company would not consent to such an arrangement, as they said they could not allow a European woman to mix up with the Chinese female passengers.

Mrs. Li Sing, who was then wearing American dress, wisely considered that if she were wearing the costume she had worn whilst in China, the Company would not look upon her as a European. She therefore retired, made a change, and appearing again before the ship's officer, said, "See, I am a Chinawoman now." Her wish was gratified.

Mr. and Mrs. Li Sing have been Mr. Cheeping's guests on Bleury [S]treet for about three weeks, during which time Mrs. Li Sing made herself quite at home amongst the Chinamen.

Mr. Cheeping says that some German and Irish women are devotedly attached to their Chinese husbands. One of his compatriots, who was once quite well-to-do and had a flourishing little business in New York, married a German woman. Shortly after the marriage, through the villainy of some men he had trusted, his business failed and he lost all his money. The man was utterly broken down, but his brave wife set to work and collected enough funds to set up a little fruit stall, which she looked after, and in that way managed to maintain both herself and husband. The latter, however, was an undeserving fellow, and his temper being warped by his misfortunes, he often scolded and beat his wife for no reason whatever. One day he struck her on the street, she cried out in pain and a policeman passing caught the Chinaman by the collar and tried to drag him to the police station. The Chinaman struggled whilst the wife begged the policeman to let him go. The policeman refused and told the Chinaman that he would have him locked up for striking his wife, and he was forcing him along when the woman cried out:

"Indeed, he did not strike me; he is the best of husbands and is always good and kind to me. I had a sudden pain in my side and that is the reason why I screamed."*

The policeman looked puzzled, but, of course, after that, what could he do but release the man?

---

* Reminiscent of the girlfriend's explanation to the police officer in "The Origin of a Broken Nose."

E.E. "The Chinese Question."
Montreal Daily Star, 16 December 1895: 4.

To the Editor of the Star:

Sir. – The Chinese question having been much discussed lately, may I take the liberty of submitting the following to your numerous readers: The law of humanity is to save, not kill, and each race must look out for itself first, and this applies particularly in this case.

Now, John Chinaman has no doubt been placed in this world with as much right to live as our own Canadians, and as he adapts himself so easily to our civilization, and makes his way amongst us – not by loud words and bluster, but by good work and quiet, dignified conduct, we are better with him.

It is well known that the Chinaman comes here alone to make money, and with the intention of returning sooner or later. See how he follows the example which we westerners set him. There are many foreigners in China, and with the exception of the missionaries, they are all there for the avowed purpose of making money. The ports of China are full of foreign private adventurers. After they've made their pile they'll return to their homes in Europe or America.

The Chinaman does not come here to settle down. If such a notion as settling here ever entered his head our treatment of him would soon knock it out.* He does not associate with our race at all – we don't and we won't associate with him.

I think J. N. Macburnie in yesterday's "Star" takes a very narrow and prejudiced view of the Chinese question. The steam laundries are taking work from the Chinese instead of the Chinese taking work from them. The Chinese started the laundry business in Canada fourteen or fifteen years ago – the steam laundries are institutions which were raised but yesterday.

There is room for all, and the Chinese do not grumble at fair competition, but when undeserved and false accusations are brought against them in order to ruin their business, why then every person who has any sense

---

* Eaton repeats several phrases from this letter in her "A Plea for the Chinaman."

of justice ought to stand up for the men who, on account of their ignorance of our language, are unable to stand up for themselves.

"K[ing] John. From whom has thou this great commission, France?"
"K[ing] Philip. From that supernal Judge, who stirs good thoughts
"In any breast of strong authority,
To look into the blots and stains of right."*

E.E.
Montreal, December 12.

Unsigned. "The Chinese and Christmas."
Montreal Daily Star, 21 December 1895: 2.†

How the Mongolians of Montreal Celebrate Yule-tide.

This is the season when the thoughts of absent ones turn towards
home, and friends and relations meet to spend the hours in happy social
intercourse; this is more than any other season a home season – a time for
children to make merry and rejoice without restraint, a time when mothers,
wives, sisters and sweethearts are made happy by thoughtful remem-
brances and grateful attentions, and husbands, brothers, fathers and sons
forget that business is before pleasure. A glimpse into the Chinese laundries in this city sets one musing. How do these men who are far away
from home and children and women kind spend their Christmas? In
weeping and gnashing their teeth?

No, indeed! A Chinaman is by nature more optimistic than pessimistic;
he is inclined to look on the bright side of life; he believes that man is born
good; he is also something of a philosopher and when he cannot get a
thing he can content himself without it. He might like to see his mother

* From Shakespeare's *King John* II Act 1, scene 2. 404–7.
† Passages from this article are recycled in Eaton's "Plea for the Chinaman," "A Chinese
Tom-Boy," and "Chinese in America, Part IV."

just as much as you would like to see yours, but if circumstances deny him the benefit of motherly counsels, it never enters his head to go on a spree for want of them; he might like to have by his side the girl to whom he was wed the day before he started for Canada, but if she be not here he sighs neither for her nor for another. The Chinaman does not carry his heart on his sleeve; he has affections, but he betrays them in actions, not words. Emigrants from other lands talk liberally and weep copiously about those they have left behind, but the Chinaman unbosoms not himself.

In sturdy silence he works and sends home every month a cheerful letter, and, if possible; some of his earnings. It is the Canadianized Chinaman who is here referred to. The Chinaman in China is Sabbathless and Christmasless; the Chinaman in Canada respects the Sabbath; and for all his loneliness rejoices when Christmas draws near.

So in many a Chinese laundry in this city are Christmas preparations in an humble way being carried on, and many are the bags of li-chee and boxes of tea which have been set aside to be given as Christmas gifts; crepe shawls, fans, curios, preserved ginger, parasols are also evidences that Chinese scholars appreciate the efforts of their Sunday-school teachers to imbue them with a faith that reaches to heaven.

At Christmas time the Chinamen visit and make presents, tell tales, crack nuts and act like sensible jolly fellows, who know how to make the best of a holiday. Turkey and plum pudding are not the great dishes with them that they are with us – they prefer a piece of roast pork, a curiously compounded gelatinous stew, and some bean cakes – but on Christmas Day the Chinaman thinks he'll be "like Canadian man," and therefore willingly foregoes his Chinese comestibles, and right joyously picks a turkey's bones and eats a Christmas pie.

The Chinese are exceedingly fond of stories and story-telling, so while the sun goes down, and long after it has set, whilst the children sing "Peace upon earth," and their elders wish, if not in their hearts, at least with their lips, "Good-will to men," the Chinese boys gather together in groups and listen to those of their number whose imaginations and experiences give them the power to portray the achievements of heroes, the despair of lovers, the blessings which fall to the lot of the filial son, and the terrible fate of the undutiful.

Themes are varied, but those which treat of magic and enchantment are the most popular. Some of the stories are said to be very exciting and considerable dramatic power must be possessed by the story tellers, for they are listened to with breathless interest. Who knows but we may have a Chinese Dickens amongst them?

Some Chinamen take advantage of the holiday to patronize our theatres. The writer asked a well-informed Chinaman if the plays in Chinese theatres resembled those he saw acted on the Montreal stage. He replied "Yes, the stories played in Chinese theatres are very much like the stories played in ours, but our actors are nearly all men. When it is necessary to personate female characters we have men dressed as females to carry on the parts. Of late years, however, a few sing-song girls have been allowed to act."

"If an audience is pleased with an actor, how do the people show their approbation – by clapping hands?"

"No," said Mr. Cheeping with a laugh, "if we are pleased we call out "Hao, hao." (Hao is the Chinese word for good.)

Gambling and opium smoking are somewhat indulged in by our black sheep Chinamen on Christmas Day. Gambling is not considered unlawful during a holiday season in China, and it may be that our Chinamen have not changed their minds on legal matters since becoming natives of Canada. A few confirmed and desperate gamblers are said to have an image made of wood on which is painted a tiger with wings.

This image is the God of Gambling, and is called "His Excellency, the Grasping Cash Tiger." The gamblers light incense and candles before it and cast lots with bamboo sticks. The gambling consists in guessing lucky characters for a specified day upon bamboo slips.

Thus, in a variety of ways do our Chinamen spend their Christmas.

The Chinese do not need to come to Canada to learn how to celebrate the New Year, because there is no country in the world where the New Year is welcomed with more rejoicing than in China. The festivities last for about fifteen days, and during the greater part of that time all the respectable hongs* and stores are supposed to close.

---

* A *hong* is a commercial establishment or place where foreign trade occurs.

Very little money except for candies and sweetmeats is spent and he who buys and sells is regarded with superstitious dread. No unnecessary work is performed and should it be necessary to hire a man to work during this season he expects two or three times as much pay as usual. There is much visiting and feasting and some wealthy families have a band of private actors at their houses for the purpose of entertaining visitors. The actors receive no wages for their services, but presents from the guests are expected. It would be a slight to the host to leave his house without giving a present to the actors.

New Year in China is a season of relaxation and rest from the cares of office and business. There is a great deal of mutual giving and receiving and not even the poorest beggar is supposed to have an empty mouth.

Games and story telling are favorite pastimes and the setting off of fire crackers affords as much amusement to a staid elderly Chinaman as it does to our wi[l]dest Canadian youngster. Chinese fire works are without doubt very beautiful. The Chinese call the darting lights "flowers."

Ceremonies too numerous to be particularized are performed during the New Year. The names of these ceremonies would cause a humorist to smile and the sober-minded to sigh. One is "Keeping Company with the Gods during the night," a ceremony which consists of making offerings and feasting before a collection of Gods or images; the Gods are supposed to graciously receive the spirit of the foods spread before them, whilst the devotees in order to be sociable with and agreeable to their august company demolish the substance of the viands.

The Chinese New Year in Montreal is like their Christmas. They spend it in resting and eating and playing games. Amongst themselves they have plenty of fun and much to say. With strangers they are timid and reserved. Some of our Chinese boys visit their Sunday school teachers and European friends on New Year's Day; others prefer to visit one another.

The Chinamen offer their callers oranges, loose skinned if possible, hot tea and baked watermelon seeds. Lady visitors are often presented with a Chinese lily.

A number of the Chinese schools, superintended by Dr. Thomson, are training the scholars in such a way that on New Year's day in Montreal the Chinaman blithely sings "Jesus Loves Me," and, whether he understands the hymn or not, is quite happy to be able to sing it. It is New Year indeed to a Chinaman when he can sing in English.

Last winter during New Year time a young girl teacher at one of the night schools, who had been teaching words and figures in a rather confusing fashion to a Chinese youth named Mark You, took it into her head to examine her pupil in the following way: "What's this?" she said to Mark You, laying hold of her left ear.

"What's this?" reiterated Mark You, pulling at his own lobe.

"Mark You," said the girl, "I told you that this was called an 'ear.' When I ask you again what it is you must say 'ear.'"

"Say ear," said Mark You obediently.

"And this," she continued, laying her finger on her forehead, "What did I tell you this was, Mark You?"

Mark You solemnly touched the forehead of the Chinaman who sat beside him, the forehead of the man in front of him, that of his teacher and lastly his own forehead. Then he arose in his seat and triumphantly announced "Four Heads."

Unsigned. "Chinese Entertainment, at Which the Chinamen Did Their Share of the Entertaining."
Montreal Daily Star, 31 December 1895: 2.*

They were all there last night – the fiddler with his fiddle, the flutist with his flute, the banjo man with his banjo and the kettledrummer with his kettledrum – all the Chinese talent of Montreal was there – in St. Paul's Church lecture room – and right merrily entertained were those who came to see and hear.

It was a gathering of thirteen Chinese Sunday schools, and the crowded room, decorated with Chinese flags and banners beautifully embroidered – presented a very animated appearance, and was in itself, as the Rev. A. B.

* The opening words of this column are recycled in Eaton's short story "Sweet Sin." See Dominika Ferens, *Edith and Winnifred Eaton: Chinatown Missions and Japanese Romances.* (Chicago: University of Illinois Press, 2002, 192).

McKay, D.D., remarked, a monument to the good work which is being done by Dr. Thomson and his wife among the Montreal Chinamen.

On the platform were seated the Rev. Dr. Barclay, chairman; Rev. Dr. Mackay, Rev. Mr. Mowatt, Rev. Mr. [James] Fleck, Rev. Dr. Campbell, Rev. Mr. Pos, Rev. Mr. Scott, Rev. Mr. Nichols, Principal [of the Presbyterian College, Donald Harvey] MacVicar, Prof. [John] Scrimger and Dr. Thomson.

After the Doxology Dr. Barclay addressed the Chinese scholars, giving them a hearty welcome. He said it gave him great pleasure to see so many of his Chinese brothers, and only regretted that he could not speak to them in their own language and tell them how sorry he was that they had met with experiences which might perhaps cause them to think meanly of the Christian faith. He wished to say that he and all the friends there assembled would endeavor to give them a different impression of Christianity.*

Then followed a reading in both languages, Chinese and English, of a portion of Scripture, Joe Gow: "The Manger Cradle," Miss Schneider; reading "The Birth of Christ," Chu Long; piano solo, Miss Amy Nichols; address, Hop Wo; hymn, "Precious Name," Wong Faw; reading the twenty-third Psalm, Mark Him; hymn, "I am so glad," Lee Tong; recitation of the commandments, Hum How Foo; Chinese song, Hoom Yen; hymn "Safely through another week," sung to a Chinese tune; song, Miss Abernethy; a short address by the Rev. Dr. Mackay: a few words from Dr. Thomson, who thanked the reverend gentlemen and teachers present for their hearty co-operation in the work he was carrying on; solo, harmonica and banjo, Mr. C. W. Stuart, which performance highly delighted the whole audience, the Chinamen in particular; Chinese melody, with accompaniment, Lee Chu; violin orchestra, Chinese violin and Chinese violinists; Oriental orchestra.

The Chinamen who helped in the entertainment betrayed very little embarrassment and acted their parts well. Hop Wo spoke in a bright and direct manner, and his earnest, grateful tones as he thanked the kind friends for their interest in himself and his fellow countrymen made a very

* This paragraph and a few phrases several paragraphs later are recycled in Eaton's "Chinese in America: Part IV."

favorable impression. The singing of "Precious Name" by Wong Faw was also good; his words were distinct and his voice pleasing.

As to the readings and recitations, they proved that, although the delivery of a Chinaman is somewhat monotonous, yet he is not destitute of oratorical power, and no doubt when these men return as Christians to China they will be able to explain the doctrines of the Bible in a clear and effective manner.

The Chinese music on Chinese instruments was the most interesting part of the interesting programme. When the flutist blew his flute and the tootist commenced to toot, when the fiddler began to fiddle and the soloist to sing, the effect was overwhelming. Smiles were on all faces, and people unaccustomed to such strange symphonies didn't know whether to be soothed or startled, especially in the intervals during which the voice of the singer was raised to a falsetto pitch to imitate a female's voice.

Dr. Thomson explained that one of the tunes was the favorite Chinese melody, and a Chinaman told the writer that the last piece of music, in which five musicians took part, was taken from a play in a Chinese theatre. The singer was supposed to be a maiden soliloquizing whilst her lover is in battle.

Refreshments were served by the ladies of St. Paul's church, and the meeting broke up, having been, in spite of the weather, a decided success.

E.E. "A Plea for the Chinaman. A Correspondent's Argument in His Favour."
Montreal Daily Star, 21 September 1896: 5.

The Mongolian Defended From the Charges Made Against Him by Members of Parliament From British Columbia.

To the Editor of the Star:

Sir. – Every just person must feel his or her sense of justice outraged by the attacks which are being made by public men upon the Chinese who

come to this country.* It is a shame because the persecutors have every
weapon in their hands and the persecuted are defenceless – for the Chinamen are defenceless. They do not understand in a full sense all that their
revilers charge them with and they have no representative men to answer
the charges. [Liberal Member of Parliament for Portneuf, PQ] Sir Henri
[-Gustave] Joly de Lotbiniere† and [Liberal Member of Parliament for
Guysborough North] Mr. [Duncan Cameron] Fraser are nobly fighting on
their side, but neither of these gentlemen are Chinese, nor have they lived
for any length of time amongst the Chinese, and so, of course, it is impossible for either of them to give back blow for blow. It needs a Chinaman to
stand up for a Chinese cause. The people who are persecuting them send
one of themselves, nay, a dozen of themselves, men who are just as prejudiced as their constituents, just as worked up over fancied wrongs and just
as incapable of judging fairly. They are all, Mr. [George Ritchie] Maxwell
[Liberal Member of Parliament for Burrard, BC], Mr. [John M.] Charlton
[Liberal Member of Parliament for Norfolk North, ON], Mr. [William
Wallace Burns] McInnes [Liberal Member of Parliament for Vancouver,
BC], [Miners' Union leader] Mr. [Ralph] Smith, etc., etc., equipped with
self-interest which is the strongest of weapons.

It makes one's cheeks burn to read about men of high office standing
up and abusing a lot of poor foreigners behind their backs and calling
them all the bad names their tongues can utter. They know that the
Chinese cannot answer them and they go on fully armed, using all their
weapons. It's very brave, I must say, to fight with the air. A fine spectacle
for the world to look at. But I suppose they don't care. They've got a party
at home to cheer them.

I will now go over the ground a little. I speak from experience, because
I know the Chinamen in all characters, merchants, laundrymen, laborers,
servants, smugglers and smuggled, also as Sunday School scholars and

* In September 1896, BC Member of Parliament George Maxwell had proposed in the
House of Commons that the head tax be raised to $500 in response to the Anti-Mongolian
League's resolution at a mass meeting in Vancouver. See James Morton, *In the Sea of Sterile
Mountains: The Chinese in British Columbia* (Vancouver: J.J. Douglas, 1974, 178).
† The Chinese Emperor made Joly de Lotbinière a member of the Order of the Double
Dragon for his efforts to stand up for Chinese in Canada.

gamblers. They have faults, but they also have virtues. Nations are made up of all sorts.

It is proposed to impose a tax of five hundred dollars upon every Chinaman coming into the Dominion of Canada. The reasons urged for imposing such a tax are that the presence of the Chinese affects the material and moral interests of the Canadian people, that the Chinese work cheap and therefore white men cannot compete with them, that they are gamblers and grossly immoral, that they introduce disease, cost the public much money and delay the development of the country.

The presence of the Chinaman does affect the material interests of this country, for he is a good and steady workman and has helped and is still helping to build our railways, mine our ores and in various branches of agriculture and manufacturing is providing a source of wealth to those who employ him. He does good to our laboring class for he acts as an incentive to them to be industrious and honest. I say honest, because he seeks to gain no advantage over other laborers, simply comes to compete with them – and competition is always good. The Chinaman stands on his merits: if he were of no benefit to this country he would soon have no reason to wish to remain here, for you may be sure, if incapable of performing the tasks required of him, he would not be given employment, for Canadians do not employ Chinamen for love; they take them for the use they can make of them.

As to working cheap, I believe if the matter was investigated, you would find out that the white men are willing to accept the same wages per week as the Chinamen, but they refuse to put in as much work for the wages. If the white man has to live, so also has the Chinaman, and I know that in Montreal the Chinese live well, and a great many of those I am acquainted with are former residents of British Columbia and have not changed their manner of living since coming East. I have seen on their breakfast tables great bowls of rice and dishes of beautiful light omelet, besides many European comestibles and I have noticed and have been told by themselves that they frequently order fowl and fish from the markets and the best of meats and vegetables. I am speaking of laundrymen, not merchants. Of course, the very poor ones are more frugal, but I can assure you a Chinaman lives merrily when he has the means.

Now, as to the charges of immorality brought against the Chinese. There are over five hundred Chinamen in Montreal, besides a transient population, and I have never heard during a residence here of many years of any one of these Chinese being accused of saying or doing that which was immoral, in the sense in which I understand the word "immoral." It is true some of the Chinamen who have been contaminated by white men and American lawyers, become swindlers and perjurers, and help their contaminators, who are just like leeches, to bleed the poor Chinese laborers who are desirous of passing into the States, and from which by a disgraceful law they are barred out, but the main body of the Chinamen are straightforward, hard-working fellows. Their worst fault is that they are somewhat cynical with regard to the honesty of white men, but that is not surprising when we consider that nearly all the white men with whom they come in contact think of nothing but squeezing money out of them by some means or other. Even the law restricting them from entering America looks as if it was got up for the sole purpose of giving unprincipled lawyers and corrupt Government officers a chance to do some boodling.*

I am surprised at the moral tone of the Chinese population of Canada. These men, far away from their homes and children and womankind, are well behaved and self-respecting. Our magistrates' hair would stand on end with surprise were a Chinaman to be brought before them charged with assault or the use of insulting language.

When Mr. Maxwell speaks of the vices of the Chinese corrupting the whole body politic of British Columbia one has to smile. It is so absurd. Surely those who are "controlled by the higher influences of civilization" cannot succumb to those who obey "the lower forces of barbarism." The Chinaman may be willing to attend Sunday school and learn all that you can teach him, but I am quite certain that it never enters his head to convert you to his way of thinking.

I am afraid Mr. Maxwell knew very little about what he was speaking when he took up the Chinese question. He knew that he wanted to get certain advantages for a party of British Columbians, and he put all his heart

* To boodle is to earn money illegally or improperly.

Selected Early Journalism: Montreal

and soul into gaining his object, forgetting that there are two sides to every story, or if he did remember, assuring himself that no one else would.

"I have but to say the word, and it will be believed," said he to his constituents on the eve of his departure for Ottawa.

The influence of the Chinese people in a moral sense is null, and I have yet to meet the man or woman who will tell me that a Chinaman influenced him or her to do that against which moral sense rebelled.

The Chinese receive instruction gladly when it comes their way, but they do not ask for it, and as to imparting to others their opinions and beliefs, the pride or humility of the race forbids anything approaching that. The quiet dignity of the Chinese is worthy of admiration, and Mr. Maxwell ought to be ashamed of himself for sneering at them for being docile and easily managed. Perhaps he does not know that the Chinese are taught to treat the rude with silent contempt. A Chinaman does not knock a man down or stab him for the sake of an insult. He will stand and reason, but unless forced, though not by any means a coward, he will not fight. In China a man who unreasonably insults another has public opinion against him, whilst he who bears and despises the insult is respected. There are signs that in the future we in this country may attain to the high degree of civilization which the Chinese have reached, but for the present we are far away behind them in that respect.

"No self-respecting people," said Mr. Maxwell, "wish to have dumped into their midst the scum of eastern barbarism."

I am sorry to have to again show up Mr. Maxwell's ignorance of his subject. The Chinese who come to our shores are not "scum." They are mostly steady, healthy country boys from the Canton district. They are none of them paupers. They come here furnished with a modest sum of money and with the hope of adding thereto by honest labor. I can prove all I say.

And do you think [visiting Chinese statesman] Li Hung Chang,* who knows all about the standing of his countrymen here would have met

* In 1896, Li toured Canada, and the US to advocate for reform of the Chinese Exclusion Act and other restrictive immigration policies.

them as courteously as he did, and send them personally kind messages, had he considered them the "riff-raff" of China.

We are not impoverished by the Chinese immigrants, for they offer us good value for our money and if any of them fall sick they are not thrown upon our hands to be cared for; they are looked after by their own countrymen.

Of course, there are a few black sheep. There are exceptions in all cases, but the Government knows that I speak soberly and Mr. Maxwell fanatically when I say that the Chinese boys who come to Canada are in the main good boys, and he declares they are "the accumulated filth of Chinese gaols and dens of vice and crime."

The Chinese have many worthy characteristics; they are good natured – all the world knows that. They have a keen sense of humor – I could tell many good stories showing that up. They easily forgive those who insult or wrong them – that is proved every day. They are hospitable, and are at heart gentlemen. In the spring of this year I visited New York's Chinatown. I went alone, and though a woman and a perfect stranger was received by the Chinese there with the greatest kindness and courtesy. For two weeks* I dwelt amongst them, trotted up and down Mott, Pell and Doyer streets, saw the Chinese theatres and Joss Houses,† visited all the little Chinese women, talked pigeon English to them, examined their babies, dined with a Chinese actress, darted hither and thither through the tenements of Chinatown, and during that time not the slightest disrespect or unkindness was shown to me. I was surprised, for I was in the slum portion of the city of New York, and dreadful tales had been told me of what I should meet and see there. I had been told that Chinatown was a dangerously wicked place; I had been warned that if I went in there alone I would never come out alive or sound in mind or body. My warners were like Mr. Maxwell and his colleagues – they did not know the Chinese people. I went there and returned the better for my visit. I had proved to my satisfaction what I had always believed, that the Chinese people are a more moral and a much happier lot than those who are strangers to them make them out to be.

* Eaton was in New York for two weeks in April 1896. Details recounted in this article anticipate "Chinese Woman in America."
† Chinese traditional temples.

Human nature is the same all the world over, and the Chinaman is as much a human being as those who now presume to judge him; and if he is a human being, he must be treated like one, and that we should not be doing were we to fine him five hundred dollars simply for being himself – a Chinaman. If a Chinaman breaks a law – a just law – a law which is a law to all Canadians, and which all Canadians are liable to be punished for, I would say at once that he should pay the penalty, but there is no justice in fining him just for what he is – a Chinaman. We should be broader-minded. What does it matter whether a man be a Chinaman, an Irishman, an Englishman or an American? Individuality is more than nationality.[†] "A man's a man for a' that."[*] Let us admire a clever Chinaman more than a stupid Englishman and a bright Englishman more than a dull Chinaman.

Why should Canadians in their own land fear to compete with foreigners, when they know that the foreigners are not liked, and if they, the Canadians, worked as well, there would be no chance for the Chinese whatever? If they really want to keep the Chinese out, let them do so by fair means, not by foul. Let the Canadians make an agreement with Canadians that Chinese labor will not be utilized in Canada. Then the Chinese would soon make themselves scarce; but so long as Canadian employers employ Chinese laborers, so long is a sign up telling all the world that Chinese labor is needed and wanted in Canada, and it is only a desire on the part of Mr. Maxwell to please the rowdy element of the Dominion which leads him to pretend that the Chinese are not of benefit to the country in which they are sojourning.

Some complain that they object to the Chinese because they will not settle here nor associate with other races. That objection is also a pretence, for we well know that if such a notion as settling here ever entered the Chinaman's head, our treatment of him would soon knock it out. "He does not associate with our race at all," they cry. Well, we don't and we won't

---

[*] Eaton deploys a version of this phrase in "Kingston Races. First Day. Descriptive Sketch" ("where individuality must ever rank higher than nationality"), "Woo-Ma and I" ("Individuality is more than nationality"), and "Leaves from the Mental Portfolio of an Eurasian" ("Individuality is more than nationality").

[†] Here, Eaton quotes the title of Robert Burns' 1795 Scots song, which expresses egalitarian ideas.

associate with him. "He comes here to make money, and with the intention of returning sooner or later," says another. In that he follows the example set him by the westerners: there are many foreigners in China, and, with the exception of the missionaries, they are all there with the avowed purpose of making money. The ports of China are full of foreign private adventurers. After they have made their "pile" they will return to their homes – which are not in China.

I believe the chief reason for the prejudice against the Chinese, I may call it the real and only solid reason for all the dislike shown to the Chinese people, is that they are not considered good looking by white men; that is, they are not good looking according to a Canadian or American standard for looks. This reason may be laughed at and considered womanish, but it is not a woman's reason, it is a man's. Women do not care half as much for personal appearance as do men. I am speaking very seriously, and if you will send a commission to investigate the Chinese trouble in British Columbia – if the Government will – they will find the matter to be as I say. That the Chinese do not please our artistic taste is really at the root of all the evil there, and from it springs the other objections to the Chinese. It is a big shame, I feel, and I think it is the duty of all enlightened men to combat with and overcome this very real and serious prejudice. Do not the sages say that beauty is a matter of opinion, and so if Wong Chang does not appear to our eyes as lovely to behold as Mr. Maxwell, there are those in his own land who would probably think the reverse. Besides, Wong Chang is here for utility and not for ornament.

I am convinced that an honest commission will find no real cause to further tax the Chinese. Indeed, if as conscientious as a commission can be, it will advise the fifty dollar tax already imposed be lifted.

Of course, there will be found many to stand up as witnesses against the Chinamen, but if watched closely it will be discovered that such witnesses belong to a class which is determined to find fault with the Chinaman, no matter what he does or does not do.

Will the Government of Canada pander to that certain class? Will it forget the debt of gratitude America and British America owes to China – China, who sent her men to work for us when other labor was not obtainable?

If it is loyal to that England, whose shores, as Mr. Fraser says, "are free to all comers, irrespective of race, creed or color," it will answer decidedly, No.

E.E.
Montreal, 19 September.

Edith Eaton. "The Chinese Defended. 'E. E.' Replies to Her Critics of Saturday and Is Supported by a Brooklyn Doctor."*
Montreal Daily Star, 29 September 1896: 5.

Both Claim that Mongolians Are Entitled to Consideration
at Canada's Hands.

To the Editor of the Star:

Sir. – Two letters referring to mine of the 19th appeared in your Star on Saturday. I wish to answer those communications at length, and if you will kindly give me space you will be giving the Chinese an opportunity to have a fair fight with those who will persist in slandering them. Up till now their enemies have had it all their own way, but "even a worm will turn."

[Letter-writer] Mr. [James] Buchanan need not affect to pass over as a joke what I brought forward as the chief cause for the persecution of the Chinese. If he has been amongst them, as he asserts, he will know that whenever they are ill used by the whites in the street they are called such names as "Yellow face," "Pig-tail," "Slanty-eyes" and so forth. I myself have heard those epithets bestowed on handsome Chinamen by men who were themselves as homely as can be made.

He says that he has been Mr. Maxwell's personal friend for thirty years. No doubt about that – "Birds of a feather flock together." He and Mr. Maxwell are like the bigots of olden time, who, in the name of religion,

* Eaton's letter was followed by a letter of support for her advocacy from Brooklyn-based Chinese medical doctor J.C. Thoms.

burnt and tortured poor innocent old women, the only reason given for
such acts being their belief that their victims were witches and liable to
harm the community in which they lived.

"It would take too much time to follow E.E. in her long attack upon
'persecutors.' I only wish to assure the public that she is all wrong about
the people who [are] different from her, and I desire briefly to show the
other side of the argument without abusing the other side as E.E. does
so consistently."

It is the party who begins the battle who "attacks." The party who
stands up for the persecuted is a defender. And, after all, where is the
"other side" Mr. Buchanan alludes to? There are a lot of men howling like
wolves after the Chinese on one side, but there is really no party to howl
back. Sir Henri[-Gustave] Joly [de Lotbinière] and Mr. [Duncan Cameron]
Fraser present the Chinese case in a fair light as just men, but they have no
thought of fighting on the same lines as the saintly Mr. Maxwell, who, with
grief at his heart and tears in his eyes, is forced by duty to explode so many
"unpleasant truths" on the backs of the Chinese. Listen to Mr. Buchanan:

"I have lived four years in the very heart of the Chinese, at the canneries,
on the Fraser River; have had them sleep in my house; have fed them; have
protected them; have striven to give them the gospel; have visited their
boarding houses, gambling dens, opium joints stores, etc.; have protested
against their vices, and have been acquainted with scores of them in every
relation of life, and my contention is that they are an unmitigated evil. So
much do I believe this that I have helped in every way the F[oreign]M[is-
sions]C[ommittee] of the Presbyterian Church to provide the only antidote
to the Chinamen's vices, the Gospel of our Lord Jesus Christ."

The artfulness of that paragraph quite staggers me. The readers of the
"Star" can see for themselves that Mr. Buchanan has advertised all his own
virtues, especially that of benevolence, and to show them off to good advantage puts them alongside of the Chinamen's vices, and all this is done,
you know, "without abusing the other side."

It makes me shudder to think of the Gospel being mixed up with a dose
of "envy, malice and uncharitableness," and then rammed into the poor
Chinese. I feel like praying, "Lord, save the poor Chinese from the Gospel."
I believe that it is infinitely better to be a heathen than a Christian such as

Mr. Buchanan. God is just, and He will provide a heaven for the heathen whom He has made heathen.

I would like to ask from whom Mr. Buchanan protected the Chinese. From himself? Surely they have no worse enemy. I am positive that he didn't find that they worked "too cheap" for him. I wish I could see and talk with those Chinese whom Mr. Buchanan fed and housed and protected.

I am a little surprised that Mr. Buchanan, who has "helped in every way the F.M.C. of the Presbyterian Church to provide the only antidote for the Chinaman's vices – the Gospel of the Lord Jesus Christ," should want to keep the Chinaman away from that antidote. It is really unkind of him – unless, of course, he has not as much faith in that antidote as he pretends to have. I know if I were a Chinaman, and Mr. Buchanan came to me with his antidote, I'd dash it to the ground, declaring it was poison.

Mr. Buchanan echoes Mr. Maxwell when he says: "The white man is under the restraint of civilization, and endeavors to hide his wrong doing, while the Chinaman has no sense of wrong and no sense of shame."

Why, the Chinese are the oldest civilized people on the face of this earth – as all widely educated people know, theirs is a grand old civilization.

The Chinese who come to Canada are mostly country boys; they have had a common school education, and from an early age have been trained to work – and the habit of working is strong on them. How, then, can they be gaol birds, dissipated characters and diseased? Such cannot work, we know that. The Chinaman by his labor here proves himself to be what he claims he is. It is impossible for a hard-working man to be an out and out bad fellow. Why, the poor things have no time to indulge in the vices they are charged with.

Then opium smoking comes up. Without going into the history of opium smoking by the Chinese, which, as we all know, would tell against the whites, I would say that if, as Mr. Buchanan says, ninety-five per cent of them smoke opium, then he must take back his statement that a Chinaman lives cheap, for opium smoking is expensive. The fascinating pipe costs each smoker from one to five dollars per day. I have certain knowledge about this, and feel justified in saying that those who smoke opium amongst the Chinese are in very small minority.

Gambling is as much a white man's vice as a Chinaman's, and the white

man has less excuse, for the Chinaman has few amusements, and I myself
have often felt glad that they could wile away an evening in a game of cards
or dominoes. "All work and no play makes Jack a dull boy."

Regarding the cost of living – he declares no Chinaman in British
Columbia spends more than five dollars per month – how can this be true
when he says his rice and tea cost $4? Will one dollar pay for all his other
necessaries such as pork, chickens, fish, vegetables and also lodging, to say
nothing of tobacco? A Chinese laborer lives as well as a white laborer in
like condition. Rice is more expensive than bread as the staff of life in this
country. We have tried it with a large family of children.

I can see nothing in collecting leavings of hotels and so forth – white
people do the same all over America. I have known respectable English
families in the city who have made very good meals out of the leavings
of hotels.

"They huddle together and live in tents three feet high and six feet
long."

Well, we always find the poor in masses. In New York the most crowded
part is where the Italians congregate. I could live in the Chinatown of that
city, but there are other places there through which I would not venture to
walk, and the denizens of such places were all white people.

"Now as to the result of all this their physical health is always bad
and they become the victims of disease, which we white people call
vice and crime."

What! when men fall sick from being badly fed and badly housed, he
calls them "vicious criminals!" On the top of a poor man's misfortunes
he pours vials of wrath and denunciation. That's what I call savage.

The majority of Montreal's five hundred have come from British
Columbia, and that is how I know all about the British Columbians. I
know just how the Chinese have made British Columbia what it is today –
it is their industry which has made it fertile and a habitable place for white
people. Yes, it is they who have made it fit for the white people to work
in – those white people who are now trying to drive them out. Why, the
Chinese are the pioneers of British Columbia; they are the true British
Columbians, and it is they and not the whites who should be claiming
privileges from the Government.

Really, the white men ought to feel ashamed to complain about the Chinese – the latter labor under so many disadvantages. A Scotch gentleman who has lived both in China and British Columbia and whose word cannot be doubted has told me how the Chinamen are taxed in every possible way. First, a head tax, then a tax for being allowed to work, and innumerable other taxes which are being imposed upon them even while they are walking down the street, getting on to boats, cars, etc. All who own a little land or a shanty are taxed over and over again. A collector of taxes told him that a Chinaman always paid his taxes, even when they were illegally claimed, for he was afraid to kick against paying them, like the white man, who generally got off.

The Chinamen too contributes liberally to the collection plate in his Sunday school. How many white laboring men in B.C. give to like causes?

It is true outside of what is needed for the necessaries of life and his taxes, the Chinaman spends little, but there is usually a wife and sometimes a father and mother and children at home to support. Chinamen marry very young, and there is not a bachelor in every two hundred of the Chinaman who come to this country – and the Chinaman does not shirk his responsibilities, nor yet does he carry his heart on his sleeve. He has affections, but he betrays them in actions, not words. Emigrants from other lands talk liberally and weep copiously about those they have left behind, but the Chinaman unbosoms not himself.* In sturdy silence he works and sends home every month a cheerful letter, and if possible, some of his earnings.

There is no danger of "the teeming population of China overflowing this fair country." The Chinaman likes his own land too well – he is an exile here – he has no wish to remove – and if some Chinamen are coming in all the time – others are going out.

I must quote Mr. Buchanan yet again. His letter is but an echo of dozens of others which have been written from time to time concerning the Chinese. Very foolish prejudiced effusions, yet at the same time calculated to stir up the ignorant. Mr. Buchanan says:

---

* Several of these phrases are recycled from Eaton's unsigned "The Chinese and Christmas."

"In conclusion, Mr. Editor, let me say that letters like that of E.E.,
while they are intended to help the Chinese, are only calculated to
do them an injustice and an injury."

If Mr. Buchanan honestly believed in his conclusions, he would never
have written the letter which was published in Saturday's "Star," which can
plainly be seen was written because he believed I had succeeded in proving
Mr. Maxwell's charges false and unfounded, and because being "personally
interested" in Mr. Maxwell, and holding the same opinions what I had said
reflected just as much against himself as against his dear friend.

I would like to make a few remarks on what [letter-writer] E.S. has
written, but have taken up too much space already. Besides I can see that
E.S. is a straight and downright hater of the Chinese and does not pose as
a "giver of the Gospel." Therefore, he or she is harmless – violent speeches
only affect us for a minute. It is the enemy who pretends to be a friend
whom one has to guard against. I should judge, however, that E.S. has
had no personal acquaintance with the Chinese people – has perhaps been
reading some dime novels in which Six Companies of Assassins play a
conspicuous part. I believe the Hoodlums have got up some such stories.*

Unsigned. "Born a Britisher. But Fifty Dollars Is the Tax on Him as a Chinaman."
Montreal Daily Witness, 27 October 1896.

Yen Moy is an Englishman by birth, speaking Chinese as his mother
tongue. Both his parents were English; he himself, by temperament,
language, intellectual and moral texture, is a Chinaman. Yen Moy has been
completely transmuted; reincarnated in a new type. In this province we
sometimes meet with French-Canadians whose names are Scotch or Irish.
Yen Moy could not utter one word of English if you gave him the world.

* Dime novels and pulp magazine fiction, beginning in the 1890s, frequently depicted
Chinatown – its opium dens and dark alleys – in sensational terms.

Yen Moy is to become a resident of Montreal. He will keep a laundry. He was born in Sydney, New South Wales, of English parents, and was taken to China when a baby. There he was brought up as a native; there he was taught the language; there he adopted the religion, the dress, the habits of the population.

And yet the hundred or more Chinamen who landed this morning at the Windsor street depot, having completed their voyage from China over the C[anadian] P[acific] R[ailway] steamship and railway system, did not recognize Yen Moy as one of themselves. Nay, they sneered openly at him. For not only has Yen Moy English features; he is an Albino. His hair and eyebrows are as white as flax. His eyes are weak, and can poorly bear the light. He has the native costume; he has the language; he has Chinese habits of thought; but the Chinese will have none of him. He stood apart; he was silent under the sneers; he trembled with doubt, and helplessness, and fear. It was pathetic.

Yen Moy hugged his little belongings, waited till all the Chinamen laughing and sneering at his peculiarity had passed down the stairs; would not have come forward at all but for the Rev. Dr. Thompson, who spoke to him kindly in his own tongue.

"Let them all go," said Mr. Ibbotson, C[anadian] P[acific] R[ailway] ticket agent. "They are free men in a free country."

"Is there not a little irony here?" suggested the Rev. Mr. Nichols, who was present.

"Yes," smiled Dr. Thompson, "free when they pay fifty dollars to be allowed to set foot on free soil. A little curious, eh?"

Mr. Ibbotson does not trouble about political or domestic economy, or even the solidarity of the race. What he understands is that when the Chinaman pays his poll tax he is a free creature.

Selected Early Journalism:

Jamaica

(1896–1897)

Fire Fly. "The Kingston Races. First Day. Descriptive Sketch."
Gall's Daily News Letter, 16 December 1896: 6.

The great event of the year, I am told in Kingston is the races, so I am very glad that I have had the opportunity of witnessing them.

Even a stranger cannot resist the contagion of enthusiasm, which seems to inspire every one during race week, and so when I sat, or rather stood upon my seat in the Stand, I came very near to clapping and shouting like the rest of 'em – just out of pure sympathy, for I must confess the races themselves had no particular charm for me. I did not know one horse from another. I did not know who were the owners and I was not betting.

Still it was pleasant to note the exuberance of spirit which seemed to dominate those who surrounded me, and when I turned my eyes on the swift coursers, each gallantly trying to out do the other, I thought, what-ever changes may happen – one thing is certain – that men and women will never cease to admire strength and courage.

You know in a crowd we can be very much alone – much more than we are sometimes in our own little room when the only bodily presence is our own small self, and so as I sat in that crowd, it seemed to me as if I were separated from it by many miles, and so being separated I began to study the people and criticize them in a way I would scarcely have dared to do had I felt them near. I can't give away the thoughts which floated through my mind, but the most important was this, that Jamaica has an individuality of its own, entirely different from English-speaking centres generally; and it is a country where individuality must ever rank higher than nationality.

The Race Stand seems to be very popular with the ladies, and a great many pretty dresses and bonnets were displayed. I am sorry to say I cannot tell you the names of the wearers of the gowns I admired so much, but I will try to find that out for you some other day.

There was a very stylish costume of dark heliotrope, trimmed with black glace ribbon, forming a pattern on it, and a bodice made with a vest and full sleeves. This was worn by an elderly lady. Very near to my side sat a young lady dressed in some light summer fabric of Dolly Varden* pattern made very simply; she wore a hat made of pink straw, the brim bent a little over the ears, and roses were twined round the crown. The young lady was a blonde, and she could hardly have found a daintier or more becoming costume.

There was a pretty pale, gray dress covered with velvet spots at my right hand, and charming white dresses and silks of many shades and qualities were noticeable.

As to outdoor raiment, there were to be seen quite a number of light capes, mostly of silk. Capes in a climate like this cannot help but be popular.

As to the attendance at the races, I am told that it was greater than it has ever been before, on account of the new railway facilities for reaching the City.

Before closing, I must say I have never seen a nicer behaved crowd than that which cheered the horses at the races yesterday. There was much talk, laughter, and acclamation, but I did not hear an abusive or insulting word.

I don't know whether I've a right to speak, but I've a deep, dark suspicion that some young men and women flirt at the races. Isn't that just too awful?

---

* A Dolly Varden pattern is a fabric print of bouquets of flowers named after a character in Charles Dickens' novel *Barnaby Rudge*.

Fire Fly. "The Kingston Races. Second Day. Descriptive Sketch."
Gall's Daily News Letter, 17 December 1896: 6.

In front, below and around me a mass of well-dressed people – a little
space below them, a line of nondescripts, happy-go-lucky creatures who
view the races free, and enjoy themselves even though they have little more
than their hands in their pockets. In the foreground, the wide grassy plain,
beyond on my left, the mountains, on my right, what appeared to be tropical gardens, though I may be mistaken, for here in Jamaica it is very hard
for me to distinguish between what is wild and what is cultivated. What
was the view which presented itself as I took my seat on the Grand Stand
yesterday, and as my eye ranged over the throng of people and rested here
and there on some "sweet bud" or charming matron excitedly betting on
some favourite horse. I became more than ever convinced that the Jamaicans are on the whole what is called a sporting people. We have sporting people where I come from you know, but I'd never dream of classing
the whole country under that head as I do the people of this Island. We
have horse races just as you do here, but the whole of our city and suburbs
do not turn out to view them. No, nor one hundredth part. One person in
a thousand may take an active interest in the races, and that's all. So, when
I send a budget of news to a foreign paper, as I may some day when I am a
little less ignorant, I shall begin with the fact that the Jamaicans are sporting people, and I'm very glad of it.

There were some very smart dresses on the Stand – some of them perhaps a little too gay – but that's not a matter of regret to the wearers, for
you know the bird of brilliant plumage is always the most in evidence, and
it needs little intuition to tell us that those who like to dress showily also
like to attract notice. We all like to be elegant, but some of us forget that el-
egance is more the result of exquisite neatness and distinguished air than
of rich materials and expensive dress-making.

One most tasteful dress worn yesterday was a white and amber striped
chiffon, around the waist an amber colored ribbon. There were several
dresses with pink glace silk, trimmed with dainty laces, and one lovely
zephyr gown of a pale blue tint was worn with a wide crest belt made of

velvet. Changeable golden brown and green silk waists became a couple of blue-eyed girls, who stood away up above me on the Grand Stand, and not far from them sat a lady in a costume of which I took special note. She wore a skirt, the foundation of which was brown, but dots of black and knots of pale yellow thread were arranged to form an irregular pattern.

The bodice was pale yellow basque with dark green velvet vest.

Another handsome dress was black silk – with a pattern of embroidery extending up in side panels.

It is, however, in hats that women seem to take the most delight. It is the same here as everywhere else, and hats of every size, material and colour gaily nodded to each other over the betting books.

Some of the girls wore dashing cavalier hats, others dainty little gipsy shapes; there was one hat of green straw with a high crown trimmed with ostrich feathers of slightly different shades of green and aigrettes to match.

Feather wreaths seem to be popular and even in this perpetual summer velvet appears to be a favorite trimming.

So much for outward apparel.

I wish I had had a bet. Everybody I have spoken to seems to have won something. I must write home and tell them that nobody loses here on a bet. All the sports in Canada will be coming down by next steamer. Poor lads! they'll think I've found the Sportsman's Paradise.

And now I'll finish with the race, hoping next year to be a first class better.

I think you have lovely horses – we couldn't get finer in Canada – It is too bad such pretty things should have to break their legs for our pleasure. If I had a horse like those I saw yesterday, I'd never allow it to run in a public race. I'd be afraid it might meet with an accident and then the Society for the Prevention of Cruelty to Animals would certainly feel justified in prosecuting me.

Jamaica is old-fashioned and romantic and lovely, and when I was a little girl, I used to dream about its coral reefs and coconut palms and monkeys and parrots, but now I've come to it, I find it just the same – in fundamentals as every other place I've ever lived in – except home.

Fire Fly. "The Firefly and Rum."
Gall's Daily News Letter, 23 December 1896: 2.

The fire fly fluttered outside of a big place used by G. Eustace Burke & Bro., for putting up rum, and as it fluttered there, some thoughts floated through its little rattled head. They ran in this wise:

Now, some people think that rum is splendiferous – the grandest stuff in the world – their affection for it is so great that they are forever hugging a bottle, and I believe, once they have it close to their hearts, they would die before they would "stand and deliver." "Oh! little brown jug, don't I love thee?"*

Others, on the contrary, rage at the sound of the name "Rum" that innocent sounding little word, represents to them the most demonical spirit in existence. Why, they would run miles to get away from what they consider its evil spells, and whenever occasion offers itself, wax mightily eloquent in the endeavor to induce others to "Touch not, taste not."

When the Fire Fly had got thus far, it peeped into the place with one eye and saw some men pouring the beginnings of rum into various vessels. The Fire Fly's eye twinkled and it pulled an idea out of its mental portfolio. The idea was, that as there seemed to be such a difference of opinion between those who knew little about the spirit in question, beyond that it was to be drunk or not drunk, as the case might be, that it would not be an unwise move to flit gracefully into the rum headquarters and enquire of the creators, they who knew all the Why's and Wherefore's of the Rum's existence, whether the same would not be "just the thing" now and then for the Fire Fly itself to indulge in. Just in a little way you know. The Fire Fly fluttered its wings and felt quite wicked. It could not have explained in a scientific manner why it felt wicked, but it did.

So feeling wicked and wise – wicked, just because – and wise well, only a wise Fire Fly would think of discovering the merits and demerits of rum from those who make it, the Fire Fly boldly flitted into Geo. Eustace Burke

---

* A quotation from an 1869 song by Joseph Winner about a couple's relationship with alcohol.

& Bro's. place. It was pleasantly received by the Bro. and after being shown
by him all the various funny processes by which rum becomes itself,
the Fire Fly which was deeply interested in it all, especially in the non-
intoxicating girls and men who were working like busy bees in the Bottling
Department, opened its mind and enquired if rum was good. It didn't
mention itself in connection with the rum; it was too innocently deep for
that. The answer came boldly in the affirmative and the Fire Fly departed.
It was perfectly satisfied; its little brain was rested, a great problem had
been solved. It had found out from those who made the rum that the stuff
was all right. Was that not a wise Fire Fly?

Fire Fly. "Fire Fly's Christmas Budget."
Gall's Daily News Letter, 24 December 1896: 7.

I am a little puzzled about what I shall write for Christmas. I wish to
amuse, but at the same time, you must acknowledge it is rather hard trying
to amuse those to whom you are a stranger. However, like Sam Walter Foss,
I believe that,
  'Tis not the greatest singer,
  Who tries the loftiest theme,
  He is the true joy bringer,
  Who tells his simplest dream.
  He is the greatest poet,
  Who will renounce all art,
  And take his heart, and show it,
  To every other heart,
  Who writes no learned riddle,
  But sings his simplest rune,
  Takes his heart strings for a fiddle,
  And plays his easiest tune;*

---

* The dedicatory verse to popular newspaper poet Sam Walter Foss's *Back Country Poems* (1892).

so think the best I can do will be to tell you something about the Christmas season at home. Canadians enjoy reading about Christmas in the West Indies because it is so different from their own, and for the same reason you may like to hear about the festive Canucks.

In Canada, at Christmas time, as you know, the snow covers the ground. If it should be otherwise, everybody is very gloomy and people go around saying: "A green Christmas makes a full Churchyard." However, we seldom have a green Christmas; and on Christmas day the children rush about with rosy cheeks sliding down hills on their sleighs or pelting one another with snowballs, and when dinner time comes they rush into the house with red cheeks and big appetites for Christmas turkey and plum pudding. Then some sit by the fire and read and chat and play games and laugh and dance and sing as the case may be, while the big fellows and the little fellows and sometimes the girls too muffle themselves in their snowshoe suits, white, blue and red blankets with bright colored woollen sashes and snow shoes strapped on to moccasins and are off for a tramp around the mountain or into the woods or across the frozen river –some of them dragging toboggans.

When I was a youngster, every Christmas morning for eight years I was to be found at a Sunday School Christmas festival. That Festival used to be the great event of the year to me, and oh, how I would look forward to its coming. I remember one year just about two weeks before Christmas day being asked by my school-teacher to write a composition on "Life." I sat me down and thought. I was waiting for Christmas and the waiting seemed long and dreary. The result of my thinking was that the composition read simply thus "Life is very long."

You can imagine the derision with which my wee literary effort was greeted. I even blush in retrospection, but, Ah me, the days when life seemed long, and dolls' dresses were of more importance than my own were the freshest and sweetest of all. ...

You Jamaicans have a lovelier country than we Canucks. God never made a fairer spot than this Island, but there's a sight which if you knew it, you would envy me for having seen. That is the Ice Palace. We generally have one in Montreal, but last year they built it in the historic City of Quebec. It is during the month of February when the Winter King reigns

Supreme that the Ice Palace arises in its glory. I was not very old when the
first one was built, and being of an impressionable temperament, immediately upon beholding its beauty, I took pen in hand and wrote a story, the
foundation of which was the Ice Palace. The "Dominion Illustrated," a
Canadian magazine, received the story and published it. During later years
I have become a little ashamed of the whole thing, but as I still retain a
certain amount of respect for the description of the Ice Palace contained
therein, I will quote it for you. [Here she quotes five paragraphs from her
story "Robin," beginning "Pushing his way…" (26–7).]

And now I want to tell you of a colder place than either Montreal or
Quebec. It is right up on the North Shore of Lake Superior in what is
called the Thunder Bay District of Canada, one thousand miles away from
Montreal. I spent a year there, and at Christmas time, the snow was heaped
high up above the door, and all the world outside looked like a great white
plain, and it was that cold that if we left water standing on the table for five
minutes it would become solid, and a Special Correspondent, with whom
I am on very intimate terms, had to keep the ink bottle on the stove whilst
she wrote a telegram to her paper down East.

Apropos of that Special Correspondent – I have a story to tell. This is
the season for stories and I am sure you would like to hear how she did
her first murder.

Well, she lived in a little Town on the North Shore of Lake Superior,
a thousand miles from her home in Eastern Canada, and some said, five
hundred miles removed from civilization. She was alone; friends and relations were far away; she was poor and earned her living, even more by
the labor of her hands than by her wits; but the depressing circumstances
of her condition seemed to have very little effect upon her spirits, for although she was small her feelings were big – and great was her vanity. Was
she not "Special Correspondent" in the District of Thunder Bay for one of
the big papers down East? Was it not a fact that every accident – fire and
small-pox scare – that excited that excitable district was faithfully recorded
by her and sent across the wires through her special agency? The consciousness of her importance was ever in her mind; it added dignity to her
step and loftiness to her brow.

One night a man was shot and killed not far from the house where this "Special Correspondent" lived. In fact, so near was she to the scene of the tragedy that she distinctly heard the report of the pistol which dealt death. Great excitement prevailed the next morning when it was found that a man had been shot and the assassin had escaped from town. There was a woman in the case, and altogether it was most interesting – especially to the "Special Correspondent" who was delighted at the chance to have a sensational story to report. The chief part of the story, however, could not be written until the murderer was caught, and as there was only one officer outside the limits of the Town who had power to arrest him, and as this officer's District extended from North Bay to Keewatin, a distance of about eight hundred miles of wild country, the chance of a speedy capture, if any at all, was uncertain.

So the "Special Correspondent" was obliged to repress her enthusiasm and wait for the murderer to return to town and give himself up to justice – which unlooked for event occurred two days after the shooting.*

The excitement of the "Special Correspondent" had by that time reached fever heat, her imagination was filled with the idea of going alone to see the Cain, having a long talk with him, and afterwards giving a graphic account of the interview, with a minute description of his appearance and so forth to the paper for which she worked. Then, thought she, they will know down East that a woman reporter is not afraid of anything. No! not even of a real, live murderer.

Accordingly, escorted by a man, for the sake of appearances,–because the good woman with whom she lived told her that if she went alone to the Public Station, everybody in town would be talking, the "Special Correspondent" inwardly grumbling at the state of society which makes an appendage in the shape of a masculine human necessary to a woman, just when she wants to show her independence – started out enterprisingly. When she reached the door of the Police Station, she turned to her companion and said: "Now

* Probably a reference to the murder of Archie Cammill (sometimes spelled "Campbell"), who was shot on the evening of 12 December 1892, in Port Arthur [now Thunder Bay], Ontario. James Rowe surrendered a few days later at a spot about twenty miles from Port Arthur and was tried for murder in June 1893.

mind, I'm to go in all alone." "Very well," said he, stationing himself at the door of the hall into which they had been admitted.

"Where is he – the man who killed the other?" She enquired of the policeman on watch.

"In his room, Miss," answered the man, pointing to a door at his side, "but you cannot see him."

"But I must," said the "Special Correspondent" imperiously. "I am the 'Special Correspondent' for——."

"Well, you can't go in, any way," asserted the stolid warder.

The "Special Correspondent" waxed indignant, but before she had time to say further, her companion interfered on her behalf and by persuasion induced the man to allow the prisoner to be seen.

The key was turned in the lock; the door opened slowly and cautiously, but strange to say, the "Special Correspondent" did not start forward eagerly to enter. No, it seemed to those who watched her that she drew back, hesitated, and her face turned pale. The policeman, however, not liking to have the trouble of opening the door for nothing, and in order to facilitate the "Special Correspondent" about her business, gave her a gentle, but decided push into the room and then closed the door, leaving her alone with the prisoner.

Now comes the mysterious part of the affair. The "Special Correspondent" instead of advancing calmly to the man whom she had come purposely to see, sitting down by his side, observing his actions and words and taking notes of the same, turned her back on him and frantically pulled at the door, shrieking "Let me out! Let me out!"

The policeman opened the door; the "Special Correspondent" rushed wildly into the street, followed by her late despised escort.

Many a moon has risen and waned o'er the Sleeping Giant guarding Thunder Bay since that "Special Correspondent" visited the man who killed another, but never yet has she been heard to explain her strange actions on that occasion. Once when the matter was broached to her she murmured that upon entering the cell, instead of seeing the medium sized inoffensive looking man who had been described to her as the murderer, she had beheld a monstrous, evil-eyed, fiery mouthed demon with blood stained hands and clothes.

Whether or no that is the case, her step is now a little less proud, her head a little lower, her voice a little meeker, herself, on the whole, a little less independent than she was "in the days that are no more."

And now I've done my duty. A Merry Christmas and a Happy New Year.

Fire Fly. Excerpt from "The Woman about Town: The Horse Car, Sarah Bernhardt."
Gall's Daily News Letter, 30 December 1896: 6.

When Sarah Bernhardt last visited Montreal I was one of those fortunate who saw her as "Cleopatra."* It was a memorable eve for me, for I had looked forward to it for some time, and what girl with the pen and ink fever who lives in the city which is to be visited by Sarah Bernhardt, does not make up her mind to see for herself and pass an opinion upon the great Diva, and swears by all the confections that were ever made that if her best fellow does not give her the chance to do so that he shall for ever-more take a back seat. However, I can't grumble, for I saw Sarah in all her glory, which was greater in my eyes than all the old time glory, of the impersonate Egyptian queen who could have been. Ah, what acting! what a voice! what graceful speaking gestures! what eloquent expression. If Cleopatra was ever half as fascinating as Sarah Bernhardt made her appear, I do not wonder that the great soldier, Antony, yielded up all his power to lie at her feet. I myself would have unhesitatingly done the same – and I am a woman.

Two years later I saw my Goddess in Boston, acting "Camille."† That heart-stirring story of a lost girl, unselfishness and sacrifice, of an honest man's great passion and belief in "All for love and the world well lost" surely never had such an interpreter as Sarah Bernhardt.

* Bernhardt performed *Cleopatra* in January 1892 at the Academy of Music in Montreal.
† Eaton's claim that she saw Bernhardt in Boston "two years" after seeing her in Montreal in *Cleopatra* suggests that she would have seen her in Boston around January 1894, but Bernhardt performed *Camille* at the Tremont Theatre in Boston only three times in the 1890s: in March 1891, April 1892, and April 1896.

Many a woman moved by the great Tragedienne's art sat crying in her seat; many a man turned pale with emotion. As for myself, though the tears did not fall, they were behind my eyes and I turned and said to my companion –

"Sarah Bernhardt is well on in years and her character has been reviled, but she is the greatest genius of the age, and if I were the richest woman in the world, possessed of youth and beauty and the love of many friends, I would exchange all and more to be a Sarah Bernhardt. One can defy age when one has genius, one can defy criticism and the carping of envious tongues when one wields the power to move the hearts of hardened, worldly wise men and women."

But what I did want to say is this, Sarah Bernhardt is just as fascinating off the stage as on it, and many who know her attribute this fascination to her taste in dress.

The most important part of Sarah's dress is her headgear. I have seen her on the street wearing a pale blue Napoleon-shaped bonnet, trimmed in front with a large purple satin ribbon bow quite in the Alsatian fashion with two loops on each side. The colors matched her wonderful eyes and the fit of the bonnet displayed to advantage her shapely head.

Now I hear that at the present time that bonnet is all the rage in Europe; every lady of fashion wears one and I am wondering if I cannot get one too. I'm pretty sure I can, for I know where the materials can be purchased, and if you will promise not to buy the same, for you know one likes to wear the only Sarah Bernhardt bonnet in Kingston, I'll let you into a little secret. The materials can be got either at the Bee Hive, Pinnock's, or Alfred Pawsey's. They have all that is required to manufacture the dainty shape, and now I come to think of it, they also have the milliners to make it up in style.

Mrs. F— called on Nathan & Co., the other day and ordered a hat which is nothing more nor less than a mass of tulle with a very full aigrette in front. It was particularly becoming and very choice. Her taste in dress is equal to Sarah Bernhardt's.

From Fire Fly. "The Girl of the Period: The Projectographe, Jamaica Lawyers."
Gall's Daily News Letter, 13 January 1897: 3.

THE PROJECTOGRAPHE.

The evening was dull one evening last week, and I thought I would go and see the new machine of Professor Edison which produces moving figures as in life, and I must say I was very much pleased.* In addition to the pictures [showman Harry J.] Daniels gave some rare specimens of ventriloquism; and altogether the exhibition of his wonderful powers as a ventriloquist was too short. It was very hard to believe when he stood before his audience with his wooden "children" seated on the table that the respective voices were solely his own. What amusing children they were to be sure. How they did delight the immense crowd which laughed as it had never laughed before. Laughter is good, it is pleasant and beneficial, and a great relief to imprisoned mirth. Mr. Daniels, I regard as a philanthropist, as indeed everybody is who puts a bit of lively color into our desperately "practical utility." It is possible to laugh ourselves content and sometimes into crying for joy!

Mr. Daniels, I congratulate you – you are "a card" and deserve to be called a Yankee McCabe!

I was allowed while the Projectographes were being displayed to take a peep into the little dark room when Mr. Daniels' "Imps of Darkness" work the "magic." Mr. [Edwin Stanton] Porter and Mr. Dows were working the wonderful machinery of Professor Edison who is styled all over America "The Wizard of Menlo Park" and exhibiting to a Kingston public these living pictures.

Just imagine, those natural photographs, life sized, moving, talking, laughing, fighting and running, which every night crowds have thronged to see, become spell bound, and when the show is over actually wish to sit

---

* Daniels and Edwin Stanton Porter toured the Caribbean in 1896–97, with the International Film Company's cheap and popular Projectograph projector, an early device for showing motion pictures.

out the whole thing gone over a second time, and sometimes a third time, because they cannot see enough to satisfy them.

The hundreds of photographs required to represent each picture (not larger than a child's finger) are run upon a belt with lightning speed by means of electricity and by their continuity produces the actual movements in reality. I need not dilate upon the pictures. Most of you have seen them and have declared them the finest things of the kind you have yet seen. But are those little dancing girls coquetting with an umbrella, those galloping cavalry men, that grand rolling tidal wave – only pictures? One can hardly bring their mind to believe it possible!!

JAMAICA LAWYERS.

I have spent six years of my life amongst lawyers and law students, so you can understand that I keep a soft place in my heart for the members of the learned and forensic profession. When I heard that I had to carry my Reporter's note book and pencil to the Magistrate's Court last week I did not quake inwardly at the prospect. Indeed, no, remembering those I left behind, I felt quite delighted at the thought of seeing their like again.

Well, I found the Kingston lawyers to be very much like my Canadian friends and as Mr. A. and Mr. C. fired their legal shots at each other with more or less telling effect – you know friction makes genius – I penned or rather pencilled the following opinion which has been in my head for a long long time, but which the piquancy of Mr. A. and Mr. C. brings out in print. Listen to it. If you are a lawyer yourself you will agree with me: –

A lawyer is a sort of Father Confessor, only instead of feeling it his duty to reprove sinners and impose penance, he aids and abets them to the best of his ability to hide their sin and avert punishment, and if that be not possible, their sins being too flagrant, he pleads eloquently in their behalf "the quality of mercy be not strained."*

One peculiarity about this Father Confessor is although he is so lenient to all those who come to him to confess, he is as relentless as death towards the persons at enmity with his own or his client's particular sinners, and after marshalling in array all their weaknesses, all their errors, he prays that

* A loose quotation from Shakespeare's *A Merchant of Venice*, Act 4, scene 1.

they be punished according to his ideas of punishment, asserting that
thereby justice will be done. That in the instance it is not mercy that
requires "straining" but that condign punishment is necessary because
prevention by example is better than cure.

My experience has taught me that lawyers make the best of politicians.
That is because they are so accustomed to taking sides that it is very easy
for them to pony up "the great principles of our party."

The bone of contention in the Court House on the day when I happened to fly in was a "Typewriter." Typewriters, I am sorry to say, though
very useful in their way, are often the causes of disputes. There are two
definitions to the word Typewriter. One means a machine, the other the
young lady that operates the machine. I won't say which of the two Mr. A.
and Mr. C. were fighting about – a woman or a machine? – but will leave
you to suppose it was the latter, for who, possessed of any sense, would
bother his mind with a mechanical apparatus when a young lady is in
question[?]

A typewriter is very much like other young ladies who have not a sur-
plus amount of that to which all men is dear, and who, unless they are able
to live on a sunflower, are forced to provide for themselves with the neces-
sities of life.

The typewriter who writes shorthand styles herself a "stenographer." If
you want to know what that is, pay a visit to the office of some gentleman
who owns a stenographer – or a typewriter. If you arrive there at the
proper hour, you may happen to see a gentleman dictating to a young lady,
who puts down a lot of funny little marks in a note book. If she has a good
memory and remembers what has been dictated to her, she afterwards
transcribes these notes; if not, her inventive powers are called into action
and somehow or other she manages to write something.

The typewriter has to exercise a great deal of control over her feelings.
For instance she may have to write four or five proposals of marriage, addressed to different ladies from the same gentleman and though she might
long to send a warning note to the poor victims who may walk into the
trap, she dare not, being bound in honour to keep silent. She is sworn to
eternal silence and cannot plead, as a certain individual did the other day,

that he wrote a letter which he said was falsehood, from beginning to end, but he wrote it to the dictation of his employer and then attached his individual signature to its truth.

Some people insinuate that the typewriter flirts. I don't know much about such things myself, but I've heard it said that many nice girls "flirt," even in Kingston, so, as typewriters are always nice, I hope all the typewriters may find pleasant and agreeable subjects to transcribe from the dictation.

I could tell you lots more about the typewriter, but time and space forbid, so I will simply end by saying that she is just like the rest of womankind; has a fair share of faults, but at the same time virtues so innumerable that you will have to go to heaven to find the end of them, and then the firm belief that if there are no Women's Rights, there are at least Women's Wrongs.*

Fire Fly. "The Departure of the Royal Mail."
Gall's Daily News Letter, 21 January 1897: 3.

"Three cheers for England, Hip-hip, hurrah!" "Three cheers for Jamaica," "Hurrah, rah, rah, goodbye, old fellows." (Why is everybody an old fellow at such a time?) "Darling, don't forget me, how I wish I were going." "How I wish you were." "Three cheers for Mr. Macdonald the Adjutant, we never will forget him." "Oh, we'll soon be rolling home to dear old England!" "Take care of yourself, do, dear, for my sake." "No. 2, good-bye, tell the folks I'm coming – some day, good-bye, good-bye, good-bye."

Then the big ship, throbbing with irresistible power, turned itself to the ocean and was gradually lost to sight. In a few days she would reach Barbados; then the screw would be turned again, and out she would speed into the sublimely lonely Atlantic, over grassy depths of green water, through wild billows of foam, and where the sea shades off into every glory of color.

* The paragraphs about "typewriters" borrow from Eaton's "The Typewriter."

The above is what I heard, and saw, and thought Tuesday afternoon. I stood on the dock witnessing the departure for England of the Royal Mail [Steam Packet Company]* steamer "Atrato," and I gazed upon the scene with much speculative wonder and more sympathy than I was conscious of at the moment. The crowd was talking, laughing, crying, advising, and shaking hands. Such shaking of hands I never saw before. I am sure today there must be many smarting palms both in Kingston and on the "Atrato."

Amongst those who were homeward bound I noticed two hundred men of the King's Own Liverpool Regiment, and of these the majority seemed in high spirits. A few, however, appeared to be somewhat saddened at the prospect of an infinite separation from those with whom, perchance, they had spent many a happy day.

Thronged on the deck were men, women and children of all conditions and of most all nationalities, whilst on the wharf with uplifted faces stood friends and relations, with, who can say, what a tumult of mingled emotions surging within their hearts.

Parting seems ever the bitterest to those who are left behind, so the faces on the steamer were on the whole more bright than downcast, whilst those on shore betrayed the sorrow and envy they could not conceal.

The tourists on the "Atrato" – they who were leaving nothing behind in Kingston save a little hard, cash – gazed like myself self interestedly and amusedly. The "Atrato's" sailors were laughing and joking. It crossed my mind that human beings are readier to sympathise with the rejoicer than with the mourner. Weep, and the world will laugh at you, laugh, and the world will laugh with you. I felt that those who were about to cross thousands of miles of roaring foaming water were to be envied, for they were going home.

"For there we loved, and where we love is home,
Home that our feet may leave but not our hearts."†

And it could easily be seen that the parting here held nothing of the

---

* The Royal Mail Steam Packet Company was established in 1839 for conveyance of mail to and from Great Britain and the Americas. The *Atrato* was designed in 1888 with state-of-the-art accommodation for passengers in the superstructure of the ship as opposed to below the decks.
† From Oliver Wendell Holmes' poem "Homesick in Heaven."

sorrow which must have weighed down the spirits of the King's Own lads
when they bade Good-Bye to old England. I was glad that yesterday I did
not witness the separation of mother from child, of husband from wife.
Such incidents may have occurred, but I did not see them.

The English voices mingled with the soft southern accents of the West
Indians as the steamer slowly glided off from the shore, and for the first
time since coming here it was borne to my mind that Jamaica is English,
and that I hardly need to quote as I do here William Watson's

ENGLAND [AND] HER COLONIES.
"O ye by wandering tempest town,
   'Neath every alien star,
Forget not whence the breath was blown,
   Which wafted you afar,
For ye are still her ancient seed
   On younger soil let fall,
Children of Britain's Island breed,
To whom the mother in her heed,
   Perchance may one day call."*

The "Atrato" is a noble steamer, and her make-up in every detail is truly
splendid both from a seaman's and landsman's point of view. I think she is
fitted up elegantly enough to merit being called "a floating palace," which
is the name we give some of the tip top American steamers. I went through
the "Atrato" yesterday admitting the little gems of state rooms, the complete smoking room, the inviting dining saloon, and luxurious music
room. I am sure the furniture and upholstery for a steamer could scarcely
be improved upon, and much artistic taste is displayed in the manufacture
of the saloons and cabins. As to the bar – Well the large number of fine
fellows I saw there yesterday was ample testimony to the fact that it is all
that can be desired.

* Watson's popular patriotic verse was included in Edmund Clarence Stedman's *A Victorian
Anthology, 1837–1895.*

Fire Fly. "The Girl of the Period: The Theatre."
Gall's Daily News Letter, 28 January 1897: 1.

THE THEATRE.

That the new Theatre will be opened this week is a welcome announcement to Kingstonians, and as considerable talent will be represented, the
success of this season's theatrical entertainment can be safely predicted.[*]

I'm a warm stage lover myself and though I have come a little in contact with the Green Room or the mimic life of the boards, I believe next
to literature it is the most potent influence that is working in the modern
world. It keeps us in close touch with all the great hopes, and enthusiasms,
and interests of the nineteenth century, links us to the past, and once in
a while, opens for us a wicket which is the entrance to a land of dreams
and forgetfulness.

I confess to a partiality for light opera, and a Vaudeville Theatre is my
delight. Why not, here's to the Vaudeville girl:

"Are you, my dear, the yellow girl,[†]
  Of all our author folks
At whom we decent people hurl
  Anathemas, and jokes?

You are a poem, or a song –
  A wicked one, they say –
A bit of colour thrown along
  A drab old world and gray.

And every well-turned ankle, dear
  Is joy to all the earth,

---

[*] Probably the New Theatre Royal, built in Kingston in 1897.
[†] The "Yellow Girl" was a stock character in vaudeville and minstrel shows – a white male
fantasy of an attractive mixed-race young woman. The source of this particular song about
the yellow girl is unknown, although Eaton's brother-in-law Walter Blackburn Harte in-
vokes the "yellow girl" as a figure for fin-de-siècle literature in his article "The Yellow Girl,"
Fly Leaf 1 (Dec. 1895): 15–20.

Except to us good folks who fear
  The smile or dance of mirth."

Now, I think I see some old lady writing to the Editor, saying that she detects an irreverence in my temperament and mind that might lead me to the commission of all the crimes that moral folk find so much joy in contemplating. There is, she avers, a flippancy in my treatment of some established things which could only be tolerated in the back-woods of Canada, but which by all means must be suppressed in such a proper place as Kingston. She is sure I am fast and ought to be kept down, and although she can discover no more heinous offence in me than a certain callousness in regard to the feelings of witless respectables, she would put me into prison had she the power.

THE PRISON. Talking of prison, leads me to change the subject – A certain interest attaches to that class of people who are punished for their sins, so last week I paid a visit to Mr. [George A.] Douglas' Hotel on Tower Street.* A most imposing edifice, I can assure you, and beautifully whitewashed, even if the faults of its occupants are not. It is not my intention to-day to describe this prison nor even what I saw there. Some other time when I am hard-up for some wholesome subject to moralize upon, I shall take up the ugly and horrible treadmill side of life, the grim irony which almost blunts charity. To-day I only wish to remark that I think the women are on a whole punished more severely than the men. And this is why. A woman no matter how low down she is, longs for some variation in her dress. Men, even free men, are accustomed to wearing uniforms. Nearly all men dress alike; but women like to have some choice in attire; they like to be able to show some individuality in the dress they put on, even if it be in but a button. It seems to me that when a woman gets into a prison uniform she loses all that is human, and so as I passed through the women's quarters of that Government Institution on Tower Street, my reflections were not so much on the sins for which these people were being punished, but on the bad effects of the yearly, and to some of the women, lifelong mortification of having to wear the same torturingly ugly uniform. I saw one uniform, however, which had a brightening influence in the place, and

* Tower Street General Penitentiary in Kingston, Jamaica.

the like of which I wouldn't mind wearing myself – that was the uniform which Mr. Reynolds, the Warden, looks so nice in.

THE BALL.

To see an arrangement of flowers and plants like that which I saw last night at Dr. Mosse's* ball, is a pleasure to the memory. There was no crowding, every plant was in itself perfect in form, colouring and development. Stiffness had been studiously avoided and the effect was that of waving, growing, beautiful life. Mr. Nunes, in his decoration, showed a decorating refinement of taste and an appreciation of the beautiful which is both marked and rare. In this land, we have many flowers to be prodigal with, but all the more so do we need to be careful when decorating, for vulgar cramming with hundreds of flowers is not beautiful. As the little Japanese flower man, Professor Choya, says, the central idea in flower arrangement is to give an appearance of growing plants, every stem must rise free and light. This effect, Mr. Nunes produced, and I for one congratulate him.

Fire Fly. "The Girl of the Period: At Alpha Cottage."
Gall's Daily News Letter, 2 February 1897: 7.

AT ALPHA COTTAGE.†

It isn't only mothers who have motherly feeling. I think when motherhood itself is denied the instinct still exists which prompts women to love little children and long to care for and protect them. Indeed, that is a "larger motherhood" which can yearn over other people's children.

That was what came home to me the other day, as I poked around the pleasant downstairs and class rooms of the Alpha Industrial School, and noted how hearty and contented appeared the children I saw there. It is a good work, – the training and bringing up of these poor homeless young ones. The Government is to be congratulated on what it has to show us at Alpha Cottage. Yet no, not the Government, it is the Sisters of Mercy who

* Dr. C.B. Moss was the Inspector of Certified Hospitals.
† A small charity orphanage and later school founded in 1880 by the Sisters of Mercy.

are carrying on this work for the Government, to whom all praise is due.
It is their power of sympathy and self-sacrifice which is transforming these
little waifs into respectable boys and girls.

Alpha Cottage Industrial and Elementary Schools are proofs of
woman's work. The coldly calculating Government, weighing reasons for
and against, fearful ever of the consequences of actions, could never have
accomplished what we see at Alpha Cottage. What has been achieved there
has been through the spirit that "believeth all things" and it is only the
women who possess that spirit. This men gladly acknowledge – they know
that women are more capable of throwing themselves into the lives of
others than they are themselves and that is why though many men object
to the woman who seeks to enter the arena of politics, law, or science, all
who are true to their consciences uphold the impulse that inspires women
to take an active part in Christian effort. Men know that women knit together like the Sisters of Mercy, by the close bond of a common vocation,
can take up a round of harsh, unlovely, discouraging duties with an enthusiasm which transfigures the work and makes it hopeful and blessed. So
the Sisters of Mercy mother the poor unshepherded waifs and strays and
there's never an urchin too dirty or naughty to find a place in their hearts.

I have been to the Convent, have conversed with the Sisters and have
roved from one school to another taking notes of the sweetness, the
airiness and the brightness of the place which has been christened
Alpha Cottage.

We have no such sunny institutions up North. If ever I have to become
an inmate of an institution, let it be in Jamaica. The open windows and
summer surroundings take away the Institution feeling, and I know if
I ever find a child that needs the shelter of an Institution I shall ask the
Sisters of Mercy to kindly take it in.

HIGH SCHOOL.

In connection with the Convent of Mercy there is a High School* and
here the daughters of some of the best and wealthiest families on the
Island are educated. I must describe my visit there.

When I arrived at the Cottage, that is Alpha Cottage or High School, I

---

* Opened in 1894 to serve upper- and middle-class girls from Kingston and St. Andrew.

was met by two sweet-faced women, Mother Aquinas [Kearns], the Superior, and Sister Agnes, the Principal of the High School. They welcomed me most courteously and kindly, and after I had viewed the beautiful grounds, stretching forty-five acres around and also observed the several adjacent buildings, I stepped into the Cottage and there beheld the girls of the High School at their studies – about sixty in all. This High School, I learnt, comprises Junior and Preparatory Schools and a division of Senior students. The Senior Division is intended to help those ambitious maidens who are desirous of preparing for public examinations.

Sister Agnes informed me that besides the usual branches of English education and in the Junior Classes, Kindergarten and Musical Drill, there are also taught piano, violin, singing, painting, drawing, French and German. A pupil could take up one or all these accomplishments by paying extra fees.

The Alpha Cottage makes an ideal school, located healthily and beautifully supplied with all the comforts and conveniences of the latest modern Academies and taught by gentle, refined ladies.

CONVENT.

From the Cottage I turned to the Convent, and whilst in the latter retreat, had the pleasure of listening to some fine music from a couple of the pupils, Miss Arch and Miss Sweetie. I do not recollect Miss Sweetie's surname, but I'm sure it cannot be as taking as her Christian.

The Convent is a handsome, commodious building, and the interior is not only very pleasant to the eye, but is pervaded with an atmosphere of comfort which makes one feel inclined to tarry. The floors are beautifully polished and the sitting-room is most tastefully furnished.

Ferns and flowers decorate tables and brackets, and on the walls hang portraits of several of the Prelates of the Church of Rome, the portrait of the late Mother Superior, and also a representation in oils of Mother Aquinas herself. The last, I scarcely recognized, the expression being very solemn and totally unlike that of the lady whose fresh youthful face beamed so happily upon me that for a moment I almost wished I myself were a member of her sisterhood.

ELEMENTARY AND INDUSTRIAL SCHOOLS.

The Mother is a young woman, still in her twenties who talks in a

pretty, illuminating manner. She has taken under her wing forty little or-
phans whom she is bringing up all herself – the Government having no
part or parcel in them. When I visited the Elementary Schools, one of their
special charges, wee Hilda Bravo, very prettily sang and played for me on
the Tambourine.

I saw 250 children in the Elementary Schools and 97 in the Industrial.
They are all under the care of 18 Sisters, four of whom I met, namely Sister
Evangelist, Sister Genevieve, Sister Xavier, and Sister Magdalin.

The very little children in the Elementary School took my fancy wonderfully; black eyes, round-headed chickabiddies. One little Coolie girl of
three or four years of age gave us a recitation in a pretty baby voice in a
manner which would have reflected credit on a child of seven.

The penmanship in all the classes showed not only careful teaching on
the part of teachers and attention on the part of the pupils, but an aptitude
for forming letters which I could not help but remark upon.

As to the behavior of the pupils, I must say I have never seen a better
and more docile appearing lot of youngsters than those Mother Aquinas
introduced to me as the boys and girls of the Alpha Elementary and Industrial Schools.

The Industrial School children are of course kept separate from those
of the Elementary School. The girls of the Industrial Schools work like
busy bees at appointed tasks one half of the day, the other half is spent in
receiving school instruction.

The boys divide their time in the same manner. The Elementary school
boys have a splendid band, composed of self-made musicians who can
pick up all kinds of tunes by ear and perform on all kinds of instruments.

They played a few selections for me and I declare I was surprised and
am quite sure I would rather hear Mother Aquinas' boys than the Grand
West Indian [Regiment Band].

Some of the children whom I saw looking bright and happy had come
to the Convent in a dying condition, but the sisters had worked hard
to restore them to the wicked world and their efforts had not been
unsuccessful.

The Industrial boys are taught gardening, carpentering and painting,
the girls everything that will make them good domestic servants.

They will never set the world on fire, but they will be able to work and get enough to eat, and what more can a boy or girl sigh for.

If they lived in America or even in the old country, it might be worthwhile to have some ambition, but in Jamaica the wise ones are they who hope for little. If they must have an ambition, let them place it on things heavenly and not on things earthly. Come to think of it – I believe that's just what they do. Being denied the opportunity of rising on earth the Jamaicans go much to church, no doubt thinking thereby to rise to Heaven.

There is no sneer in my remarks. I merely write my thoughts as they come to me, and I can assure you I felt real good as I stood in the pretty Convent of Mercy Chapel and confessed to myself that happiness is possible even to those who dare not try their wings.

"Where Nature's harp are all in tune,
A calm or a still on life's rough sea.
A place where is always afternoon.*

A Canadian Fire Fly. "The Girl of the Period: A Veracious Chronicle of Opinion."
Gall's Daily News Letter, 8 February 1897: 3.

A VERACIOUS CHRONICLE OF OPINION.†

I have not the fine, whimsical positiveness of opinion of Mr. Andrews, but this is what I think of the interesting case of Nunes vs. Moulton and vice versa, which came up in the Police Court on Friday, and of which I was an amused witness.††

* From popular contemporary writer Cy Warman's poem "Give Me Not Riches."
† Eaton may have borrowed this phrase from the subtitle of Walter Blackburn Harte's regular *Lotus* editorial column "Bubble and Squeak: A Veracious Little Chronicle of Individual and Fantastic Opinion." See *Lotus* 2.2 (August): 132; 3 (September): 172; 4 (October): 212; 5 (November): 253; and 6 (December): 296.
†† Robert Nunes was a white Officer of Customs and Moulton was a lower ranking black officer. Nunes assaulted Moulton with racist slurs while the latter was on duty; Moulton lost his temper and hit his senior officer. Both were injured and both charged with assault. Though the judge found both parties guilty, he fined Moulton ten shillings and Nunes only one shilling.]

I think it was a case in which both men gave evidence against themselves, Nunes admitting having spoken to Moulton in a decidedly aggressive manner, and Moulton acknowledging having hit back his superior
officer.

I think the judge could have done no less, and no more than find them
both guilty of assault, and according to the justice which passes current in
modern law courts, both men were fairly dealt with by the presiding Judge.

But thinking deeper, I have come to the conclusion that whilst Nunes
acted like a blackguard, Moulton's conduct was that of a man. Who would
not refuse to obey an order delivered in the manner in which Nunes delivered his to Moulton? Who possessing the spirit of a man would not have
resisted being pushed out of the place like a dog?

Moulton would have been beneath contempt had he meekly put up
with Nunes' bullying, and I should have despised him just as I despise the
"British workman" who blushes and pulls his forelock when his master
condescendingly calls him "My honest fellow" "My good fellow" etc.

I notice that Jamaicans are continually complaining about "the lazy
nigger," the lazy labouring class – I myself think there is good cause for
this. But the cause of the cause is this: the labouring people here have little
respect for themselves; they are the most humble and servile lot of humanity I have ever come in contact with. Sometimes I pity them – sometimes
I feel like saying – "If you will get down on the ground, you must expect
others to put their feet on you."

Now these people, in order to become an intelligent working class
should be made to see the dignity of labour, and the only way to attain this
end is by educating them to labour. Free born, educated men regard work
as a blessing. Slavish and ignorant people regard it as degrading and something to be shunned whenever this is possible.

I do feel so sorry when I hear people declaring that education destroys
the children of the labouring class. It is untrue of industrial education. The
highest type of workingman is he who wants the best education for his
children, I mean by that the education which fits them for the position
they are destined to fill. For himself he naturally seeks the comforts of life
as well as the necessaries, and good wages, but only the educated and

skilled workman has the right to ask for this, and only the educated workman makes himself worth this.

At the same time I am no Socialist. I do not believe that all men are
equal, either in the sight of God or man; they are not born so, whatever
they may try to make themselves. A man may buy himself a dress coat to
adorn his exterior but that will not give him brains to furnish the inside.
So I consider the true artist, the true poet, and the philosopher far away
and above ordinary men and the society of wits is higher society than the
society of fools.

You see, I don't feel like preaching "the brotherhood of man" because I
don't believe in it, but I do believe that every man should respect the manhood of his fellow and that every man should try to live up to the best that
is in him, and should not be debarred from the opportunity of doing so.

The educated workman is the most industrious in the long run, and
until Jamaica realizes this and makes an effort in the right direction the
country will continue to be dragged down by a lazy, worthless population.
There is plenty of room on the Island for the educated workman – they
are like needles in a bundle of hay!

But to return to Moulton and Nunes. There is a humorous side to the
story, and for all my declaration that Nunes acted like a bully, and Moulton
like a man, to a certain extent, my sympathies were with Nunes.

I can understand how exasperating such comfortably pious people like
Moulton can make themselves to men like Nunes. Moulton's complacency,
and his belief in his own impossible virtues was too funny for anything.

Fire Fly. "The Girl of the Period: At Church."
Gall's Daily News Letter, 16 February 1897: 5.

AT CHURCH.

I had a glimpse of piety last Sunday, and by its light strolled churchwards,
accompanied by a lady who, like myself, was desirous of trying a pulpit
discourse as a change from tabletalk.

We arrived at the Church in good time and modestly sat ourselves
down in a seat which appeared retired enough to attract our attention, and
were just beginning to congratulate ourselves on being able to see without
being too much seen, when a nicish, elderlyish female leaned over from the
pew in front and informed us that we had better change our seats as the
one in which we were ensconced belonged to certain parties. We took the
hint and proceeded to another likeable pew, only to find that we were
again trespassing on forbidden ground and were again accordingly turned
out. Nothing daunted we tried another, and this time an usher came up
who appeared quite shocked at our having taken seats without asking the
Church members' permission and so without delay requested us to "vacate
the premises" at the same time pointing us out another pew.

Obediently we crawled into the seat designated by him and submis-
sively "shoved on" when the intimation came to "sit in the middle."

Our limbs were just beginning to feel reposeful when again came the
order to "move" and breathing a prayer for peace I squeeze myself up to
the edge of the bench whilst my companion whispered to me that she felt
like getting up and leaving the place.

These proceedings took place in the Parish Church, and I just make
them public because I am of a communicative nature and would like
other tourists to hear of the amusing manner in which Jamaicans welcome
strangers into their places of worship. I shall advise all my friends who
desire "change" to seek it in the Parish Church.

WEDDING BELLS.

What a lot of couples will be happy soon. I never heard so many banns
published at a time as I heard last Sunday, and as I noticed that most of the
contracting parties were termed widows or widowers, I could not refrain
from whispering to my friend that marriage in Kingston was evidently
not a failure.

LOVE OR LITERATURE.

In answer to a young and enquiring spirit who hails from – well –
somewhere not very far from Kingston, and who writes in a vein of frank
and cordial ingeniousness, asking my opinion on the advisability of his de-
voting himself to writing stories, or to making love, either one of which

pursuits he vows he must take up, but which "both at a time" he cannot settle his mind to, I would say:

In the first place, I can give absolutely no encouragement to the story writing; but one out of a thousand writers has the satisfaction of seeing his stories in print, in any kind of a respectable magazine; as to getting paid for them, that is only to be thought of as a wild, wild dream. Editors are singularly dense men and very seldom appreciate the work of a genius, and of course my correspondent is that. Besides Jamaica is a long way from any of the literary workshops, and who knows what might happen to the precious manuscripts, whilst en route to their destination – they might even be swallowed up by a shark, and though of course, the shark might get fished up and forced to disgorge its swallowed treasure, as Jamaica history tells us is sometimes done with Jamaica sharks, still there's a chance that it mightn't.

So I will say to this young man who is earnest and worthy and deserves to be met with the kindly patience due to true and generous ambition that he had better occupy his time exclusively with love. In these days of his youth he can certainly make love much better than he can write and who knows, the experience may equip him for success in literature, if in say, ten or twenty years from now he still has a desire to wield the pen. Love-making itself is a good preparation for literature. So many of us have to get to work to earn our bread and butter early in life that we find no leisure for the fine education and spiritual stimulus of a period of youthful and ardent love making, and can only take in "between whiles" that which is really the champagne of life.*

---

* A significant part of "Love or Literature" recycles and revises a section of the "Bubble and Squeak" column in the October 1896 issue of *Lotus* (2: 216–17). As Doyle notes, "Grace [Eaton Harte] had to take over most of the editorial chores on the *Lotus*" (117) while [her husband, editor Walter Blackburn] Harte was ill in the fall of 1896. It is possible, since a story by her was also published in this issue, that Edith Eaton also helped craft some or all of the *Bubble and Squeak* column for October. Certainly, another section of *Bubble and Squeak*, a tribute to "a young woman of my acquaintance" who "bustl[es] between her kitchen and her [reviewer] husband's little study adjoining," seems more likely to have been written by Edith about Grace than by Harte himself.

Youth does not last long, and he whose young manhood is not made
easy should not waste that period in scribbling.

Put a few hours of love's illusion in the balance against a heap of imma-
ture manuscripts, and who can doubt which will give the most satisfaction.
After this plain exposition, I shall lose my respect for my correspondent, if
he does not stick to love and have a good time.

Fire Fly. "The Union Poor House."
Gall's Daily News Letter, 26 February 1897: 3.

The old Admiral's Pen in St. Andrew is, as everybody now knows, the
Union Poor House. I paid it a visit the other day and had a little talk with
the kind and genial Superintendent, Mr. Davidson, and afterwards followed in the wake of the cheery Matron, Mrs. McKillop, as she made her
rounds of the wards.

To my mind the Institution is more of a hospital than a Poor House for
nearly all the inmates are suffering from some kind of disease – in many
cases simply from old age.

The wards are light and airy and surprisingly clean. In one I found
some very aged people, several of them over ninety years, and very shriv-
elled up.

The Superintendent informed me that since the Institution opened in
1870, 3,258 of those who were admitted have died and have been buried at
the Institution's expense. Indeed, most of those who apply to be taken in
are at death's door.

Many of the sick, some of them young girls, were suffering from paraly-
sis; and skin disease seemed to be quite prevalent. Two young women with
enormous heads made me feel that life is a terrible thing to some of us; –
the horror of the painful sight has not yet been overcome, yet the unfortu-
nates appeared to be moderately cheerful.

The grounds of the Institution are extensive and give the impression
of being well kept. It can easily be seen that reformative influences are at
work in the place, but I think if some light and suitable employment could

be given these people – that is, those of them who are suffering from a lingering illness which yet leaves them a certain amount of strength and energy – that they would find more interest in life, and at the same time the Institution would be helped towards becoming self supporting.

Mr. Davidson lives on the premises and bestows unceasing care on the poor people. He seems to know all his charges by name although the number is altogether 260.

The Matron, Mrs. McKillop, also treads her way amongst them with a footstep that is welcomed, and she is assisted in her duties by two nurses.

As to myself – the ugly realities of life irritate me, and I think I would need to become a Saint, before I could consent to pass a week amongst those who seem to have grubbed amongst the muck heaps of the world, and lost what I consider the secret of happiness.

But this only makes me have the more respect for those who consult the feelings of others before their own. Practical charity is salted with heroism.

Fire Fly. "Our Visitors: Myrtle Bank."
Gall's Daily News Letter, 5 March 1897: 1.

MYRTLE BANK.*

Myrtle Bank is like a big bee-hive at present. It is filled with wealthy Britishers and Americans. Amongst the latter are R[oswell] P[ettibone] Flower, ex-Governor of New York and H[erman] D. Armour, one of the multi-millionaire Armours.† These big wigs are both in the prime of life: grey haired and grey whiskered and as they are accompanied by the chief ladies of their families the atmosphere around their table d'hote is most lively and invigorating.

* Kingston's Myrtle Bank Hotel, run by the wife of Scotsman James Gall, who also owned *Gall's Daily News Letter*, was a private hotel frequented by Americans. Eaton took her board there while working for the *News Letter*.
† With his brother Phillip Danforth Armour, Herman D. Armour founded the Armour Meatpacking Company in Chicago in 1867.

Apropos of the Armour family, I hear they are noted, not only for their wealth, but for the kindness and consideration which they manifest towards their employees.

I was told a little story last night by an American gentleman. He said that some time ago Phil D. Armour, the head of the great pork packing business, visited his San Francisco office. Few of the clerks knew him by sight, so feeling at liberty to abuse his own name, he began to pull the Armours and the Armour business to pieces. This, to a girl clerk there. She listened in silence, but when he had finished, turned upon him and showed how she resented his conduct by lecturing him in a way he never forgot. She was not going to stand having the Armours or any of their business concerns raked over the coals in that way.

The result was that shortly afterwards, the girl was surprised to receive a cheque for fifty dollars with the compliments of Phil. D. Armour.

These gentlemen and their party will remain on the Island for several days. They have been visiting all the other Islands, but have yet much to see. Their longest stay will be at the City of Mexico. They will reach New York, their cruise being then over, on the 22nd day of March.

I see that several United States Judges and Attorneys at Law are resting their weary brains at Myrtle Bank, and the Register tells me that Doctors and Ministers are also in evidence. I spied the Hon. Dr. Johnston, Member for St. Ann, and the Hon. Rev. Carey Berry, Member for St. Andrew, sitting in a corner of the verandah the other night discussing political matters, with the Hon. Mr. Gideon. I'm not sure that it was politics with which they were occupying their leisure hours – what I heard may have been simple jokes, for Legislative Councillors are not always as grim as their titles would seem to suggest, and I have been told by some, although I myself am a little skeptical on that point, that the one subject under Heaven most infrequently discussed at their meetings out of the Council room, is politics.

Such pretty blouses are worn by the fair tourists from the "Ohio." They are mostly made of diaphanous stuff but I discovered in the dining room of the Hotel a very dressy blouse of black surah trimmed with row after row of cream lace insertion. Then there was an uncommonly smart blouse of blue striped from collar to waist, back and front, with three rows of coarse white lace.

Her Excellency, Lady Blake [wife of the Governor], passed through Myrtle Bank yesterday in order to take the launch which was to convey her to the "Partridge." I noticed that the gown she wore was red in color and trimmed with cream lace, which lace colour seems to be very fashionable.

The Bay looked lovely yesterday with the Fleet and the small boats and everything else that was there.

Ex-[New York State] Governor [Roswell Pettibone] Flower, who had strolled down to the pier, gave me the impression from some remarks which I tried my best not to hear, and which he was making to some gentleman who sat beside him, that he and his party were enjoying the scene immensely.

Mr. DePass tells me that on Monday [excursion operators] Raymond and Whitcomb's tourists will arrive. Amongst the list of names is the well-known one of Hoyt. Their rooms in the Myrtle Bank Hotel are already engaged. They come in charge of [popular journalist] Mr. Luther Holden, who was here to make arrangements for their reception a few months ago. Mr. Holden has lately been writing articles descriptive of Jamaica for the Boston "Home Journal."

CONSTANT SPRING HOTEL*

It is pleasant to record that the Constant Spring Hotel is also enjoying great popularity. All who love the sound of the sea will cling to Myrtle Bank, but all who love the hills and mountains and the beauty of distant ocean views will abide at Constant Spring. There too will be found some of New York's "Four Hundred" and many an English aristocrat. Mr. [A.A.] Priestley's Cricket Team will put up there on arrival, the 12th of this month, and will remain during their sojourn in the Island. Another Ball is on the Lapis.

When last at Constant Spring I saw displayed some beautiful views of the scenery of the Lake St. John District in Quebec, Canada. The scenery of Canada may not be quite as summery and gorgeous as what we have before us in Jamaica all the year round, but I prefer the former; it is grander and more varied. There we have the beauty of the changing seasons; the

---

* The Constant Spring Hotel was built in St. Andrew, six miles from Kingston, in 1890 in anticipation of the hundreds of thousands of tourists who attended Jamaica's Great Exhibition in 1891.

sweet freshness and greenness of the spring time, when the trees burst into
bloom and the air is filled with the fragrance of apple blossoms and
hawthorn; the bright skies of summer, when the fields are sweet with
blooming clover; the magnificent glory of Autumn, when the leaves change
their color and the maple tree stands conspicuous amongst all the trees of
the forest in her bright robes "a type of our young country in her pride
and loveliness."* There is no tree in all Jamaica which can compare either
in form or coloring with our Canadian maple tree. Last of all we have winter, my favourite season, when the rivers and lakes become ice-bound,
when the air becomes frosty and exhilarating; when the blood bounds
quickly, when the eyes become bright and the cheeks red; when one feels
that one could live forever. But although up there we are not worn out by a
"perpetual summer," yet our summer is hot enough to cause all Canadians
who can afford it to leave the cities for country homes, and so many of
them fly off to the Lake St. John District, views of which I have told you I
saw at Constant Spring, and seek refuge there in a hotel called the Island
House, a large and beautiful structure, beautifully and conveniently situated. It is always cool in the Lake St. John District; the Lakes, Falls, and
Forests are wonderful, sweet wild strawberries and raspberries grow in
abundance, and it is a paradise for the hunter and fisherman. The hotel is
filled during the summer months with Canadian and American visitors,
and I could not help wondering whilst thinking of the comfort of the
place, and the pleasure to be enjoyed there, whether it wouldn't be of benefit to some of our wealthy Jamaicans to take a trip up that way during the
summer months. It would put fresh life in them; there's so much "snap" in
the air in Canada, and up near Lake St. John, it is so deliciously cool and
fresh. You have a country for our tourists in the winter months, but in
summer they say it is not enticing. Then will be the time to see Canada.
One lady told me she would like to go, if only to bring some brightness to
her eye, some lightness to her step, and some colour to her cheek.

---

* A loose quotation from Henry Faulkner Darnell's "The Maple," a mid-nineteenth-century
poetic tribute to Canada that was frequently anthologized.

Fire Fly. From "Woman's Gossip: Don't Tax Bicycles, Civil Service Examination."
Gall's Daily News Letter, 17 March 1897: 6.

Like the Hon. S[amuel] C[onstantine] Burke, I do not think that bicycles should be taxed, and for this reason – a great number of the silent steed riders are women and girls, and as the members of my feminine gender seldom have money of their own, however are they to raise funds for a bicycle tax? It is hard work to squeeze a ribbon and lace fund out of male relatives, and the girl who summons up courage enough to ask that her pocket money may be increased so as to allow of paying for a bicycle tax will not only be refused but will lay herself open to receive a good lecture on the frivolity of bicycle riding. Ye men who make the laws of this country, consider the woman on the wheel, she toils not, but she spins, and Solomon in all his glory was not arrayed in a skirt forming knickerbockers with a long basqued coat, the basque being so full and lengthy as to form a skirt allowed to fall loosely all around; he did not wear blue silk stockings with russet shoes, laced to the ankle, and a white cloth cap. The above is a description of a natty bicycle suit I was admiring the other day. It was speeding down the road to Constant Spring.

Fire Fly. "Another Pleasure Party. Mr. John Jacob Astor."
Gall's Daily News Letter, 5 April 1897: 1.

Mr. and Mrs. J. J. Astor,* of New York, with a small party of congenial friends, Miss Blight, Mr. Rutherford, Miss Goddard, and Mr. Wadsworth, are enjoying a southern cruise in the "Nourmahal," Mr. Astor's Yacht.

I visited it last Saturday whilst it lay in Kingston Harbor, and had quite a pleasant chat with Mr. Astor, who cheerfully told me all about the trip.

---

* John Jacob Astor IV (1864–1912) was a US businessman, developer, and investor. He was a lieutenant colonel in the Spanish-American War.

The "Nourmahal" is 250 feet long, 30 feet beam and 15 feet draught. It is a model steel yacht, barque rigged; the wood work of mahogany. It is 1,600 tons and was built in Delaware – a true America beauty, bearing gaily the "Stars and Stripes." The interior is luxuriously furnished, lighted by electricity, heated by steam, and affords, beside the usual yacht and steamboat accommodations, all the comfort of parlour, club room and private boudoir. The ladies' sitting room and staterooms are marvels, everything seems to have been got up with an eye to beauty, regardless of expense. As to the dining room and sitting rooms with their wonderful rugs and esthetically tinted upholsterings – let the day be what it may, let the storm burst and the sea beat, there one is "rose lined from the storm."

Everything that can make life worth living has been gathered together in the "Nourmahal," and there I saw rare and artistic curios, books, the latest – and in an air-tight case an array of shining old-fashioned guns and spears such as would make British General [Henry Jardine] Hallowes green with envy. But I can't begin to tell all I saw – that would take too long. On the deck, chattering for all they were worth, were a number of fine parrots. These have helped to beguile away some of the happy tourists' golden hours. I should calculate those birds were worth a little sum. Some distance away from the parrots were a couple of "connecting links," monkeys, you know. Mr. Astor told me that he had bought them in Jamaica, but they didn't at all seem to mind the prospect of separation, and were scampering about, and making love to the stewards in fine style. I might say that the boat is manned by sixty seamen; Master – Captain Curtis.

The party left New York by special car on the 10th of February. They reached Tampa on Sunday the 23rd, and left there on the 26th by the "Nourmahal," which Mr. Astor had ordered to be sent on ahead of him. From Tampa they proceeded to Key West, where they stayed for about four days, from Key West to Port-au-Prince, Haiti, then St. Thomas, St. Croix, St. Kitts, St. Lucia, St. Domingo, Guadeloupe, St. Vincent, Granada, and from there to Trinidad. Martinique, they passed over on account of yellow fever.

At each of their stopping places they remained for a couple of days, and whenever it was possible, brought out their bicycles and enjoyed a spin. When roads were bad and wheeling out of the question horseback riding was indulged in. Mr. Astor remarked that wherever English people were settled, he found the places the cleanest, next to be prominent in the virtue which ranks next to Godliness were the Danish, then the French, and last the Spanish – Indeed the latter people were more marked for their love for mother earth than for the cleansing spring.

"And what else did you do and what else did you see?" I enquired.

"Well sometimes we played tennis," replied Mr. Astor. "That was while we were staying on the Island."

Mr. Astor, speaking of Kingston, said he thought it a very pretty little City, and though far from spotless, much more savory than the chief settlements on the other Islands. On Friday evening he and his party had taken a drive towards Morant Bay. In the scenery they had found much to admire. They had brought a stack of bicycles with them and on Saturday morning had cycled around Kingston, making a short stay for a refreshing drink at the Myrtle Bank Hotel, which, he said, he found to be a very cool and pleasant resort. They had intended going to the Theatre in the evening, but having heard that the Theatrical Company had not yet arrived in Town, of course, that was off. Mr. Astor said he would have liked to remain long enough to see all that was to be seen in Jamaica, but arrangements for his yacht to leave on Sunday evening for Florida were already made. He thought our Harbour beautiful and was pleased with the whole prospect before him.

The weather had been fine during the whole of the cruise and he, his wife and his guests had enjoyed the best of health. The heat in Trinidad they had felt to be more oppressive than at the other places visited.

Mr. Astor has an American figure, tall and agile, though not very muscular, he appears to be a little over thirty, is fair with blue eyes and light, straight hair; at present he is somewhat sunburnt; his features are sharp, his manner easy and courteous. Everything about him evidences the possession of great wealth and refined tastes, but he is pleasant enough to prevent one from begrudging him his good fortune.

All his officers are from Maine, and he said they had been agreeably surprised to find that the Captain of the ship alongside came from the same place. In connection with the "Nourmahal" Mr. Astor has a fine steam launch.

Selected Later Fiction

(1896–1906)

Sui Seen Far. "The Gamblers."
Fly Leaf 1.3 (February 1896): 14–18.*

The rain splashed in his face, soaked through his garments, ran down his
back and trickled through his wide sleeves in an almost vindictive manner.
But he shambled on indifferently, slowly and heavily, apparently totally
unconscious of physical discomfort. Looking into that bald face one could
not penetrate its placidity, and even the eyes seemed expressionless. The
small, well-shaped hands did not look as if they were accustomed to man-
ual labor; nevertheless his clothing consisted of the ordinary blue blouse
and pantaloons of a working Chinaman, and it was a very dilapidated
Yankee hat around which he had wound his queue. The peculiar means
by which he prevented the last mentioned part of his costume from being
blown off by the wind and rain attracted some little attention from the
passers-by; but to jocose remarks and amused smiles he paid no heed.

Ah Lin was proceeding to a gambling resort, and his thoughts were not
with the scenes and faces about him.

When he reached his destination, he slipped a key from out of his
sleeve and admitted himself into a large low room furnished with a long
table, a couch and some wooden chairs. Two men sat on the couch, and
about a dozen were grouped around the table – all Chinamen. There was

* Reprinted as "The Gamblers" in *The Traveler* and as "Gambling Cash Tiger: A Chinese
Story" in *The Westerner*.

but one small window in the place, and the day being dull, the gloom of the room seemed to be made palpable and visible by the light of two oil lamps. On the window ledge was a pipe, a small lamp and a tiny porcelain cup full of jellified opium.

One of the Chinamen arose, took the pipe, dipped a pin into the opium, turned it around until a quantity of the sticky drug adhered to it, then inserted it into the pipe, held the pipe over the flame of the lamp, and drew two or three long breaths. Here was peace and a foretaste of oblivion – a vapor was seen to exhale out of his mouth and nose.

Ah Lin walked up to the smoker, and the two held a short confab.

"Well," said Ah Lin at length, "I have fifty cents left; with twenty-five cents I can draw a lot, and with the balance I will see if I can win half a dollar on a red cord stick."

"All right," returned the smoker, "and I'll do the same; but first let us worship the tiger."

In a corner of the room on a small table stood a wooden image of a tiger with wings grasping an immense cash between its paws.

Ah Lin and Hom Lock lighted some sticks of incense and bowed themselves before the image – the Chinaman's gambling god.

Some of those who were at the head of the centre table called to Ah Lin, and tried to prevail upon him to stake some money in a game which was played by means of a round board with a hole in the centre through which a slender stick was passed and fastened underneath to a larger board. The top piece of wood was designed to be moved around like a wheel; it was marked off into many parts upon which cabalistic figures were painted. Ah Lin had no inclination to spin the wheel, and turned to another man who sat near holding three sticks in his hand. Those three sticks were three lots; three ends projected outwards; three ends were grasped and hidden by the man's hand, hanging down from which was a red tassel or string professedly attached to one of the sticks. The sport consisted in guessing which stick had the red string.

Ah Lin ventured twenty-five cents on one of the lots or sticks, but lost. The head gambler pocketed the twenty-five cents and Ah Lin moved silently away. If he had won he would have received his quarter back with another quarter added.

At the other end of the table was a deep earthen vessel, and around it were grouped the major part of the men in the room. One man was tying up small bundles containing sums of money from one cent up to twenty-five dollars. Each package was marked with a sign word. When his task was completed, the man cast all the bundles into the vessel, and in a loud voice announced that all who wished could cast lots and for twenty-five cents have the chance of making twenty-five dollars.

A number, including Ah Lin, paid twenty-five cents and marked their names on a list of signs. Then the vessel and its contents were shaken up. All in turn were then invited to take at hazard from its portentous belly, the parcel for which they had staked. As he opened his, Ah Lin's face turned grey; it contained but one cent.

"What have you got?" asked Hom Lock, in an excited whisper, leaning over Ah Lin's shoulder. "Just one cent, eh? Well, I have the twenty-five dollars – the Tiger favors me – he's a great God."

There was a crash; the lamps were knocked down and extinguished. Ah Lin had leapt across the table and was dragging the Gambling God around the room, striking it repeatedly with a stick.

"It's a great God, isn't it," he yelled. "See how it likes to be insulted. Oh, it's a great big God."

"It's a great God," shouted Hom Lock; there was a knife in his hand; he pressed close to Ah Lin.

Ah Lin saw the knife, and something slipped from his sleeve and two knives gleamed – then disappeared.

Some one struck a light. The owner of the place picked up the fallen God and placed it on the table. It calmly looked down upon two dead men.

Sui Seen Far. "Ku Yum."

Land of Sunshine 5.1 (June 1896): 29–31.

Ku Yum, the bride, who was to start on her long journey to America on the morrow, sat in her room and wept. Young maidens, her cousins and friends, wept with her, as is the custom in China on the eve of a wedding,

but the tears which Ku Yum shed were not merely waters of ceremony;
her heart ached sadly, for tomorrow she would no longer be reckoned as
belonging to her father's family, but then and for evermore would be the
chattel of a stranger.

Tie Sung, who was living in San Francisco and had become wealthy,
had sent to China for a wife, and Ku Yum, the daughter of Ha You,
was chosen.

All the formalities of betrothal and marriage by proxy had been gone
through. The go-between, an uncle of Tie Sung, had arranged everything,
even the favorable prediction of the fortune teller, who had prophesied a
bright and happy future for the young people. A card on which a dragon
was painted assured the parents of Ku Yum that all was well with their
daughter; and another card with a phoenix satisfied the family of Tie Sung
that their son was provided with a wife after their own heart.

So there was nothing more to do but weep, and this Ku Yum did copiously – until her friends had one by one departed and left her alone. Then
she brightened up and dried her tears. She was not wholly miserable. The
prospect of a new life in a new country was not without its charms, and as
she caught a glimpse of her rich attire in a mirror and saw that her hair
was done up for the first time like a married woman's, a change came over
her and she felt glad that things were as they were.

She was indulging in some bright day dreams when the voices of her
father and mother in the next apartment fell on her ears. They were talking
about herself, and this is what they said:

"I am pleased," said her father, "to know that Ku Yum is at last disposed
of. She is so plain that I was afraid we should never find a husband for her;
and it was a bright idea to present A-Toy as our daughter when Tie Sung's
uncle visited us. If he had seen Ku Yum he would have sought elsewhere
for a bride for Tie Sung, who, they tell me, is particularly well favored."

"Yes," replied A-Chu, the mother, smiling through her tears. She was
grieved at the thought of losing her daughter, and yet like a dutiful wife,
felt bound to smile when her husband was pleased. "Yes, dear husband, I
rejoice that our daughter is well married, but I shall miss my little girl."

"I have provided her with a suitable outfit," continued Ha You, "and as
a parting gift shall present her with the gold bracelets which belonged to

my mother. A-Toy will accompany her as maid. What a pity it is that Ku Yum is not as good looking as A-Toy."

"Oh, do not speak like that," cried the mother. "Ku Yum is pretty enough for me, and she has the Golden Lily feet, which A-Toy has not."

"True," said the father, "but the Golden Lily feet are the result of art, not nature."

Ku Yum pressed her hands to her heart. What was this they were saying? Her thoughts flew over the past few weeks. She remembered how, when Tie Sung's uncle had first come to her father's house, A-Toy, her handmaid, had been sent for in great haste and presented to him, whilst she, the daughter of the house, had been bidden to remain in her room. She remembered also, how on the day of the proxy marriage her mother had laid on her particularly strict injunctions to keep her veil tightly drawn down.

Ku Yum stood up, her lips compressed, her face flushed with shame.

"I will not," said she, "do aught that will disgrace my father. But I will die before I hear Tie Sung say: 'I have been deceived; my wife is not the wife I desired – not she whom I was told would be given me.'"

II

Just two days more and Ku Yum and her maid would behold the shores of America. Sadly Ku Yum gazed on the blue water. Gladly would she have thrown herself into its depths – but the ship must bring a bride to Tie Sung and she was the daughter of a Chinaman and dared not shame her father.

"A-Toy," she called.

A-Toy approached. She was a beautiful girl. Her figure was plump, also her face; her mouth was small and round, her eye long and bright; her brows finely arched and penciled, her hair of the deepest black and very abundant.

Ku Yum sighed as she gazed on her. "Why is she so well favored whilst I am so plain?" she asked herself. And A-Toy thought: "Why is Ku Yum a mistress and A-Toy a slave?"

"A-Toy," said Ku Yum, "how would you like to take my place, dress in my clothes, and be Tie Sung's bride?"

A-Toy's eyes sparkled.

"Oh, mistress," said she, "you are mocking me."

"Nay," said Ku Yum, "I am serious. When we reach America I will be A-Toy; you will be Ku Yum; you will marry Tie Sung, and I will be your maid and you shall be my mistress."

Upon arrival of the ship at San Francisco, Ku Yum and A-Toy were met by Tie Sung, accompanied by a brother and another relative. A-Toy, robed as a bride and closely veiled, was helped into a cab by Tie Sung, Ku Yum following, and the whole party drove off to a Joss house.

III

A week had elapsed since A-Toy became the wife of Tie Sung; and she and Ku Yum were together in the upstairs apartment of Tie Sung's house. A-Toy was attired in a richly embroidered blue silk tunic and gay trousers; her hair was built up into a flat structure and adorned with imitation jewels and flowers. She looked very well indeed, but Ku Yum, who was very poorly clad and whose little feet were concealed in a large slipper with a sole like a pyramid, looked pale and thin. She was engaged in washing some cups and saucers, and every now and then she would lift her hands to wipe away the tears which ran down her cheeks.

A-Toy, observing the action, called her angrily.

"Why are you crying? If you do not stop I will tell Tie Sung to whip you."

"Tie Sung will never whip me," answered Ku Yum. "I will not allow him to do so, and he would not even if he could, for he has a kind heart. It is you who are hard and cruel. Ah! that I had never wished to change places with you!"

"Slave! do you dare to speak thus to me – and of my husband?" cried A-Toy, and struck her former mistress with a small carved stick which lay on the table beside her.

Ku Yum left the room and went and stood on the veranda outside. It was evening; the veranda was high, and looking down one could perceive nothing but a soft darkness.

Ku Yum stretched out her arms to the faint moon.

"Beautiful ladies in the moon," cried she, "close your eyes for a little while. Life is too hard to bear."

"A-Toy! A-Toy!" called Tie Sung's wife, "come in and prepare my bed." But there was no answer.

IV

"I have received a letter from Tie Sung," said Ha You to his wife.

"He seems to be very pleased with Ku Yum's appearance, and compliments us highly on her beauty."

"I always thought Ku Yum lovely," replied A-Chu, complacently.

"He says, however," continued Ha You, "that her temper is not as good as he would like it to be."

"He's out of his mind," retorted A-Chu with asperity. "Ku Yum's temper is of the sweetest."

"What do you think he means when he says he is surprised to find that her feet are large, not at all like a lady's?"

"I think he must be joking! Ku Yum's feet could not possibly be smaller."

"In the postscript to his letter he informs me that A-Toy, Ku Yum's maid, fell from a high veranda and was picked up dead. He is sending the body to China so that we may have the pleasure of burying it. By the way, he says that the men who discovered A-Toy's body discovered also that her feet were the Golden Lily feet. My dear, do not scream so; our friends will be running in to see if I'm killing you."

Mr. Ha You assisted Mrs. Ha You, who had fallen on the floor and was emitting loud screams, to rise; and as she rose he forced her eyes to meet his. What she saw in those placid depths had an effect, for she immediately became calm and quiet.

"Now listen to me," said Ha You.

"My daughter, my little daughter is dead!" sobbed the mother.

"That is so," replied Ha You, "but remember, no word of this to a living being. The body that arrives must be buried as the body of A-Toy, the slave. I will not be disgraced."

So Ku Yum was buried among the slaves, and the mother stood afar off and wept.

Montreal, Canada.

Sui Seen Far. "The Story of Iso."
Lotus 2 (Aug. 1896): 117–19.

"A talking woman will come to a sad end," said old Tai Wang dolorously.

"Why so, Tai?" questioned my cousin. "Don't you think that a little sharp exercise of the tongue benefits the general health?"

"No, not when the tongue belongs to a woman," answered Tai. "Listen and I will tell you the story of Iso: "Iso lived in the Chinese country outside Kiahing,* among the mulberry-trees and rice-fields. Her parents were poor, but respectable, and as a great number of children, mostly boys, had been born to them, they were much esteemed by their neighbors, for in China it is believed that none but the eminently virtuous are blessed with many sons.

"Iso was the eldest, and after reaching the age of six she was seldom seen without a chubby baby strapped on her back, and thus she moved about washing dishes, sewing, and performing other necessary tasks. But even when a child her tongue got her into trouble.

"Once, when her mother bade her take the boys out, she led them to a place where they could amuse themselves with weeds, rock-work, and small ponds, and seated herself with the baby on a grassy mound. To her then came a woman called Mai Gwi Far.

"'Dear me!' said Mai Gwi Far, looking around; 'what a number of little brothers you have! Your father and mother must be very good.'

"'Yes,' said Iso, 'they are good, but they are not good just because they have given me so many brothers. I love my brothers now that I have them, but if they were not here, I should not want them. I would not be so often hungry and my bones would not ache from working so hard. If Kuang Ing Huk† offers my parents so many children and they accept them without considering whether they can keep the new ones without taking the rice from those they already have, I can not see why they should be praised for doing so. To me they would seem wiser and better if they had fewer children.'

* Now Zhejiang, eastern coastal province just south of Shanghai.
† The Chinese Goddess of Mercy.

"These words so horrified Mai Gwi Far that she ran with great haste to Iso's father and told him of the unfilial disposition of his daughter. Iso, being then thirteen years of age, was too old to be whipped, so her father took her and locked her up in a room and kept her there without food for a day and a half, which was indeed a mild punishment for one whose tongue babbled so much foolishness.

"One morning Iso was sent to sweep the tomb of her grandfather and to pull up the grass and weeds which might be growing around his grave. In the afternoon the whole family would meet at the tomb for the purpose of worshiping the dead. Iso carried with her a quantity of incense-sticks and different kinds of food, such as fish, pork, fowl, and vegetables; these she placed around the grave; also some cups of tea.

"Just as she was finishing her task a 'red-headed' stranger came her way and spoke to her in the Chinese language. Iso, only too glad to have the opportunity to rattle her tongue, answered back; consequently the 'red-headed' stranger filled her mind with many senseless ideas; and when her relations came to burn mock money and offer food to the departed spirit who was supposed to partake of the spiritual essence of the offering, Iso refused to worship, saying that she did not believe that the spirit of her grandfather cared whether she worshipped at his grave or not, and if it did care, it was not worth worshiping.*

"Ever after that day Iso was regarded with suspicion and aversion by the members of her family, and once, when she returned from marketing with a cat following at her heels, her father became so incensed that he ordered her to leave his presence forever, and so she would have done had not her mother put in soft words. The coming of a cat to a house is regarded by the Chinese as an omen of approaching poverty.

"Negotiations for the marriage of Iso were commenced ere Iso was six-teen. A go-between who had been engaged by a respectable family in the neighborhood tendered a proposal of marriage to her father, which pro-posal was in behalf of the eldest son of the family. The young man being considered eligible, Iso's father consulted a fortune-teller, and was told that

* The phrase "red-headed stranger" is Eaton's shorthand for an Anglo-American adven-turer, a figure that reappears in her 1902 story "The Coat of Many Colors."

the signs were favorable for a happy marriage; the betrothal was then sealed by the families exchanging cards. Iso's family were given a card on which a dragon was painted, and the family of the young man received a card with a phoenix. Presents were sent and the material for the bridal dress was brought, and, forty-eight hours before the time fixed for the marriage, Iso was told that she must prepare to become a bride.

"Now, instead of thanking her parents for providing her with a suitable husband, as any proper or dutiful daughter would have done, Iso tossed her head at the news and said: 'I cannot marry any man whom I do not know well. Let him come here and see me; let me become acquainted with him before marriage, and after the passing of two months I will tell you whether I will become his wife or not. My husband must be pleasing to me, and whether or not he will be so no one can judge save myself; for we all look through different glasses.'

"It is impossible to describe the anger of Iso's parents when they heard much monstrous ideas expressed. Her father said: 'You are mad; nevertheless, you shall marry the man I have chosen for you and at the time appointed.'

"So Ting Sean, Iso's father, hushed up his daughter's words and preparations for the bridal went on, and the event might have been consummated had not one of Iso's little brothers repeated her sayings to a young friend, and thus they were carried to the family of Hop Wo, Iso's betrothed.

"Who would allow a son to marry a woman with a tongue like Iso's? The proposal of marriage was withdrawn, the engagement declared broken. Ting Sean had the mortification of seeing the daughter of his enemy, Lee Chu, borne as bride through the streets to the home of Hop Wo. As to Iso, she was everlastingly disgraced; there were no more proposals of marriage for her and she died in a strange land, far away from China – the country which heaven loves."

"How did that come about?" inquired my cousin.

"Some 'red-headed people' took her across the sea, and right glad were her parents to be rid of the shame of her presence. That is the story of Iso, the girl who talked too much."

"And it's a very good story, too, Tai, said my cousin. "She who is called in China 'The woman who talks too much' is called by us 'The new woman.'"

Sui Seen Far. "A Love Story of the Orient."
Lotus 2 (October 1896): 203–7.*

Two men were carrying a coffin slung with ropes to a pole. Within the coffin was the corpse of an old man sitting in an upright position – a cloth was bound around its head and a few straggling gray locks fluttered in the breeze; the eyes were closed; the expression on the face was that of calm contempt. Six shaven yellow-robed priests, crooning a monotonous death-chant, followed. This was in the heart of an Eastern forest.

The procession halted in front of a small building surrounded by cryptomeria;† one of the priests swung open an iron door and disclosed to view a large oven: he muttered a few words and the men who carried the coffin thrust it into the oven and piled around it a quantity of wood. To this they set fire and closed the door.

The priests moved a short distance off and commenced chanting again. In about an hour's time the oven was opened and some ashes and unconsumed bones were raked out, placed in an earthen vessel, and carried away. The priests returned to their monastery, but as they left the spot where they had consigned their brother to ashes, one, almost a boy, said to the portly brother who walked beside him:

"I am filled with ardent curiosity concerning the life in the world of him who has at last attained to perfection. 'Tis said you know his history."

"Hush! speak not so loud," admonished the portly one, "but to-night when all the rest are sleeping or praying, come you to my cell and I will tell you the life-story of Ku Lau."

* Revised and recycled in "The Bonze" in *The Westerner.*
† Tree in the cypress family.

The little cell in which the monk Tai Shun was supposed to fast and do penance presented an inviting appearance at the midnight hour. A dark red cloth was draped over the iron bars, and bowls of rice, minced pork, chicken, and two small jugs of samshu* set on a little table caused the young priest to hesitate and look around in a scared way before entering.

Tai Shun motioned to a cushioned seat.

"I dare not," said Yenfoh, regarding with longing and yet frightened eyes the table. "Are we not taught that the consumption of anything that has had animal life is a sinful act and that he should abstain who hopes to sit upon a lotus flower when transmigration shall cease, gazing for all eternity upon Buddha?"

"My son," replied Tai Shun, "when you have lived a little longer, you will know that people seldom practice what they preach – besides, if we were actually to follow out the theory of abstaining from animal food, we should have to reject all sustenance whatsoever, for the water and vegetables which you have been taught to regard as proper food for those who desire to be pure, are full of living things."

Thus speaking, Tai Shun lifted with one hand his own chopsticks and with his other tendered a pair to Yenfoh, who finally yielded to temptation.

When the last tiny bowlful of samshu had been tested, Tai Shun said:

"Fifty years ago Ku Lau was one of the handsomest youths in Suchau,† in the province of the Happy River, and Mae, the daughter of Wong T'sae, was above all the maidens the loveliest in the land of lovely women.

"How these two came to love one another I am unable to say, but this I know, when Ku Lau was sent to finish his studies at the Imperial College in Pekin, he carried in his sleeve one of Mae's tiny golden shoes.

"Ku Lau's family were poor, but he was a remarkably clever youth and had earned his own college expenses. It was his ambition to gain the third literary degree, after which he hoped to be appointed a teacher in one of the schools in his own province and receive a salary.

"Mae's father was a wealthy merchant."

Here the old priest produced a small box, unlocked it, and took therefrom two letters, yellowed by age; the tracing of the characters on one was

* Chinese rice liqueur.
† Now spelled Suzhou, a major city in Jiangsu Province near Shanghai.

much finer than on the other, but both had evidently been written by persons skilled in the use of the hair pencil.

"These letters are one from Ku Lau to Mae and the other from Mae to Ku Lau," said Tai Shun.

"Where did you get them?" asked Yenfoh.

"This is Ku Lau's," went on Tai Shun, ignoring the question. "Now, listen," and taking up the epistle which bore the heaviest characters, he began:

"'My dearest friend and my heart's love, – I hope your sweet and beautiful self is well in mind and body. I am working hard and have many new and difficult branches of study to master, but if for a moment I lay down my book or pen and pencil, I see your face before me, giving me courage and hope. For your sake I rejoice in the thought of success; and for your sake I dread failure.

"'I often ask myself whether I deserve my fate. If, before I had met you, I had been married by my father to some girl chosen by him and to me unknown, to what a dull existence I should have been doomed! for there is no joy or life where there is no love, and there is no love in such marriages.

"'It is love which causes the tender interest and sympathy between us two. Do I not find happiness in reading your letters, which tell us what you do, what you say, what you think – and am I not assured that it never wearies you to hear from me? That is love.

"'I have now the happiness to inform you that the literary Chancellor has seen fit to single me out as one the best competitors and I see that I rank high on the list which has been posted up of the comparative merits of the compositions. They also give me credit for writing four verses during the burning of the candle, which, indeed, I found an easy task, you being my inspiration.

"'Some of the other students are sending in their cards as an expression of thanks to the high Mandarin who presided at the examination, but I shall not follow their example, for this Mandarin is a very ignorant man. I laugh in my sleeve when he pompously puts questions to me, knowing that he himself could not tell whether they are answered rightly or wrongly. He is said to have obtained his office by purchase.

"'Do you remember me writing to you of one of my classmates, a very brilliant fellow named Wong Chow? He has been banished from College because it was discovered that his great-grandfather was a play actor. It seems that any one related to a person who has earned his living as an actor is not permitted to aspire for literary honors. I think such a rule is most unjust. Wong was the cleverest student in the College.

"'I am tired of the "Five Classics" and the "Four Books."* I wish so much importance were not given to these studies. I prefer mathematics, which branch of learning is little regarded by the teachers.

"'However, I must do my best to please those in authority, for thus shall I hasten our union.

"'Ah! Mae, will you not be proud when you behold your Ku Lau with the gold flowers in his hat and the red sash. 'Tis then I shall kneel before my father and say: "Choose no wife for your son, for his heart has already chosen;" then you will approach, and your sweetness and gentleness will win my father and your father also to say: "Let it be as our children wish."

"'And now with lingering pen I say farewell. Forever with you is the heart of your Ku Lau.

"'P. S. – If you wish to see me now or at any time, send word by the carrier-dove and I will come. Do you want me? Say yes.'"

During the reading of this letter Yenfoh's youthful face had assumed a sad and earnest expression. Was he regretting a joy renounced before revealed?

"Would you care to hear the woman's letter?" enquired Tai Shun.

"Yes, ah! yes."

Then the old priest read:

"'Beloved, – I am full of fears of I know not what. You will smile when you read this, but when the other day I found the leaves of the beautiful rose geranium you gave me becoming of an unpleasant hue and all of the blossoms withering, I cried until sundown – my heart felt so heavy and sad.

* The authoritative books of Confucianism (c. 300 BCE).

"'The owl, which our people call "the constable from the dark land," has also been giving warning of some approaching calamity.* Last night I heard its cry, faint and indistinct as though afar off.

"'Oh, hasten back to me, my dear one – I need your presence – without the warmth of your smile I cannot live. Do you think of me? The sing-song girls, they who laugh and dance and sing and paint their faces – do they ever cause you to forget your Mae? Sometimes I fear me that your heart may change and that another may be dearer than I have been. Let me hear at once if it be not even now so. Let me hear so I may die.

"'But I am foolish and wicked to write thus – forgive me, forgive me.'

"'So you are meeting with success in your studies. I rejoice with you. Did I not always believe that you could achieve all that you attempted? How proud I am – how happy! I entreat you to remain at Pekin until the final examination. You must not think of leaving now. Such an act would be madness, and I should never forgive myself were I to stand in the way of your success. But I live in the thought of your return. What a day that will be! Oh, I think my heart will stop beating with rapture!

"'A man who has had his ability recognized in a province not his own is always afterwards very highly appreciated and made much of by his own people. I have heard my father say so. He says also that a man may have the wisdom of a god, but until he proves it in a strange city his own people will regard him as a fool. Yes, you will rise to be a man of influence and honor, and you will be a just man and will not use your rank and power to oppress the people as father says so many officers do.

"'Of myself, there is little to say. I walk with my mother and cousins in the morning; I sew and embroider in the afternoon, and Sung Sung tells me fairy tales, and sometimes my father makes me read some of the writings of Confutze.† He wishes me to have more learning than my cousins, and though I have no taste for study, I will try to be a wise woman for your sake. Ah! for your sake, what would I not do? Mae.'

---

* This phrase is used in Justus Doolittle's 1864 *Social Life of the Chinese*, a book Eaton knew well and relied on as her "primary source of information on Chinese culture." See Dominika Ferens, *Edith and Winnifred Eaton: Chinatown Missions and Japanese Romances* (Chicago: University of Illinois Press, 2002, 28).
† Another spelling of Confucius.

"It seems," continued Tai Shun, "that shortly after Mae sent this letter, her parents agreed with the parents of Ku Lau to betroth their children – that is, the parents had decided to do what, unbeknown to them, the children had done for themselves.

"Mae was told by her father that he had betrothed her to a very worthy young man, and a letter was written to Ku Lau apprising him that a bride awaited his coming.

"Ku Lau received the tidings with a happy heart – he had been given the name of his prospective bride. Mae, who had only been told that she was to wed her father's choice and who never dreamt that his choice would be her own, wept bitterly, and wrote a pitiful note telling her lover of her father's wishes, and ending with 'Oh, what shall I do?'

"Ku Lau, exulting in his knowledge and smiling whilst he wrote, answered: 'Marry the man whom your father has chosen for you.'

"So it came to pass that the morning after her carrier-dove had fluttered with its message into Mae's room, she was found dead. Her lover's thoughtless jest had caused her to believe that he no longer loved her and was willing that she should be claimed by another.

"Her parents mourned and sent the news to Ku Lau. He returned home raving, and after the wildness of his grief had spent itself, a deep melancholy settled upon his mind; he gave up all his brilliant prospects and entered our monastery, where he has remained for half a century, spending his time almost entirely in his own cell.

"This is the story of Ku Lau, a priest of whom the Brotherhood is proud, for whilst the majority of us seek the seclusion of a monastery in order to avoid arrest and punishment for crimes or in consequence of adversity in business, Ku Lau banished himself voluntarily from a world which found no fault with him."

"And he became a true priest of Buddha," murmured Yenfoh dreamily – the samshu was beginning to affect him. "Through years of complete mental abstraction and yearning after perfection he was indeed purified from all human sentiments."

"It is supposed so," replied Tai Shun; "but sometimes whilst passing his way I have heard the whispered name of her who died, and have questioned, 'Is his mind indeed given to Buddha, or can it be that he has sought the solitude of a cell in order to be able to think, undisturbed, on his lost love?'"*

Sui Seen Far. "A Chinese Feud."
Land of Sunshine 5.6 (November 1896): 236–7.

Fantze stood behind the counter in her father's store, listlessly rolling up and down the balls in the counting machine; she was thinking of the feud between the Sam Yups and the See Yups.†

Fantze was an American born, and though she wore the Chinese dress and ate with chopsticks, she was in many respects an American girl; for her mother had died when she was in swaddling clothes and her father had allowed the ladies of the Mission to have much to do with the bringing up of his little daughter.

And Fantze had a lover – just as any American girl might have had – and he, too, was an American Chinese, having been brought to the states when but nine years of age. His father, a boss laundryman, had returned to China but a short time since, leaving his business in charge of his son, who managed it so successfully that he bade fair to make his "pile" in a much shorter time than his father before him.

But Wong On had no intention of following his parent to China. Degenerate Chinaman! He preferred the land of his adoption to that of his forefathers, and cherished the hope of building a little home for himself and Fantze in America.

---

* Eaton revisits this narrative in "The Bonze" in "The Chinese in America – Part III."
† Two member groups of the Six Companies (also known as the Chinese Consolidated Benevolent Association), the most powerful organization in Chinatown, authorized to represent the interests of immigrant Chinese. The Sam Yups were a group of Cantonese-speaking merchants from the Third (i.e., "*sam*") District; the See Yups were a larger group of labourers, mostly speakers of a rural dialect, from the Fourth (i.e., "*see*") District. In 1895, the murder of a See Yup by a Sam Yup led the See Yups to withdraw from the Six Companies and boycott Sam Yup–owned businesses. Eaton offers a revised version of this narrative in "The Story of Tai Yuen and Ku Yum," in "The Chinese in America–Part III."

Wong On and Fantze were engaged – not betrothed as boys and girls in China are without having anything to say themselves in the matter, but engaged just like ordinary Americans who pledge themselves to marry the one (they believe at the time) they love the best.

Wong On was never seen with Fantze on the street, and he dared not venture to ask for permission to visit her in her rooms, but he was forever finding excuses to call at her father's store, behind the counter of which she spent much time, poring over her picture books, sewing and at the same time keeping an eye on any customers who might enter during her father's frequent absences. The two young things had been very happy in one another's companionship, and Fantze's father had smiled and approved. But happy days go by.

There are ten districts in the Province of Kwangtung. When the Chinese say "a Sam Yup man," they mean a man from the Third District, and when they say "a See Yup," they mean one from the Fourth District, and so on.

Some time ago in Southern California a Sam Yup murdered a See Yup. All the See Yups knew that one of their number had been killed by a Sam Yup; but though they thirsted for revenge, they could not discover the murderer. It therefore became a case, not of man against man, but of district against district, and as a result a Sam Yup man soon went the way of the murdered See Yup. The See Yups, however, proved better detectives than their enemies, and traced the crime so that the actual murderer, a man belonging to one of the See Yup's secret societies, was convicted and punished by the law of the land. At this the See Yups became so bitterly incensed that notice to boycott all Sam Yups was sent by their chiefs to the See Yups all over the continent. The boycott spread and became a serious matter, for the See Yups are much more numerous than the Sam Yups, the See Yups being chiefly laundrymen and laboring men, and the Sam Yups merchants, who depend for the success of their business upon the trade of the See Yups.

Any See Yup seen in the store of a Sam Yup after the issuing of that notice was regarded with suspicion by his clan. Indeed, his life was not safe, for it was whispered that trusted emissaries of the Brotherhood were on the keen lookout for delinquents, who would be dealt with summarily and secretly.

So Fantze had good cause to feel sad. Supplies being now ordered to be sent direct to the chief laundries in the city where her father did business, her father's trade was ruined, and her lover, though he visited her as often, did so at great risk.

The door bell rang. It was Wong On; he stepped across the store and stood by Fantze's side.

"My pearl is misty today," said he, taking her hands and looking into her face.

"Ah, Wong On," she replied, "I fear for you – visit me no more, I entreat."

Wong On's face became stern. "Am I a cur?" he made answer.

She shook her head, and a quaint little smile flickered around her mouth as she said: "In my eyes you are a superior man."

"Then how can you expect me to leave you when you are in trouble and need me?"

"Because, Wong On, your life is precious, and or my sake you must be discreet."

"Look," said he, turning over the leaves of a bound *British Workman*** which lay on the counter.

The girl peeped over his shoulder and saw a picture of Queen Victoria presenting some soldiers with medals.

"Those men," explained Wong On, "are receiving a reward for bravery. So some day shall I be rewarded, and my medal will be you."

Long and earnestly Fantze gazed – then the words came slowly: "The bravest soldiers receive no reward – they do not live long enough."

It was a wretched night. The wind blew in wild gusts and drove the rain savagely. Wong On emerged from his warm room and started for Fantze's home. He pulled down his cap and turned up his collar and walked quickly along, not noticing the footsteps behind him, muffled in the downpour.

He had made up his mind to marry Fantze without further waiting, for she and her father were almost destitute, and the lover in him yearned to take care of the girl. That very evening did he intend to persuade old Lee Fee to allow the Presbyterian minister to perform the ceremony. Though

---

* An English Protestant socialist and temperance broadsheet published between 1855–92.

the old man burnt sticks of incense to Chinese gods and worshipped before an ancestral tablet, both he and Fantze were Christians.

The To-come appeared before Wong On – the wonderful To-Come. He saw therein the most beautiful little woman in the world moving about his home, pouring out his tea and preparing his rice. He saw a cot; and kicking and crowing therein a baby – a boy baby with a round shaven head and Fantze's eyes. He saw himself receiving the congratulations of all the wifeless, motherless, sisterless, childless American Chinamen. "Ah!" thought he, with a pitying thrill, "I will invite them by the half dozens to spend evenings with me, and Fantze shall entertain them as I have sometimes seen the wives of my American friends entertain their husbands' company. How very happy I shall be!"

A fire kindled in his heart. Just a few more steps and he would be with Fantze. But then there was a swish. Long, skinny arms threw a bleeding body against the door, on the other side of which sat Fantze dreaming of someone. Then Quong Sin, agent of one of the See Yup's secret societies, thrust a bloody blade up his sleeve and slunk silently away.

Time brings changes. In time the feud between the Sam Yups and the See Yups died out, and Fantze became the wife of a proud old Confucianist who took her home to China. She renounced Christianity; but the last heard of her was that she had shown to some travelers as her most precious possession a picture torn from a Christian book. Underneath the picture is said to be written in Fantze's round hand: "These are brave men, but where are the bravest?"

Montreal, Can.

Sui Seen Far. "The Daughter of a Slave."
Short Stories 25 (January–March 1897): 218–23.*

"He that has wine has many friends," muttered Koan-lo the Second, as he glanced backwards into the store out of which he was stepping. It was a Chinese general store, well stocked with all manner of quaint wares and about a dozen Chinamen were sitting around, whilst in an adjoining room could be seen the recumbent forms of several opium smokers who were discussing business and indulging in the fascinating pipe during the intervals of conversation.

Noticeable amongst the smokers was Koan-lo the First, a tall, middle-aged Chinaman, wearing a black cap with a red button. Koan-lo the First was cousin to Koan-lo the Second, but whereas Koan-lo the Second was young and penniless, Koan-lo the First was one of the wealthiest Chinese merchants in San Francisco, and a mighty man amongst the people of his name in that city, who regarded him as a father.

Koan-lo the Second had been instructed by Koan-lo the First to meet Sie, the latter's bride, who was arriving that day by steamer from China. Koan-lo the First was too busy a man to go down himself to the docks.

So Koan-lo the Second and Sie met – though not for the first time. Five years before in a suburb of Canton City they had said to one another: "I love you."

Koan-lo the Second was an orphan and had been educated and cared for from youth upwards by Koan-lo the First.

Sie was the daughter of a slave, which will explain why she and Koan-lo the Second had had the opportunity to know one another before the latter left with his cousin for America. In China the daughters of slaves are allowed far more liberty than girls belonging to a higher class of society.

"Koan-lo, ah, Koan-lo," cooed Sie softly and happily as she recognized her lover.

* Reprinted as "The God of Restoration" in *Mrs. Spring Fragrance* (1912).

"Sie, my sweetest heart," returned Koan-lo the Second, his voice both glad and sad.

He saw a mistake had been made – that Sie believed that the man who was to be her husband was himself – Koan-lo the Second.

And all the love that was in him awoke and he became dizzy thinking of what might yet be.

Could he explain that the Koan-lo who had purchased Sie for his bride, and to whom she of right belonged, was his cousin and not himself. Could he deliver to the Koan-lo who had many friends and stores of precious valuables, the only friend, the only treasure he had ever possessed. And was it likely that Sie would be happy eating the rice of Koan-lo the First, when she loved him, Koan-lo the Second.

Sie's little fingers crept into his. She leaned against him.

"I am tired; shall we soon rest?" said she.

"Yes, very soon, my Sie," he murmured, putting his arm around her.

"I was too glad when my father told me that you had sent for me," she whispered. "I said: 'How good of Koan-lo to remember me all these years.'"

"And did you not remember me, my Jess'mine flower?"

"Why, need you ask; you know the days and nights have been filled with you."

"Having remembered me; why should you have dreamt that I might have forgotten you?"

"There is a difference; you are a man; I am a woman."

"You have been mine now for over two weeks," said Koan-lo the Second. "Do you still love me, Sie?"

"Look into mine eyes and see," she answered.

"And are you happy?"

"Happy! Yes, and this is the happiest day of all, because to-day my father obtains his freedom."

"How is that, Sie?"

"Why, Koan-lo, you know. Does not my father receive to-day the balance of the price which you pay for me, and is not that, added to what you sent in advance, sufficient to purchase my father's freedom. My dear, good father – he has worked so hard all these years; he has ever been so kind to me. To think that he will no longer be a slave. Yes, I am the happiest woman in the world to-day."

Sie kissed her husband's hand.

He drew it away and hid with it his face.

"Ah, dear husband!" cried Sie. "You are very sick."

"No, not sick," replied the miserable Koan-lo, "but, Sie, I must tell you that I am a very poor man, and we have got to leave this pretty house in the country and go to some city where I will have to work hard, and you will scarcely have enough to eat."

"Kind, generous Koan-lo," answered Sie, "you have ruined yourself for my sake; you paid too high a price for me. Ah, unhappy Sie, who has pulled Koan-lo into the dust! Now let me be your servant, for gladly would I starve for your sake. I care for Koan-lo, not riches."

And she fell on her knees before Koan-lo, who raised her gently, saying:

"Sie, I am unworthy of such devotion, and your words drive a thousand spears into my heart. Hear my confession. I am your husband, but I am not the man who bought you. My cousin, Koan-lo the First, sent for you to come from China; it was he who bargained for you and paid half the price your father asked whilst you were in Canton, and agreed to pay the balance upon sight of your face. Alas, the balance will never be paid, for as I have stolen you from my cousin, he is not bound to keep to the agreement, and your father is still a slave."

Sie stood motionless, overwhelmed by the sudden and terrible news. She looked at her husband bewilderedly.

"Is it true, Koan-lo; must my father remain a slave?" she asked.

"Yes, it is true," replied her husband, "but we have still one another, and you say you care not for poverty, so forgive me and forget your father. I forgot all for love of you."

He attempted to draw her to him, but with a pitiful cry she turned and fled.

Koan-lo the First sat smoking and meditating.

Many moons had gone by since Koan-lo the Second had betrayed the trust of Koan-lo the First, and Koan-lo the First was wondering what Koan-lo the Second was doing and how he was living. "He had little money and was unused to working hard, and with a woman to support, what will the dog do?" thought the old man. He felt injured and bitter, but towards the evening after long smoking his heart became softened and he said to his pipe: "Well, well, he had a loving feeling for her, and the young I suppose must mate with the young. I think I could overlook his ungratefulness were he to come and seek forgiveness."

"Great and honored sir, the dishonored Sie kneels before you, and begs you to put your foot on her head."

These words were uttered by a young Chinese girl of rare beauty who had entered the room suddenly and prostrated herself before Koan-lo the First. He looked up angrily.

"Ah, I see the false woman who made her father a liar!" he cried.

Tears fell from the downcast eyes of Sie, the kneeler.

"Good sir," said she, "ere I had become a woman or your cousin a man, we loved one another, and when we met after a long separation we both forgot our duty. But now I repent and come to you to give myself up to be your slave, to work for you until the flesh drops from my bones, if such be your desire, only asking that you will send to my father the balance of my purchase price, for he is too old and feeble to be a slave. Sir, you are known to be a more than just man. Oh, grant my request, 'tis for my father's sake I plead. For many years he nourished me with trouble and care, and my heart almost breaks when I think of him. Punish me for my misdeeds, dress me in rags and feed me on the meanest food, only let me serve you and make myself of use to you so that I may be worth my father's freedom."

"And what of my cousin? Are you now false to him?"

"No, not false to Koan-lo, my husband – only true to my father."

"And you wish me, whom you have injured, to free your father?"

Sie's head dropped lower as she replied.

"I wish to be your slave. I wish to pay with the labor of my hands the debt I owe you and the debt I owe my father. For this I have left my husband."

Koan-lo the First arose, lifted Sie's chin with his hand and contemplated with earnest eyes her face. "Your heart is not all bad," he observed.

"Sit down and listen. I will not buy you for my slave, for in this country it is against the law to buy a woman for a slave, but I will hire you for five years to be my servant, and for that time you will do my bidding, and after that you will be free. Rest in peace concerning your father."

"May the sun ever shine on you, most gracious master," cried Sie.

Then Koan-lo the First pointed out to her a hallway leading to a little room, which room he said she could have for her own private use whilst she remained with him.

Sie thanked him and was leaving his presence when the door was burst open and Koan-lo the Second, looking haggard and wild entered. He rushed up to Sie and clutched her by the shoulder.

"You are mine!" he shouted, "I will kill you before you become another man's."

"Cousin," said Koan-lo the First. "I wish not to have the woman to be my wife, but I claim her as my servant. She has already received her wages – her father's freedom."

Koan-lo the Second gazed bewilderedly into the face of his wife and his cousin. Then he threw up his hands and cried:

"Oh, Koan-lo, my cousin; I have been evil. Always have I envied you and carried bitter thoughts of you in my heart. Even your kindness to me in the past has provoked my ill will, and when I have seen you surrounded by friends I have said scornfully: 'He that has wine has many friends,' although I well knew the people loved you for your good heart. And Sie, I have deceived. I took her to myself knowing that she thought I was what I was not. I caused her to believe she was mine by all rights."

"So I am yours," broke in Sie, tremblingly.

"So she shall be yours – when you are worthy of such a pearl and can guard it and keep it," said Koan-lo the First – then waving his cousin away from Sie, he continued:

"This is your punishment; you shall not see Sie again for five years. Meanwhile, go and work."

"Your husband comes for you to-day; does the thought make you glad?" questioned Koan-lo the First.

Sie smiled and blushed.

"I shall be sorry to leave you," she replied.

"But more glad than sad," said the old man. "Sie, your husband is now a fine fellow; he has changed wonderfully during his years of probation."

"Then I shall neither know nor love him," said Sie mischievously. "Why here he –

"My sweet one."

"My husband."

"My children, take my blessing, be good and be happy. I go to my opium pipe, to dream of bliss, if not to find it."

With these words Koan-lo the First retired.

"Is he not almost as a god?" said Sie.

"Yes," answered her husband, drawing her on to his knee; "he has been better to me than I have deserved. And you – ah, Sie, how can you care for me when you know what a bad fellow I have been?"

"Well," said Sie, contentedly, "it is always our best friends who know how bad we are."

Sui Seen Far. "Sweet Sin: A Chinese-American Story."
Land of Sunshine 8.5 (April 1897): 223–6.*

"Chinese! Chinese!" A small form darted across the street, threw itself upon the boys from whom the derisive cry had arisen, and began kicking and thumping and scratching and shaking, so furiously that a companion cried in fright, "Sweet Sin! Oh, Sweet Sin! Come away, you will kill them!"

But Sweet Sin was deaf to all sounds save "Chinese! Chinese!" Before her eyes was a fiery mist.

* This story explores a scenario similar to those explored in "Half-Chinese Children" and later in "Leaves from the Mental Portfolio of a Eurasian."

A quarter of an hour later Sweet Sin with a bandaged head was being led to her home by a couple of much scandalized Sunday-school teachers, her little friend following with a very pale face.

Sweet Sin was the child of a Chinese merchant and his American wife. She had been baptized Wilhelmina, but for reasons apart from the fact that her father was Hwuy Sin, a medical student had, in her babyhood, dubbed her Sweet Sin, and the name had clung.

On arrival at the house, they were met by the mother, who was much perturbed at the sight of her offspring.

The Sunday-school teachers explained the case and departed. The mother bathed Sweet Sin's face. The child liked the feeling of the cool water; her head was feverish and so was her heart.

"I'm so sorry that this happened," said the mother. "I wanted you to go to Mrs. Goodwin's party tonight, and now you are not fit to be seen."

"I'm glad," answered Sweet Sin. "I don't want to go."

"Why not?" queried the mother. "I'm surprised, she is so kind to you."

"I do not think so," replied Sweet Sin, "and I don't want her toys and candies. It's just because I'm half Chinese and a sort of curiosity that she likes to have me there. When I'm in her parlor, she whispers to the other people and they try to make me talk and examine me from head to toe as if I were a wild animal – I'd rather be killed than be a show."

"Sweet Sin, you must not speak so about your friends," remonstrated the mother.

"I don't care!" defiantly asserted Sweet Sin. "Last week, when I was at her house for tea, she came up with an old gentleman with white hair and gold-rimmed glasses. I heard the old gentleman say, 'Oh, indeed, you don't say so! her father a Chinaman!' and then he stared at me with all his might. Mrs. Goodman said, 'Do you not notice the peculiar cast of features?' and he said 'Ah, yes! and such bright eyes – very peculiar little girl.'"

"Well, and what did you do then?"

"Oh, I jumped up and cried: 'And you're a very peculiar, mean old man,' and ran out of the house."

"They must have thought you a little Chinese savage," said the mother, but her cheek glowed.

"They can think what they like! Besides, it isn't the Chinese half of me that makes me feel like this – it's the American half. My Chinese half is good and patient, like all the Chinese people we know, but it's my American half that feels insulted for the Chinese half and wants to fight. Oh, mother, mother, you don't know what it is to be half one thing and half another, like I am! I feel all torn to pieces. I don't know what I am, and I don't seem to have any place in the world."

Sweet Sin had been brought up in the Methodist Church and her mother sent her to Sunday-school regularly. Sometimes she felt a missionary spirit. One day, to an old laundryman, she told the story of the creation of Adam and Eve, the first man and woman. The old man listened attentively, but when she had finished, said:

"No, no, I tell you something better than that, and more true. The first man and woman were made like this: Long, long time ago, two brooms were sent down from the sky. They were brooms while they were in the air, but as soon as they touched earth, one became a man, the other a woman – the first man and woman."

Sweet Sin was greatly shocked, and for several days could think of little else than the broom theory. At last, she asked her father if he would not, as a special favor, enlighten Li Chung as to his true descent, but her father merely smiled and said:

"You had better leave Li Chung alone; his theory serves him as well as your Sunday-school teacher's serves her. Each is as reasonable as the other."

"Father!" exclaimed Sweet Sin, "are you a heathen?"

"That is a matter of opinion, my daughter."

II

"Forget me," commanded Sweet Sin.

"Not while I have breath and blood."

"You must; I tell you to."

"But one always remembers what one's told to forget."

Dick Farrell's grey eyes looked pleadingly into Sweet Sin's. She was seventeen now. California sunshine and the balmy freshness of Pacific breezes had helped to make her a bewitching woman.

"I thought you liked me, Sweet Sin."

"So I do."

"But I thought you cared for me as I do for you."

Sweet Sin turned her face aside. She would not let him know.

"I like, but I do not love. As to you, why, next week there will be some-body else to whom you will be telling the same old tale. Don't interrupt. I know all about it. Besides, even if you did love me, as you say, the life of love is short – like all that's lovely. Yesterday, we hailed its birth, today we mourn it – dead."

"Sweet Sin, come to me – don't be wicked!"

"I told you I did not care for you."

"I will not believe it."

"Well, whether you believe it or not, I must leave you now, as I have something to do for father. Dick, do you remember once asking me if my father was a Chinaman; and when I replied yes, you said, 'Doesn't your flesh creep all over when you go near him?' You were about twelve then and I ten."

"I cannot recall the things I said so long ago," replied the young fellow, flushing up.

"No! Well, you see this is the day when I remember – the day when you forget."

III

They were all there – the fiddler with his fiddle, the flutist with his flute, the banjo man with his banjo, and the kettledrummer with his kettledrum. All the Chinese talent in that California city were assembled together, and right merrily was the company entertained.*

Hwuy Sin was giving a farewell banquet to his Chinese friends. He was about to return to China after an exile of about twenty-five years, and Sweet Sin, the child of the American woman, now dead two years, was to accompany him. His daughter was of a full marriageable age, and like every good Chinese father, what he desired for her was a husband – a husband such as could be found only amongst his cousins in China.

---

* This entire paragraph recycles a part of Eaton's journalistic "Chinese Entertainment."

Hwuy Sin thought tenderly of his child; she had been a good daughter – a little more talkative and inquisitive perhaps than a woman should be, but always loving to him. Suddenly he arose from his seat; he had not seen her that evening and there were some instructions about the packing of his caps which he would like to give before the night closed.

Rat, tat, tat. Hwuy Sin stood outside Sweet Sin's door and waited. As it was not opened to him, he called softly, "My child, it is your father."

But Sweet Sin heard him not.

IV

When Hwuy Sin returned to his guests he walked heavily.

"My daughter has gone to the land of spirits; mourn with me," he said.

And in Chinese fashion they mourned with him.

Hwuy Sin went back to China, and the mid-ocean received a casket containing what had once been called Sweet Sin. As he watched it sink, he said, "In all between the four seas, there was none like her. She belonged neither to her mother's country, nor to mine. Therefore, let her rest where no curious eyes may gaze."

Sweet Sin's farewell he carefully laid away. It was written in the beautiful Chinese characters he himself had taught her, and the words were:

"FATHER, SO DEAR: I am not tired of life, and I dislike death, but though life to me is sweet, yet if I cannot have both it and honor, I will let life go. Father, stand up for me, and no matter what others may say, do not feel hard against me. My Christian friends will shake their heads and say, 'Ah, Sweet Sin!' their faces will become long and melancholy, and if you ask them to give me Christian burial, for my mother's sake, probably they will refuse. They will talk about right and wrong, and say that I have gone before my Maker with a crime on my soul. But for that I do not care, as what is right and what is wrong, who knows? The Chinese teachers say that the conscience tells us and they teach the practice of virtue for virtue's sake. The Christians point to the Bible as a guide, saying that if we live according to its lessons, we will be rewarded in an after life. I have puzzled much over these things, seeking as it were for a lost mind.

"Father, I cannot marry a Chinaman, as you wish, because my heart belongs to an American – an American who loves me and wishes to make me his wife. But, Father, though I cannot marry a Chinaman, who would despise me for being an American, yet I will not marry an American, for the Americans have made me feel so that I will save the children of the man I love from being called 'Chinese!' 'Chinese!'

"Farewell, father. I hope God will forgive me for being what He made me.

"Sweet Sin."

Montreal, Can.

Edith Eaton. "Away Down in Jamaica."
The Metropolitan 7.12 (19 March 1898): 4, 13.*

Early morning; the sun glorifying the mountain tops, the valleys shrouded in mist. Two riders were wending their way up a mountain side; the path was narrow and the woman rode ahead of the man.

"Is it not lovely?" she cried. Her eyes were shining.

"I am glad you think so," he replied.

They rode on, contenting themselves with calling gaily to one another until they reached a widening in the path, when the man rode forward and seizing the bridle of the woman's horse, turned its head around.

She drew a deep breath.

The mist had cleared from the valleys and down below were green depths of irrepressible verdure, the glow and color of unknown trees and brilliant blossoms and fruit; orange groves, banana plantations and acres of cane fields stretched far away; vistas of loveliness opened up on all sides, revealing glimpses of dazzling sea and shining beach.

"It is an enchanted country," she murmured.

"And see that line of mountains; the topmost peak seems a part of the

---

* Although Eaton wrote *Land of Sunshine* editor Charles Lummis from Kingston on 30 January 1897, saying she was "scheming to write some West Indian stories," "Away Down in Jamaica" and "The Sugar Cane Baby" (*Good Housekeeping* 1910) are the only West Indian stories by Eaton that have been located.

sky." He had dismounted and stood beside her horse; his hand guided her wondering eyes. How near to one another they seemed in that fair solitude!

"May I tell you what I feel," said he.

"Ah, no, not now," she replied, frightened, she knew not why.

"Pardon me, but I will."

And thus Wickliff Walker and Kathleen Harold became engaged.

When not under Wickliff Walker's influence, Kathleen Harold rebelled against her engagement to him; but when he was near, when he talked to her in that low sweet voice of his, all strength of mind deserted her, and though words which might have set her free hovered behind her lips, they ne'er came forth.

Reclining on a lounging chair on the balcony of the hotel in Kingston, she gave way to vague and melancholy musing. Before her stretched the sparkling, ever changing sea. Just over its horizon a ship was sailing. Oh! to be in that ship! Strange imaginings, undefinable and inexplicable floated through her mind as she gazed on that great circle of water.

"Of what are you thinking, Kathleen Mavourneen?"

Wickliff Walker raised her hand and retained it while she murmured something about being tired of Kingston.

"We must go to the mountains then."

There was a strong emphasis on the "we."

"I can go alone," the girl answered with sudden spirit.

"But I will not permit it. My dearest, what are you thinking of? I will make you mine by special license next Monday and then for the mountains. My wild bird is not frightened."

She looked up and shuddered. It seemed to her that his human shape was magnified to a giant in size. It was only a fantasy, but it proved his power – her head fell meekly.

When evening came he drove her to a place some miles out of Kingston – an old fort standing on a high, rocky promontory running out into the sea. Down below the windows the rocks descended in broken heaps, and there they rested, watching the slumbering sea; he talking lover's talk, and she, under the glamor of the time, the place and the person.

"I think the sea fascinates you," he remarked, noting how her eyes dwelt always on the waves.

"It does," she answered. "So great, so free, so mysterious; I adore it. Ah, see! there's a chapter from Revelations."*

She started to her feet as she spoke; he rose with her, and they stood gazing on the grandest and most gloriously beautiful sight that human eyes could witness. Great flaming waves surged to their very feet, and as far as the eye could reach, rolled a magnificent sea of fire.

The mingling together in great numbers of the phosphorescents had caused a phenomenon which occurs about once in thirty years in the West Indian waters.†

But hark, what was the cry which seemed to echo from the cliffs behind them.

"Wickliff Walker, Wickliff Walker."

Weirdly the name fell upon their ears, and the man who bore it paled in the moonlight.

"Someone is calling you," whispered Kathleen Harold. She dared not trust her voice aloud.

"I see nobody," he answered in suppressed tones.

"Neither can I. I am afraid; let us go back."

CHAPTER II.

Miss Harold stood before the glass, brushing her long shining hair. Rachel, one of the serving maids belonging to the hotel, stood near, watching the process with admiring eyes.

"Well, Rachel, my hair is rather straight, is it not?" queried Miss Harold, gaily.

"Lovely, Missus," replied the girl. "Missus is lovely all over."

"Nonsense," laughed Miss Harold, "but I can assure you, Rachel, if my hair was only like that which grows on your head, I would be quite happy. How do you manage to make yours so nice and crinkly?"

Rachel laughed heartily, showing her white teeth.

"Missus is so funny," said she.

---

* "And I saw what looked like a sea of glass glowing with fire." Revelation 15:2.
† "Occasionally at night the sea becomes illumined with the phosphorescent light emitted by tiny animalculae and by species of medusae." Silver S.W. and Co., *The West Indies: Book 1* (London: R. Clay, Sons, and Taylor), 29.

"You think I'm joking, Rachel, but indeed, I am not. Don't you see me rolling my hair in papers every night. That's to make it curly, like yours. But perhaps you think my hair is cold, and I wrap it up to keep it warm."

"Missus is so funny," again repeated the girl.

Miss Harold, having finished brushing her hair, coiled it round her shapely head; then, taking a cream rosebud from a bowl of flowers that stood on a table near by, pinned it coquettishly above her left ear.

"B-e-a-u-t-i-f-u-l!" exclaimed the maid.

"You are a flatterer. By the way, Rachel, who sends me such lovely flowers every day?"

"'Tis Clarissa brings them."

"Clarissa! Who is Clarissa?"

"Clarissa is a brown girl, Missus. She was adopted when a little child by some rich white people. They brought her up like a lady, but some years ago she ran away from them."

"Indeed! Quite a romantic history! Next time she comes I would like to see her."

So saying, Miss Harold tripped out of the room, down the long hall and on to the balcony where the balmy freshness of the ocean could be enjoyed.

CHAPTER III.

The members of the Legislative Council were deep in the estimates, and in the press gallery sat young Everett, taking down the proceedings for his paper. Now and then, when an honorable member became particularly heavy and tedious, he rested his head on his hands – that head of his was aching horribly, and the droning of men's voices seemed intolerable. Late hours, drink and hard work in a tropical climate were telling on him. He had changed greatly; one could hardly recognize him as the bright-eyed, bright-spirited young fellow who had arrived in Jamaica just a year before, fresh from Canadian snows. It was not all his fault either. False hopes, born of deluding letters, had been his, and when those hopes one by one had fallen to the ground, there seemed nothing left for the boy to do but to fall also. If he had been able to pay his passage to a northern port, he would have fled the island, but save for his weekly wages he was penniless. Too proud to ask for aid, he drudged on, but so despairingly that there could be but one end. A few weeks of happiness had been his, during which, despite the grind, a woman's companionship had been more than wine, but of that he had also been bereft. Alas! alas!

"The honorable member for W— may remember that this Council by yesterday's vote, rejected any section of this bill that had for its object the re-imposition of certain duties. If, therefore, the Honorable Colonial Secretary places on the Order of the Day a notice that the Council resume in a committee the consideration of what was decided upon yesterday and the Council concur, we will be stultifying, gentlemen, our action of a former occasion. Eh! What?" –

The black member in white clothes broke off his speech and stared with round eyes at the press gallery, which scarcely seemed to be absorbing as it should his flow of eloquence. Young Everett had fallen from his seat in a dead faint, and the other two reporters were bearing him away.

"Will the Honorable Member for B— proceed with his remarks."

The Honorable Member for B— mumbled a few words, then sat down. He could not afford to waste his breath when there was no hope of being reported fully in the local papers.

They brought young Everett to the hotel in Kingston and the kind-hearted Manager had him laid on a couch on the breeze swept verandah.

He recovered consciousness just as Miss Harold stepped daintily from her room. She looked at the two men who were preparing to depart, and at the yellow haired lad lying low; so pale, so weak, so altogether broken. Her eyes filled; she stepped impulsively to his side.

"Are you sick? Oh! I am so sorry," said she.

The men withdrew. Everett covered his face with his hands as if he wished to shut out all sights and sounds.

"Can I do anything for you?" A very agony of sorrow and remorse took possession of her.

He did not answer, nor by motion nor sound betrayed that he was aware of her presence; she might have been in the invisible moon, instead of standing by his side, almost touching him with hands that once in a fit of passion he had smothered with wild kisses.

"Oh, will you not even speak to me?"

"It's this beastly Jamaica," he muttered hoarsely.

So much being gained, Miss Harold pushed a low cane seat towards his couch and began fanning him.

"Don't fan me; I can't bear it," he cried, moving his head restlessly.

Meekly she furled her fan and they sat in silence; he, lying still, his haggard young face turned seawards; she, with her heart growing weak within her and thinking sad, sad thoughts. This was her love whom she had encouraged only to disappoint, for when she had wooed him with her eyes, he had answered like a man, and like a woman, she had turned and rated him soundly for his presumption. "She encourage a boy! What nonsense!" she had cried in well feigned indignation. "She had been kind to him as a friend – that was all." Then came Wickliff Walker whose attentions had gratified her vanity and who, to her surprise, became her master, though not through her heart. How she wished she had never met him! How she wished she had been true to herself. She stole a look at the stricken face beside her – Suddenly her mouth quivered and a tear rolled slowly down her cheek on to the sleeve of his coat.

Everett saw that tear and in a second it had blotted from his mind all but the one absorbing passion of his life.

"Kathleen – Then you do care."

"Why, of course."

His face became light, yet he would not be too sure.

"But you are engaged to him; I heard you were to be married on Monday."

"What is an engagement?" she asked with fine scorn. "As to marrying him on Monday; some business called him to Port Antonio last night, and though he wanted to put it aside until after we were married, as it would keep him there a week, I urged a delay, and now I shall break altogether."

"When? Today?"

"Yes, I shall write him at once. Lend me your note book. What shall I say? 'Wickliff Walker, I hate you, I detest you.'"

"Write this: 'Sir, as I do not love you, I have decided not to marry you. This puts an end to our engagement.'"

Miss Harold took down the words dictated, and a few minutes later a messenger was dispatched to the post office with a missive addressed to Wickliff Walker, Esq., Port Antonio.

"Now, I feel as if I could live forever," said Phil Everett. An elixir stronger than life itself for the time being was coursing through his veins.

Yet, poor lad! even as he spoke, the gates of death were opening for him, and each hour thereafter found him weaker. The next day he could not sit up, and the following morning he received a notice from his employer that his services were no longer required. This did not affect him; the necessity for work was over. The fever had been in his system for months. Its poison had been coursing through his veins as he tramped the hot, dusty streets of Kingston, amidst the rabble of the market place and the docks; when reporting at dinner, council and court, long had it striven with his youth and his strength, and at last had overcome. There was no pain, only a constant, never-ceasing fatigue, a strange, dull sleepiness. After the first flush of joy that the assurance of Kathleen Harold's love had brought him, he had settled into a dull, lethargic state, and though she whom he had so longed for was constantly by his side, he seemed neither to know nor care, which was bitterness, indeed to her. Now and then his eyes would rest on the big black buzzards with their long beaks and pink feet, hovering around in search of food.

"I don't like them," he said one day.

"What dear?" asked Kathleen Harold.

"The buzzards – they draw life from death."

"Do not look at them, Philip. Look at me."

But his mind, despite her entreaty, dwelt on the birds, and she despairingly sank on her knees and laying her cool cheek against his hot parched lips called him by the dearest of names. Whereupon he closed his eyes and slept. So near to the grave was he.

CHAPTER IV.

Wickliff Walker smiled, but it was a smile that was not good to see.

He thrust Kathleen Harold's note into his breast pocket, ordered a "Buss'" and leaving his breakfast of naseberries,* turtle steaks and white yam, untasted, drove quickly to the Railway Station, arriving there just in time to catch the train for Kingston, which he boarded. He smiled again

---

* The nasberry is a popular sweet fruit in Jamaica.

as he stepped off the train; on his dark, handsome face was written "What I will shall be accomplished." "What I desire I shall obtain."

A distinguished looking brown girl with wonderful eyes confronted him. She was clad poorly, but her form was superior to dress.

"Clarissa," he exclaimed in a voice which betrayed both annoyance and surprise.

"Yes," answered the girl, "It is Clarissa."

"And what are you doing here?"

"What does it matter to you? Our meeting is an accident. Nevertheless, now that I see you, I have some words for you to hear."

"Well," leading her to where they could not be observed. "What is it? Speak quickly. I have no time to waste."

The girl pressed her hand to her heart. Hearkening back to the past, she heard the voice now in her ears, but the words were, "Do not run away; stay awhile, so that I may tell you how I love you."

She looked him proudly in the eyes.

"I wish to know," said she, "whether I am really nothing to you now."

"Oh well, Clarissa, that's a queer question to put to a reformed man. You must know that I have given up all my wild ways, drinking, gambling and so forth, and am settling down to a respectable old age – am going to be married in fact."

The man spoke embarrassedly, but with an attempt at lightness.

"So I surmised," answered the girl very quietly. "I saw you one night on the rocks. I called you by name, and you heard me."

"Yes, you are right, we heard you. What were you doing there?"

"Like the Devil, I wander to and fro upon the earth."

"Hush! You should not talk like that."

"Should I not? That's because you don't like to hear about the Devil who puts to shame reformed men, and who, after all, is a nobler creature than such as you. He's not a coward at any rate, and if he does send people to Hell he enters himself with them; whereas you push in your victims, then fearing the flames totter away to be saved."

"I will listen to no more of this."

"No. Well. Good bye, reformed man. You have answered my question. May you be happy with your bride. I go to the Obi man."

Wickliff Walker had won the battle. At the sound of his voice; at the touch of his hand, Kathleen Harold's new born courage had deserted her and the flag over her heart's fortress had gone down.

She stepped across the verandah to where for the last few days she had been in the habit of watching beside Phil Everett. She had no intention of telling the truth to her young lover – had this fair, frail woman, but her feet carried her to where he lay, for despite her apparent falseness, she loved him.

How still was the recumbent form – his arm hid his face, but the beautiful, broad forehead, lovingly caressed by his soft fair hair which stirred now and then in the breeze, was as white as marble. Kathleen Harold bent over him and gently moved the arm. There was a strange heaviness about it which terrified her. It seemed dead. It was dead.

And above the hot sun shone and the buzzards flapped their wings.

Rachel held forth to her friends in the country. The following was her discourse.

"Master Phil; he died of the fever. Miss Kathleen, she found him dead and lost her head. She said nothing to nobody, just came to her room and took the flowers. She put them on his breast and laid her head down upon them like a broken hearted lamb. She must have died in a few minutes – that was what the doctors said. They said the flowers were poisoned and asked me where they came from and who brought them. I told them that Clarissa used to bring them every day. Someone found Clarissa and she said she was glad Miss Kathleen was dead and that she had sent the flowers on purpose to poison her. The doctors said Clarissa was mad and ordered her to be locked up, but she got away from them and has hidden where no one can find her. Mr. Walker, he looked very black when he saw Miss Kathleen lying dead near Master Phil. Miss Kathleen was to have married him very soon, but I think she loved Master Phil the best. Miss Kathleen's body was fixed up and sent to her people in the States. Mr. Phil he was buried that day in Kingston; his folks up North are poor. Two such beautiful corpses I never did see. I feel like singing." Rachel dropped into hymn and the others joined in:

"Oh, there'll be mourning, mourning,
Oh, there'll be mourning, mourning,

Oh, there'll be mourning, mourning,
At the Judgement seat of Christ."*

Sui Sin Fah. "The Smuggling of Tie Co."
Land of Sunshine 13.2 (July 1900): 100–4.

Amongst the daring men who engage in contrabanding Chinamen
from Canada into the United States, Jack Fabian ranks as the boldest in
deed, the cleverest in scheming and the most successful in outwitting
Government officers.†

Uncommonly strong in person, tall and well built, with fine features
and a pair of keen, steady blue eyes, gifted with a sort of rough eloquence
and of much personal fascination, it is no wonder that we fellows regard
him as our chief and are bound to follow where he leads. With Fabian at
our head, we engage in the wildest adventures and find such places of
concealment for our human goods as none but those who take part in
a desperate business would dare dream of.

Jack, however, is not in search of glory – money is his object. One day
when a romantic friend remarked that it was very kind of him to help the
poor Chinamen over the border, a cynical smile curled his moustache.

"Kind!" he echoed, "Well, I haven't yet had time to become sentimental
over the matter. It is merely a matter of dollars and cents, though, of
course, to a man of my strict principles, there is a certain pleasure to be
derived from getting ahead of the Government. A poor devil does now
and then like to take a little out of those millionaire concerns."

It was last summer and Fabian was somewhat down on his luck. A few
months previous, to the surprise of us all, he had made a blunder, which

* In Harriet Beecher Stowe's *Uncle Tom's Cabin* (1852), Cassy sings this hymn from the attic
of Simon Legree's house to make Legree think his house is haunted.
† In a 16 September 1900 letter to Lummis, Eaton writes that Fabian's character is "drawn
from life." Her unsigned article, "They Are Going Back to China: Hundreds of Chinese at
the C[anadian] P[acific] R[ail] Station," published in the *Montreal Daily Star* on 21 August
1895, mentions "Arthur Fabian, who ha[s] charge of the Chinese branch of the passenger
department of the CPR."

resulted in his capture by American officers, and he and his companion, together with five uncustomed Chinamen, had been lodged in a county jail to await trial.

But loafing behind bars did not agree with Fabian's energetic nature, so one dark night by means of a saw he made good his escape, and after a long, hungry, detective-hunted tramp through woods and bushes found himself safe in Canada.

He had had a three months' sojourn in prison, and during that time some changes had taken place in smuggling circles. Some ingenious lawyers had devised a scheme by which any young Chinaman on payment of a couple of hundred dollars could procure a father, which father would swear the young Chinaman was born in America – thus proving him to be an American citizen with the right to breathe United States air.* And the Chinese themselves, assisted by some white men, were manufacturing certificates establishing their right to cross the border, and in that way were passing over in large batches.

That sort of trick naturally spoilt our fellows' business, but we all knew that "Yankee sharper" games can hold good only for a short while, so we bided our time and waited in patience.

Not so Fabian. He became very restless and wandered around with glowering looks. He was sitting one day in a laundry, the proprietor of which had sent out many a boy through our chief's instrumentality. Indeed, Fabian is said to have "rushed over" to "Uncle Sam" himself some five hundred Celestials, and if Fabian had not been an exceedingly generous fellow he might now be a gentleman of leisure, instead of an unimmortalized Rob Roy.

Well, Fabian was sitting in the laundry of Chen Ting Lung & Co., telling a nice looking young Chinaman that he was so broke that he'd be willing to take over even one man at a time.

The young Chinaman looked thoughtfully into Fabian's face. "Would you take me?" he inquired.

"Take you?" repeated Fabian. "Why, you are one of the 'bosses' here.

* Many Chinese entered the US during the Exclusion Era by using fraudulent documentation that identified them as US-born, or as the sons of Chinese who had already been granted US citizenship.

You don't mean to say that you are hankering after a place where it would take you years to get as high up in the 'washee, washee' business as you are now?"

"Yes, I want go," replied Tie Co. "I want go to New York and I pay you fifty dollars and all expense if you take me and not say you take me to my partners."

"There's no accounting for a Chinaman," muttered Fabian, but he gladly agreed to the proposal and a night was fixed.

"What is the name of the firm you are going to," inquired the white man.

Chinamen who intend being smuggled over always make arrangements with some Chinese firm in the States to receive them.

Tie Co hesitated, then mumbled something which sounded like "Quong Wo Yuen" or "Long Lo Toon," Fabian was not sure which, but did not repeat the question, not being sufficiently interested.

He left the laundry, nodding good-by to Tie Co as he passed outside the window, and the Chinaman nodded back, a faint smile on his small delicate face lingering until Fabian's receding form was lost to view.

It was a pleasant night on which the two men set out. Fabian had a rig waiting at the corner of the street; Tie Co, dressed in citizen's clothes, stepped into it unobserved, and the smuggler and would-be smuggled were soon out of the city. They had a merry drive, for Fabian's liking for Tie Co was very real; he had known him for several years, and the lad's quick intelligence interested him.

The second day they left their horse at a farm-house where Fabian would call for it on his return trip, crossed a river in a row-boat before the sun was up, and plunged into a wood in which they would remain till evening. It was raining, but through mud and wind and rain they trudged slowly and heavily.

Tie Co paused now and then to take breath. Once Fabian remarked: "You are not a very strong lad, Tie Co. It's a pity you have to work as you do for your living," and Tie Co had answered:

"Work velly good! No work, Tie Co die."

Fabian looked at the lad protectingly, wondering in a careless way why this Chinaman seemed to him so different from the others.

"Wouldn't you like to be back in China? " he asked.

"No," said Tie Co decidedly.

"Why?"

"I not know why," answered Tie Co.

Fabian laughed.

"Haven't you got a nice little wife at home? " he continued. "I hear you people marry very young."

"No, I no wife," asserted his companion with a choky little laugh. "I never have no wife."

"Nonsense," joked Fabian. "Why, Tie Co, think how nice it would be to have a little woman to cook your rice and to love you."

"I not have wife," repeated Tie Co, seriously. "I not like woman, I like man."

"You confirmed old bachelor," ejaculated Fabian.

"I like you," said Tie Co, his boyish voice sounding clear and sweet in the wet woods. "I like you so much that I want go to New York, so you make fifty dollars. I no flend in New York."

"What!" exclaimed Fabian.

"Oh, I solly I tell you, Tie Co velly solly," and the Chinese boy shuffled on with bowed head.

"Look here, Tie Co," said Fabian; "I won't have you do this for my sake. You have been very foolish and I don't care for your fifty dollars. I do not need it half as much as you do. Good God! how ashamed you make me feel – I, who have blown in my thousands in idle pleasures, cannot take the little you have slaved for. We are in New York State now – when we get out of this wood, we will have to walk over a bridge which crosses a river. On the other side, not far from where we cross, there is a railway station. Instead of buying you a ticket for the city of New York, I shall take train with you for Toronto."

Tie Co did not answer – he seemed to be thinking deeply. Suddenly he pointed to where some fallen trees lay.

"Two men run away behind there," cried he.

Fabian looked round them anxiously; his keen eyes seemed to pierce the gloom in his endeavor to catch a glimpse of any person; but no man was visible, and save the dismal sighing of the wind among the trees all was quiet.

"There's no one," he said somewhat gruffly – he was rather startled, for they were a mile over the border and he knew that the Government officers were on a sharp look-out for him, and felt, despite his strength, if any trick or surprise were attempted it would go hard with him.

"If they catch you with me, it be too bad," sententiously remarked Tie Co. It seemed as if his words were in answer to Fabian's thoughts.

"But they will not catch us, so cheer up your heart, my boy," replied the latter, more heartily than he felt.

"If they came, and I not with you, they not take you and it would be all lite."

"Yes," assented Fabian, wondering what his companion was thinking about.

They emerged from the woods in the dusk of the evening and were soon on the bridge crossing the river. When they were near the center Tie Co stopped and looked into Fabian's face.

"Man come for you; I not here, man no hurt you." And with the words he whirled like a flash over the rail!

In another flash Fabian was after him. But though a first-class swimmer, the white man's efforts were of no avail, and Tie Co was borne away from him by the swift current.

Cold and dripping wet, Fabian dragged himself up the bank and found himself a prisoner.

"So your Chinaman threw himself into the river. What was that for?" asked one of the Government officers.

"I think he was out of his head," replied Fabian. And he fully believed what he uttered.

"We tracked you right through the woods," said another of the captors. "We thought once the boy caught sight of us."

Fabian remained silent.

Tie Co's body was picked up the next day. Tie Co's body, and yet not Tie Co, for Tie Co was a youth, and the body found with Tie Co's face and dressed in Tie Co's clothes was the body of a girl – a woman.

Nobody in the laundry of Chen Ting Lung & Co. – no Chinaman in Canada or New York – could explain the mystery. Tie Co had come out to

Canada with a number of other youths. Though not very strong he had always been a good worker and "very smart." He had been quiet and reserved among his own countrymen; had refused to smoke tobacco or opium, and had been a regular attendant at Sunday schools and a great favorite with mission ladies.

Fabian was released in less than a week. "No evidence against him," said the Commissioner, who was not aware that the prisoner was the man who had broken out of jail but a month before.

Fabian is now very busy; there are lots of boys taking his helping hand over the border, but none of them are like Tie Co; and sometimes, in between whiles, Fabian finds himself pondering long and earnestly over the mystery of Tie Co's life – and death.

Seattle, Washington.

Sui Sin Far. "Woo-Ma and I."
The Bohemian 10 (January 1906): 66–75.

Introduction

Woo-Ma and I were the daughters of a Chinaman who had been brought up and educated in California, where, when he had at attained to the age of twenty-four, he married my mother, then a pretty American girl of Irish and English descent. We were therefore Anglo-Chinese. We were not at all alike, either in appearance or character. I was small and chubby with scarcely any nose to speak of, black eyed, black haired, brown skinned and rosy cheeked. My eyes were pointed at the corners like Chinese eyes, and on the whole, I favored my father, only, of course, much prettier than he could ever be. When born, I was so small, so dark and so queer, that the nurse actually forgot to exclaim, as is the custom on such occasions, "What a fine child!" Indeed, my mother, as soon as her eyes fell on me, cried, "Oh, nurse, what a homely little creature, take it away." And my mother's

opinion was approved of and endorsed by all who beheld me, and even my
father, who gave me perhaps my warmest welcome, could not refrain from
mournfully prophesying, "It will never get a husband."

However, as the vanity of a young female, whose age is summed up by
days and hours, is scarcely as sensitive as when the years are added to its
life, the uncomplimentary remarks had very little effect upon my constitu-
tion. In fact, I laughed in the face of them, and by the time my mother
had become accustomed to my homeliness, had grown quite a good
looking child.

Woo-Ma was more like mother; she was taller than I and slenderer. Her
features were straight and her eyes wide open and gray-blue in color; her
hair was a pretty soft brown and curled naturally; she had dear little hands
and her skin could almost have been called fair.

On account of our parentage childhood's days had not been made easy
for Woo-Ma and I. It is a dreadful confession to make, but from the age of
seven to twelve, I believe I hardly ever went out of the house without getting into trouble and returning with scratched hands and face and disor-
dered hair. For me to be a "proper" little girl was an absolute impossibility.
The sneers and taunting words which seem to be the birthright in America
of any child who has a drop of Chinese blood in its veins used to madden
me beyond endurance, and I would turn upon my tormentors and scratch
and bite until utterly exhausted.

As Woo-Ma did not feel constrained to twist her hair into a tight pig-
tail, constitute herself the champion of all unfortunate Chinamen, and
state at the beginning of an acquaintance in a defiant and aggressive manner that she was Chinese, she naturally escaped many of the misfortunes
which befell me. Nevertheless, I have seen her turn white and tremble with
excitement and pain on hearing the mocking cry, "Chinese! Chinese!"

Mother was a Methodist and Woo-Ma and I were brought up in the
Methodist church, but Father seemed to have no religion at all, which fact
greatly disturbed my peace of mind.

"Father," I said one day, "are you a heathen?"

"Run away and don't bother me," answered Father.

I, however, carried my perplexities to Woo-Ma and asked for her opinion as to whether or not Father was a heathen. Woo-Ma reflected for a few

minutes, then replied: "No, I don't think he is exactly a heathen; I believe he is what is called a Free Thinker."

I was not satisfied with this answer and continued troubled in spirit until the next day, when I prevailed upon Woo-Ma to write two poems, one entitled "The Dying Christian," the other "The Dying Atheist." The former depicted in glowing words the happiness of dying a Christian; the latter, the awful horror which a man who has lived the life of an unbeliever experiences when his last hour has come. These two poems I addressed to my father and mailed the next morning. I expected to hear from him concerning them, but was disappointed, and evidently my delicate attempt to convert him was unappreciated.

And thus Woo-Ma and I grew up – in the outskirts of Chinatown.

I

We had visitors. They were: Mr. Christopher Hartley, a man of about thirty years of age, with manners ingratiating and smile fascinating; Jim Nesbit, an old school friend of ours; Joo Pei, my betrothed; Wong Lee, a friend of his; and Richard Forman, introduced by Jim as "one of the boys."

The conversation had been general until Mr. Hartley and my sister separated themselves and, withdrawing to the large window seat at the end of the hall, began to converse together in low tones. This I did not like at all. I knew that Woo-Ma was deeply in love with Christopher Hartley and I had come to the conclusion that he was only making her miserable.

"I suppose," said Jim Nesbit, addressing Wong Lee, "that you have not lately come from China."

"I have come here ten years ago," replied Wong.

"You are naturalized, then," rattled on Jim, who was trying to divert his mind from Woo-Ma.

"I got a 'high up' lawyer to make me natural two years after I first come," calmly asserted our Chinese friend.

"And is this little boy your eldest son?" continued Jim, pointing to a cute little fellow in long braided queue and a broidered silk blouse who stood by Wong Lee's knee.

"No, my eldest is the son of my first wife," replied Wong Lee. "This is the son of my third wife, I wrote to China for them to send her to me here and I paid one thousand dollars to her grandmother for her, and sent as well eight hundred dollars with which to buy her trousseau."

"Were you not married in China?" Jim asked.

"Yes, three times," replied Wong Lee.

"How long is it since your first wife died?"

"She is not dead; she is living in China with her mother," Wong Lee answered.

"Are you divorced from her?" ventured Jim.

"How can you be so inquisitive, Jim? You shall not ask Mr. Wong Lee any more questions," I put in.

"He does not care," answered Jim. "When I want some information and a person is willing to give it, I do not see why I should remain in ignorance. You have no objection to answering my question, have you, Wong Lee?"

"I like to tell what you like to hear," said Wong Lee politely.

"So it is all right," said Jim triumphantly. "Are you divorced from your first wife, Wong Lee?"

"No."

"Then, how is it that you have been married three times?" asked Jim.

"In China, a man can have as many wives as he can afford to keep, but if he cannot keep one wife he cannot have one."

"Can a Chinese lady have more than one husband?"

"No," answered Wong Lee very decidedly. "That would not be right at all."

Said Jim, "Is it true, Mr. Wong Lee, that Chinese ladies are so averse to marriage that there is a custom prevalent amongst them of gathering together, when any of their young friends is about to become a bride, for the purpose of weeping and mourning over her impending fate?"

"I think sometimes the Chinese women do that, but men don't bother about it," returned Wong Lee.

"Ah, then," mused Jim aloud. "The Chinese women, poor things, cannot be very happy."

Father, who had entered the room very quietly, now ranged himself, with Wong Lee and answered for him. Father could talk well when he wished. This is what he said:

"The Chinese women are happy enough. You see, a daughter has no inheritance, neither does she receive any marriage portion from her parents. She is bought from them by her future husband and his relations, who send presents according to their means. I read in the Bible of Abraham sending a steward to buy a wife for his son, Isaac, and that the steward took with him jewels of silver and gold and raiment which he presented to Rebekah's friends when he asked for her as a bride for his young master. It is just in that way that the Chinamen get their wives, and after they are sent to them they are obliged to support and care for them. A Chinese girl is obliged to marry whenever her father or guardian so wishes; she has no option."

"Poor Chinese brides!" I softly said.

"Well," said Father, turning to me. "Perhaps the Chinese do not show quite as much consideration for their women as daughters and wives as do the people of this country, but as mothers the Chinese women are treated with the greatest respect by their children, who, even when themselves advanced in years, pay the utmost deference to the commands and counsels of an aged parent."

There was somewhat in Father's expression as he made the last remark which made me feel that his conscience was reproaching him for deserting in his early youth his own parents. Father had run away from his home when only ten years of age and had been brought to California by a troupe of strolling players.

"How did you become acquainted with these Chinese gentlemen?" inquired Richard Forman in an undertone.

"They are my father's friends," I answered. "My father is a Chinaman."

"Indeed, I am deeply interested."

Quick to resent being patronized I retorted: "Thanks for your interest, but I am afraid that I cannot pay it back."

I was ashamed of myself immediately; but Richard Forman did not seem to heed the flash and sitting down beside me, said: "You remind me of a sister of mine who died two years ago in England."

I made no reply, and he continued: "She was just about as old as you when she died. She was then my only living relative."

"Did she live with you?" I inquired.

"Yes," said he. "She was always with me. She was the only person who ever felt for me a spark of affection."

"You must miss her."

"Rather."

"Are you English?"

"Well, I'm as much English as anything, though I call myself American. I'm a mixture. My father was half German, half English; my mother was French and Irish, I was born in the United States, but we returned to Europe when I was about ten years old, and since then I've lived all over. My father was a professor of music, my mother was, at one time, an actress. They both died when I was a lad and left me with Alice. She, as I told you, died last year when we were in England. There, you have my whole family history."

"Thank you for giving it to me; but I did not ask you to," I answered gaily, for I was touched.

"Who said you did?" brusquely replied Richard Forman. "An hour ago we were perfect strangers; but you looked so unsympathetic, so unlikely a person to condole with me, so unsentimental, that I felt drawn towards you, and am crossing with you at our first meeting the bridge which leads from acquaintanceship to friendship."

"Oh!" I ejaculated.

"Yes, we are great friends," said Richard Forman with conviction.

Again I became suspicious.

"I never flirt," I said.

"Neither do I," he answered. "Shake hands."

"Do you like the Chinese?" I inquired irrelevantly.

"I do," replied Richard Forman most impressively.

I felt that I had made a mistake and tried to rectify it by another.

"Oh!" I said, "I mean as a nation."

"I'm afraid," said Richard Forman reflectively, "that I am not capable of liking any nation. A nation is too large; my heart is not capacious enough to take it in – but I tell you what – to my mind a clever Chinaman is more than a stupid American and a brilliant American is more than a dull Chinaman. Individuality is more than nationality."

"That's a nice speech," I approved. "Mr. Forman, tell me, what do you
do – who are you? Jim has introduced to us so many of 'the boys,' as he
calls them, but none of them is like –"

"I'm a failure," Richard Forman interrupted with a queer smile. "Does
that suit you? I have failed in all I ever attempted. I have built many castles
in the air – but all have fallen to pieces. I have no money, no friends, no
hopes even."

"You have no wife to bother your life, no lover to prove untrue," I
laughingly replied.

Just then Joo Pei came up and I introduced the two men. Joo Pei was
the best looking Chinaman I have ever known, He was also a perfect gentleman and we were to be married in less than two months, when I was to
return with him to China. I was sure that as his wife I should love him
devotedly; he was so clever, so good and so kind.

That night I spoke long and earnestly to Woo-Ma and warned her
about Mr. Hartley, but she seemed neither to hear nor heed and her expression was that of a person in a happy trance.

II

"Farewell," said Joo Pei; "your father you obey, and I go to return never."

"Farewell," I replied, whilst the tears blinded my eyes.

Joo Pei lifted my hand. I could not see him, but I felt his gaze and
heard: "My desire in this world, little bird, is for you a cheerful heart
to have."

Then he was gone, and for me the sun had ceased to shine.

Just one month before the day fixed for my wedding, Woo-Ma had
disappeared and father had become an embittered man. His love for me
assumed a strange form, for he broke my engagement in order to keep
me with him. Poor Father! I saw the years creep over his face when they
told him Woo-Ma was gone, and when I at first refused to do as he wished
and said that the betrothal he himself had sealed should not be broken,
he had answered with a glance of the eye that was so eloquent of pain
and sorrow that I had felt myself a criminal, and despite Joo Pei's loving
arguments, refused to return with him to China when he was recalled
by the government.

III

Woo-Ma had written to me. After more than two years' separation I was
to see her again, my dearly loved only sister. I went to the meeting place
she had designated, and found her changed almost beyond recognition.
I embraced her in a passion of grief. Then we talked.

"It was just about two months before father betrothed you to Joo Pei
that I forgot you, Father, everything, every one but him, and gave up all."

As Woo-Ma spoke, a wave of swift and sudden anger swept over me.

"What," I cried, "you gave up all knowing him to be the man he was?
Without excuse of any kind you became – a bad woman?"

Woo-Ma laughed mirthlessly.

"Yes, without excuse of any kind I became that which you name."

"Oh, my God, my God," I cried – "and this is my sister – and I have
been so proud!"

"I did, however," went on the clear voice, "believe that he loved me, and
I thought that by the sacrifice of self, I would save him from the wiles of
worthless women, teach him to believe in the unselfishness of love, and in
a sense, bind him to me. He looked forward to rising to a high position,
and I knew that in order to succeed politically, he must succeed socially,
and to succeed socially a man must not have a wife who will cause curious
smiles to appear on the faces of his friends. I loved him too well to subject
him to the humiliation of having a Chinese wife."

"Shame on you, Woo-Ma, for that speech," I cried. "Shame, shame to
be ashamed!"

"Have mercy, A-Toy, I can stand this no longer," pleaded Woo-Ma.

I had not known until then how cruel I could be.

"Never mind me," I said penitently. "We are sisters, Woo-Ma, and it is
because I am so sorrowful and indignant for your sake that I speak as I do.
Tell me all and I promise that no bitter word shall escape my lips."

She went on: "For a brief period I lived in Paradise. None knew of my
sin, and I – I could not regard it as a sin. I was so sadly happy. But before
long I perceived a change which drove me frantic. From different sources I
learned that he was paying attention to other women. I became wild with
jealousy. I wrote imploring him to come and see me. What had I done to
offend him – was he offended? He did not reply. I went to him and he re-

ceived me as ever, called me his darling and offered to kiss me. How loath-
some are such caresses. I would have none of them, for I clearly perceived
I had been but the 'love of a day,' with whom he had finished forever.

"Long before it had come to that, yet after I was his, Father had told me
that he had made arrangements for a marriage between myself and Joo Pei.
Had I any objection to the proposal? If I had, he would substitute you as
bride in my place; but he preferred to keep you. You were always Father's
favorite. I was bewildered. What! I marry Joo Pei, I, who belonged to
Christopher Hartley. No, such a marriage could never be! but if I refused,
you would be sacrificed, and you, I knew, would not say no. I shuddered to
think of my sister being wife to one whom I believed then you could never
love. The customs and manners of the Chinese people were not ours; you
were not born to be the toy of an Oriental, and such you would be if you
married the man Father had selected. I scarcely knew what to do or say;
but finally I told Father I could never be wife to any man. He did not
understand and was disappointed. Then you became engaged to Joo Pei,
and I disappeared – disappeared because I knew father would not part
with his one daughter and my loss would save you. As to me, what
mattered my fate?"

"Then it was for my sake you left home?"

I could not add to Woo-Ma's pain the knowledge that her sacrifice had
but injured me.

"Yes, A-Toy, but not wholly for your sake. I had proof of Christopher's
unfaithfulness. I could not bear my life at home and sooner or later I
would have had to leave – or die."

"Oh, Woo-Ma," I cried. "Whatever has happened, you are still the best
and dearest. You are not bad; the sin does not lie with you; it is with that
Christopher Hartley whom I hate."

"Nay, A-Toy," replied my sister sadly. "Affection prompts you to speak
thus; but my own conscience tells me that I have done evil. I would never
have left Christopher Hartley had he not first abandoned me, and what
he has brought home to me is my just punishment."

"Well, Woo-Ma," I asserted. "Christopher Hartley is a devil. It was
satanic of him to win your love for pleasure and throw it away for the
same reason. The loss was all yours."

And poor Woo-Ma answered: "There are times when to lose is a pleasure. I loved to lose for him. Some human beings have a genius for painting, some for music, some for poetry. I had a genius for loving."

"And I have a genius for hating," I retorted. "No, Woo-Ma, defend him as you please, worship him as you please; be a worm under his feet forever; but do not expect me to act and feel likewise. Because I am half white you thought that I was too good to be the wife of a Chinese gentleman. Because you are half Chinese I think that you are too good for such a man as Christopher Hartley."

Then remembering my promise to say no bitter words and overcome with remorse, I laid my head on my sister's shoulder and burst into tears. As to Woo-Ma, she threw her arms around my neck and bending her head over mine, wept with me. Thus, with mingled tears and mingled feelings we became sisters once more. Ah! poor, romantic Woo-Ma! Sweeter and more unselfish, lost girl as she was, than any other woman in this hard cold world. Well do I remember when we were girls of fifteen and sixteen reading together [Thomas Babinton] Macaul[a]y's account of the Duke of Monmouth's execution, and how in his last moments, the "darling of the English people" had spoken of his beloved Henrietta, the Countess of Wentworth, as being pure and good beyond other women and as having reclaimed him from a life of debauchery by the sacrifice of herself. Woo-Ma had remarked on that occasion, "I would have been prouder to be that lady than the most honored wife in England." And I had replied, "But every man is not the duke of Monmouth."

IV

I made Father comfortable in a big arm chair in my own room and seating myself on an ottoman at his feet, laid my head on his knees. We remained silent for some minutes, but I felt his hand stroking my hair and there was balm in the touch, for my heart was aching, for loving kindness and unshared troubles had lately made us seem almost like strangers to one another. We were in the apartment which had been given over to Woo-Ma and me after mother's death. Mother had it furnished in half Chinese, half American style, and silk panels, incense burners, Chinese mattings, jade stone and ivory curios, and more than all, the sweet perfume of the

Chinese lily, impressed me always with the fact that I was not an ordinary American girl.

"Does the fan which I bought you for Jim's sister please you, A-Toy?" Father asked.

"Yes," I replied, "It is beautiful and Polly will wear it at her wedding."

"When will that be?"

"Eh? Oh, I think next Wednesday."

"Your mind is not with your words," remarked Father.

I knew it was not. 'Twas far away – with Woo-Ma.

Father understood and asked very gently if she was coming home.

"Yes," I replied. "she said she would – some day."

Father's face worked strangely; but he bade me say no more, and then a visitor was ushered in – Jim Nesbit. He had a letter to deliver to me from one who was on his way to South Africa. I knew the handsome writing, and on opening it, read: "Dear little A-Toy:- –

You will never see or hear from me again, and this letter is simply to re-peat once more that I love you, though I have no right, knowing all to say such words. Do you remember when we first met – three years ago? Well, even at that first meeting, I felt the impulse to ask you to love me; there was something so fresh and genial in your manner, so shy yet trustful in your glance. I knew you were not for me and I left you. Chance brought us together again. I became too fond of you. I can picture you curling your lip and saying half aloud with you shrewd, yet innocent, smile, 'Oh, he's been drinking'; but if ever I was sober in my life, I am now, as I write, as many a poor fellow has done before, 'Good-bye, sweetheart, good-bye.'"

With all his cleverness Richard Forman had been unable to compre-hend that it was just as natural for a daughter of a Chinaman to love a Chinaman as it is for the daughter of a white man to care for one of her father's race. He had made a great mistake. Nevertheless, a tear fell on that little one. How criss-cross the lines of life run!

"A-Toy," said Jim, when he rose to go. "I have seen Woo-Ma."

I followed him into the hall and closed the room door behind us before I said:

"And will she come home to us? Father wants her more than ever. She promised to come some day; and why not now?"

Jim's brow clouded and he sighed heavily.

"A-Toy," said he, "Woo-Ma is with the smugglers of Chinamen. She has taken to that reckless adventurous life because she says it helps her to forget and she believes she would go mad were she obliged to live quietly at home. Dressed as a youth, with a peaked cap pulled over her pretty brown hair which she has cut short, she takes many a boy over the border."

I covered my face with my hands. "Oh, Woo-Ma!" I moaned.

That night there was little rest for me; but about three o'clock in the morning I fell asleep and dreamed. This was my dream: A dark, starless sky, a road unlevelled and desolate, a lumbering van, from under the rough covering of which peered the faces of three men with Mongolian features. Two men, in the uniform of custom house officers, riding at full speed after the van.

My dream changed; the van, the custom house officers had disappeared. I saw but a youth; he was alone and dying. Turning a face that I knew to the sky, he cried: "Oh. God, Thou who gavest me my life, forgive me that I do not seek to preserve it. Thou knowest my strange origin, the forces that blend in me, the forces that war in me. Thou knowest my weakness, my pride, my jealousy – Thou knowest that I was loved – that I believed I was loved – Thou knowest I loved. Is it Thou or the Devil that sayest, 'Thou shalt love'? Thou knowest that all has been taken from me – Thou knowest my shame and my grief. Thou knowest that I am in much pain and there is nothing left for – Thou knowest – only Thou knowest--"

Here my dream became indistinct and I knew no more, until out of a dark blur there appeared to my dream-consciousness a face – the face of Woo-Ma – dead.

That was all of my dream. I was awakened by the mechanical repetition by my own lips of the last line of [Thomas] Hood's "Bridge of Sighs":

"Owning her weakness – her evil behavior,
And leaving with meekness her sins to her Saviour."

A heavy shadow seemed to oppress me all of that day. Dreams are such mysteries. I could not get the "Bridge of Sighs" out of my mind. I found the poem and read it through from beginning to end, thinking thus to work it off; but the gloom would not be dispelled. The piteous spectacle of the wronged girl rose ever before me – with Woo-Ma's face.

Toward evening Jim Nesbit came in, followed by Father; so haggard, so old, so stern-looking, that the words on my lips were arrested.

Then Father spoke, and if his face was changed, so also was his voice.

"I have a telegram," said he. "Woo-Ma is coming home."

He paused and stared fixedly at me. I felt my blood congealing. But though I tried to speak, words refused to come.

"My God Almighty!" cried Jim, *"You know!"*

The blackness of night encompassed me.

* * *

They buried Woo-Ma whilst I lay deliriously babbling of childhood's days – of pleasures which leave no sting. When I was able to sit up, they brought me a youth's suit of clothes and a peaked cap. They had been worn by my sister and I keep them in memory of her. How criss-cross the lines of life run!

Cross-Continental
Travel Writing
(1904)

Wing Sing. "Wing Sing of Los Angeles on His Travels."
Los Angeles Express, 3 February 1904: 6.*

[Note–Wing Sing is the pen name of a well-known Americanized Chinese merchant of this city. He recently left Los Angeles to make a visit to his old home in China, going by way of Montreal. Before starting he promised *The Express* to write a series of articles in his own untrammeled style, telling of his travels. Appended is the first contribution. – Ed.]

I am a Chinaman. My name is Wing Sing. I got a wife and boy in China, but for ten years I live in America. I learn speak American. Some time white man laugh at my speaking and I say him, "Perhaps you not speak my Chinese talk so well I speak your talk. Perhaps I laugh more at you try to speak Chinese man's language." That American man not laugh any more. Los Angeles very nice place – like China some. I got big store opposite the Plaza. You know North Los Angeles Street? That where my store be. For ten year I work very hard. Then I say to me, "Wing Sing, not good work too hard. Perhaps you may take holiday."

My cousin in Montreal write me very long letter – say plenty good thing. I laugh. He say, "Come see me. This city very fine city. You take railway car or steamboat all the way to San Francisco. Then you take railway

---

* In 1903, the editor of the *Los Angeles Express* was Samuel Clover, who had first published Eaton's work in 1900 when he was editor of the *Chicago Evening Post*.

car or steamer all the way to Vancouver, just what you please. Vancouver, Canadian city up north. When you get there, you take one big train name Canadian Pacific Railway train, Imperial limited; that train fly fast with you to me. Four day, four night go by you see one big fine building, same Emperor China palace. That Canadian Pacific Railway station, Montreal. Then you see me."

So I say to my partner, "I go see my cousin in Montreal. Take good care of business till I come back. Good bye."

White man's New Year night I take the train to go to San Francisco. I sleep all night in the sleeper, very good and comfortable. Southern Pacific train all right for Chinaman. Next morning I see the country through the window of the car and what I see give much pleasure to me. Very fine farm and very fine cattle. That good for country.

Lady, She Have No Sense

People in the car they look at me and old man say to his friend: "See that Chinaman," and his friend look at me and laugh at me. So I look at him and I laugh at him – plenty funny people in America.

One lady have a nice full-moon face look at me, and then she walk to me and then she smile at men, and then she say to me, "Mr. Chinaman, won't you please me all about Mr. Confucius?" I say to her: "I not teacher, I not scholar, I business man. Confucius to Chinaman same as Jesus to white man. I not go to white business man and ask him to tell me all about Jesus, for he not know. I go to American preacher to know all about your sage, Jesus. So you got Chinese teacher and scholar to know about Confucius."

Lady she go back to her seat and I say to me that she was very nice American lady, but too bad she have no sense.

Plenty place go by I get to San Francisco and I go see my cousin in San Francisco. He have cigar factory on Commercial Street and he make big dinner for me.

Next morning I go to steamship agent and I tell him I want take Pacific Coast steamer "Puebla." He say, "She just sail, you too late." Then he tell me to buy ticket on steamer name "Coronado," she sail first steamer from San Francisco and she not cost much money to take her ride. I go on the

Coronado, and she roll up against a big wind on her way to Seattle. She little steamer, but she very good. All the other passengers were white men. The captain and the mate, they make big jokes, which I not understand to say, but I understand to think.

All the men make voyage pleasant to me. I think sailor very good man, he not drink, he have no girl and he look solemn at the sky and the sea and think big thanks and talk big talks. I tell the captain I go visit Montreal, Canada. He go tell me my fortune and he say I marry when I go to Montreal. I put on face to believe, for it not polite not to believe the captain to his face, and I not tell him I got little wife in China. The engineer, he say he find Chinaman thumb in can of tomatoes. I say, "How you know Chinaman thumb?"

He No Can Eat Much

Some passenger very sick stay in berth all time. I sick too, but me Chinaman and so not say I sick – just say I not can eat much. The steamer, she stop at Aberdeen [Washington]. I go take train from there to Seattle. It very bad day – rain, rain, rain all the time. I think I leave the sun behind me in California. I look out window and see very green country and plenty good tree. The air very nice and clean. I say to me, "Los Angeles fine sun, this country, fine air. In China, fine sun and fine air too."

Two men take seat in front of me and one say, "Are you natural Chinaman?" I say, "Yes, I got high up lawyer to make me natural two years after I first come." Then he say to me, "Are you marry?" I say "Yes." He say, "How many times?" I see that he think he have some fun so I think I have some fun too so I say "Four time."

He laugh and say "Are three of your wives dead or did you get divorces?" I say "No. In China a man can have as many wives as he has money to keep." He say, "Oh, that not right. When you go back to your country, you must teach them to do as we do in America."

I say, "Now, my turn. I know American man, clerk in my store. One day I see him walking with a lady. I say to him, 'Who that lady?' He say, 'She my girl.' Another day I see him walking with another lady, and I ask him again, 'Who that lady?' and he say, 'She my girl.' 'That very funny,' I say. American man not think it right to have two wife. Chinaman not think it right to have two girl."

But the train then come to Seattle and I go see my cousin.

Wing Sing. "Wing Sing of Los Angeles on His Travels."
Los Angeles Express, 4 February 1904: 6.

After I have visit with my cousin in Seattle I go up to Vancouver, British Columbia. The C[anadian] P[acific] R[ailway] agent he tell me I can change for car for Montreal at Mission junction, but I say I want to see Vancouver. I travel in parlor car that be very good to see and very good to feel, and I think myself one Chinese mandarin.

I see a man write with a pencil in a book. I say: "What you do?" He say: "I make note of my trip." I say: "I make note too." So I tell the conductor to give me paper and pencil, and I look see what the man put in his note, and I write the same. He say the car we ride in Canadian Pacific car on Northern Pacific system. He say we come through Washington that be very fertile country for cabbages and grass and timber; that it rain all the time in winter, and very fine in summer, and that it so green and fresh that he thought he back again in the Emerald Isle.

I show him what I write, and he laugh and say: "Oh, you must not copy what I write, just put down what you think yourself." I say: "Oh, that all right. I think same as you." He say: "Then you must be an Irishman," and I tell him that I think Chinaman be all kind of man in the states. He say: "But you not be in the states – very soon you be in Canada – we just come to Sumas. That the border line – I change my pin here." Then he pull his pin out of his tie and put in another. I see the one he pull out was made like the American flag, stars and stripes, and the one he put in was made of straight pieces of color – red, white and blue.*

---

* Canada's official flag until 1946 was the Royal Union Flag, better known as the "Union Jack."

He Fancies Vancouver

When I get to Vancouver, Canadian Pacific agent show me big hotel to go to, and I get room and go to sleep. Next morning I look out of window I see plenty of mountain – one very tall and white. I see river too. That river called Fraser river. One time my cousin wash gold in Fraser river, and some day he go out catch plenty of fish. At 10 o'clock I go see Canadian Pacific Empress steamer sail to China. Some day I go to China in that steamer. She look so that I be not afraid to sail all the four seas in her. Then I go inspect the railway train.

Plenty railway train run to Vancouver. Every place want to go can take train or steamer to. I speak to Canadian Pacific man, and I say: "How many mile I travel in your car to Montreal – 1,000, you think?" He laugh and say: "Oh, more near 4,000." I sit down and try to put 4,000 mile railway track in my head, but my head not can hold it. Then I go walk around Vancouver, and I find out that city not many year old, but very strong. It can do business as if it was as old as Canton. The air smell good like Seattle air, and the rain very glad change from Los Angeles sunshine. I see plenty my countrymen – two my cousin. Some day I think I start business in Vancouver. My cousin say I sure make money.

Feels Like a Mandarin

One more night go by, then I take Canadian Pacific train to go straight through to Montreal. The agent he tell me that my cousin make mistake, and that the Imperial Limited train not run in winter, so I say that all right, I not care wait till summer, so I take Canadian Pacific train, not Imperial limited. I go in the Pullman, name "Narbonne." I now very big mandarin with very high degree. I sit on a plush seat and I see everything splendid around me – carpet, lamps, furnishings.

Chinaman like to see everything nice. I look in mirror side me, and see myself look more nice than before I come on car. All the day I watch out of window. British Columbia all same Washington, with grass growing, cattle feeding, rivers running, mountains snowing. My friend with the note book he travel with me in the Pullman, and he tell me when we come to place call Yale, that some Chinaman there build Joss house. One time he say he see Chinaman wash gold in the river there.

When the night arrive the porter come and make up bunk for me to sleep. When I go lie down in it I find it comfortable. The porter he pull the curtain around me and it dark, but I turn a round hole above my pillow and the place fill with electric light. I fold my silk jacket and I put it on shelf at the foot of where I be. Then I go to sleep – I know no fear, the train travel so smooth.

Wing Sing. "Wing Sing of Los Angeles on His Travels."
Los Angeles Express, 5 February 1904: 6.

We are at a place call Revelstoke [British Columbia] when I get up next morning: The Irishman he up before me. I think he up all night. He show me his notes. I copy: "In the night we passed much splendid ranching and mining country. Darkness has also hidden from us most beautiful lake and mountain scenery and many a sportsman's paradise." I say "that too bad, but one must have sleep. If you lose your sleep you lose your mind, and if you lose your mind, that too bad, for then you got no left to look for it as you would if you lost your hat."

Irishman tell me have plenty time to sleep after he finish his journey and he not think he got much mind to lose. He tell me that when I sleep I miss see the Gold Range of mountain and some beautiful lake call Shushap lake, mountain passes and valleys and water that roar like lion. I say that too bad too, but I content, as the day before I see plenty beauty in the Cascade mountains and the Columbia river.

Irishman he tell me to see how the railroad curve here and wind itself like a snake around the mountain, taking us up high all the time. He say that very big engineering trick. I very much interested and impress. He say: "You Chinaman you not know the value of western machinery, steam and electricity. You think all the time about your grandfather's grandfather, and how to get money to build a Joss house."

I very indignant. I say to him: "That is not true one little bit. The Chinaman he man like other man, but the other man he not be kind to the Chinaman like he be to himself. He go make up a wooden image in his head, and he call that a Chinaman. The Chinaman he always take an interest in what is good for his business, and when he hear of a fine railway like Canadian Pacific, and how it do much good for the Canada country, and bring plenty of people in there to settle it and to grow it, he want see that railway. He think some day the Chinese build railway like that in their own country.

Irishman say he not think same me. The Chinese people too much prejudice. Sometime they destroy railway after people build. "That true," I say, "but that because the people build it not make good impression on our people." The Canadian Pacific railway people different – they know plenty Chinaman and they do plenty business with them. "Why not the Chinese people build railway?" I say. "They build small railway already; they do mining like American people; they trade with the other countries. If the other country people treat Chinaman proper he do business with them just same friend."

The porter come and say we soon be at Glacier house at the foot of "Sir Donald." I say, "Sir Donald Smith?" for that I hear the name of very great Canadian man. He say, "No, Sir Donald." I too polite to contradict him, but I think he make mistake, and I tell the Irishman to look see if he can see Sir Donald Smith.* He laugh and say he not have to look to see, he have to see. He say "Sir Donald" one of big peak of the Selkirk mountains. He point it out to me, and something shining and high he call a glacier. My breath and my blood stand still as I look. All the time we go higher and higher, and the air it become colder.

I travel in California and China, but I never see mountains and between mountains like I see on this road. Many beautiful hours I keep my eye on them. They make all kinds of shapes and the ice and snow that ornament them I not can describe sufficient.

One place we come to the Irishman tell me Columbia valley and he show me to look one way and say "That mountain over there Selkirks." Then he tell me to look other way and say "That mountains it is the Rockies."

I not can say nothing. My expression it not express me.

* Sir Donald Smith, 1st Baron Strathcona and Mount Royal, headed the Canadian Pacific Railway. .

Wing Sing. "Wing Sing on His Travels."
Los Angeles Express, 6 February 1904: 6.

ON THE CAR, EN ROUTE TO MONTREAL, Winter Time. – We go on all
day and night and another day and night and it all one "magnificent" sight.
The Irishman tell me the word "magnificent." He say I write that I relieve
my feelings. He tell me the name of the place we pass as Field, Banff,
Canmore, Calgary [Alberta], Moosejaw, Regina [Saskatchewan] and some
others I forget. He tell me better to see the country in summer when all
the trees have their leaves and the river run free, but I think, "What for
Chinaman from Los Angeles want see summer place?" That he see all
the round year in California.

When a man travel he want change and it be more good for Los Angeles man to travel through winter country than through summer. I like see
and feel the cold winter and the trees that are dress in snow; they are more
beautiful to my eyes than the trees with the leaf. In the Rockies I see plenty
big white flowers everywhere, in the water, in the air and on the trees.

I say to the Irishman, "Oh, I see that big white water lily come float
down that water." And he say, "That water lily is the snow and the roses
and the grasses and the leaves are all snow and that old woman with the
cap on her head over there, she is made by the snow."

I say, "What old woman?" He say, "Why, nearly all the trees look like
old women with white caps on their heads, don't they?" I say, "She be very
straight old woman."

When we come to that part of the country which he call the prairie I be
very much interested for I always hear that very good country for business.
It hot in summer and it cold all winter and it grow much wheat, plenty
enough to supply all the people in Canada, and all the people in Europe
and all the people in America. That why there be so many big buildings
call grain elevators all along the eastern part of the Canadian Pacific railway line. He say plenty room for poor people to come and take farm and
grow rich in this and, so I think when I go back to China I tell some of

my countrymen to come. My countrymen good farmers, make things grow in all land they touch. I think the wheat land the same to the white man as the rice land to the Chinaman.

There not much snow on the prairie land and some place we come to we see plenty cattle graze. My friend point to them and say they cattle ranch. They near Calgary. He write in his note book that this be fine climate, and that all along the foothills in the distance there be good game for sportsman.

When we come to the place called Regina he tell me that some policeman soldiers are there to look after the Indians. He say they call "Mounted Police," and ride on big horses and dress in red coat. I see some Indian at that place. I think he look like Chinaman with bad temper.

All the people that I see wear big coat and plenty fur, their face red, and they look as if they had much blood. The Irishman tell me it is the climate make them so juicy. I think the climate make me have big appetite. I go into Canadian Pacific dining car and I eat first-class breakfast, rice dry and not mildewed, and the fish and the meat not turned and served with proper sauce.

You want to know good man? You watch see what he eat. Good man eat good, clean food.

Wing Sing. "Wing Sing of Los Angeles on His Travels." Part 5.
Los Angeles Express, 10 February 1904: 6.

When I finish eat I go to Winnipeg, and the Irishman he come with me to take a walk, and he tell me that Winnipeg very important city, and he show me so many railway tracks and stores for merchandise. It has no sea, but it has river, and it do business with the east and the west country. One time it be one part of the prairie, but it grow very fast. The street all white with the snow, and I think they be soft, but I find they be hard and good for walk. All the carriage have no wheels, but they have little bells in front. They ring as the horse run and make pretty sound to my ear.

I say, "What sort of carriage you call that?" The Irishman tell, "That sleigh. When the street be covered with snow in Canada wheel no count." I look at the sleighs and admire them much. I think when I go to Montreal I get sleigh and take ride with the bells. After we walk we come back to Pullman car. I feel much superior man. The cold air so much beneficial to me and the car it much agree with the sense. I think I gain six pounds since I leave Vancouver. I take nap, and when I wake I hear two lady talk behind me. The car go very fast, but I think six Canadian Pacific cars not near so fast as two lady tongue.

Next day the Irishman tell me that when I sleep in the night I pass plenty forest and land from which the copper and the silver come, but he say he see all, and he tell me much that I listen to hear.

Wing Sing Sees the Big Lake

Then we come to Fort William and Port Arthur, two town close to-gether on the north shore of Lake Superior.* When we pass them by we see more of beauty than where the Selkirks and the Rockies take us up to the heavens. That is the beauty of the scenery that belongs to Lake Superior. We ride by the north shore in the morning, and in the evening we see the sun set over the big white lake.

It is the sky of heaven then. The Irishman say it be only where the rivers and lakes are ice-bound that sunsets like that be seen. One time we see big part of lake shining like the best glass, and then it is the frosted glass we see, and then we see small part of lake, for the trees they hide it, and the rock they hide it, but it come again until the dark not suit my eyes to see. I say to the Irishman I very glad behold what I hear is the biggest lake in the world. He say "Very grand country, fine mining region."

Last day of the trip come the city of Ottawa, the capital city of Canada. The Irishman point to me the government buildings and the building he call the parliament house. He say the man call governor of Canada live there and his house call Rideau hall – very fine place to see. The Irishman ask that some day I go with him to visit Ottawa and hear the men in parliament make laws and see the Chaudiere Falls near there.

* Eaton worked in the twin cities of Port Arthur and Fort William, northern Ontario, for about a year in 1892–93.

He Hears Habitant French

I hear some people talk very strange talk in the car. It is not Chinese – it is not American. Sometime I think it be same talk as the talk of the Spanish people in Los Angeles, but no, it is not. The Irishman he say "That is the French talk. We have plenty French people in Canada." I say, "I glad to see the French people. All the people of all countries that have a big railway like the Canadian Pacific be very happy. When I see the big railway cross the continent, and the big steamer that go to China for my countryman to see, I feel that the people of China and the people of all countries belong as it were to one great circle of kindred, and that all beneath the sky are as one great family." The Irishman he say he approve my sentiment.

It was great delight to me all day what I see, hundreds and thousands of white fields and hills, and plenty little black trees and bushes. This the Irishman tell me very good farm. He say the snow keep the earth warm in winter. I say, "California like happy, cheerful, smiling friend;" Washington and British Columbia like one sympathizing friend: cry when we cry and laugh when we laugh; but most part of Canada like one good firm friend that keep cool outside but never lose warm heart.

Then the conductor call "Montreal" and I see my cousin.

Wing Sing. "Wing Sing of Los Angeles on His Travels."
Los Angeles Express, 24 February 1904: 6.

MONTREAL, Feb. 19. – Gung Hee Sun Neen,* Happy New Year. Now we have the Chinese New Year in Montreal and I keep it with my cousin and my cousin's friends. We visit much and we have plenty feast, and my cousin he pay all that he owe and all the people owe him some bill they come pay him. The New Year big time with the Chinese. It not the same as the American New Year that come every time first day January. The Chinese New Year sometime January, sometime February. It according to the months in a year. Sometimes twelve months in a year, sometimes thirteen.

* "Gung hee" is "felicitations," "sun neen" is "new year." The phrase is Cantonese and a variant of "gung hei fat choi" – Happy New Year.

The time the moon go round the earth – that one month. The moon go round the earth thirteen times in the last Chinese year. One moon to a Chinaman same as one month to American. See!

First New Year day we have big ceremony call "Rounding the Year," and in the night we have another ceremony call "Keeping company with the gods during the night."* Pardon me if not explain what that mean. There be some things to write about and some things to be quiet about. The American people not yet come to understand all the Chinese ceremony. Next day all the Chinese people are merry. They enjoy pleasant food, they get pleasure from music and they live comfortable and not think of what make them mourn. All the week they are like that.

My cousin he take me see many of his friend. Lee Chu very fine fellow. He bring his wife out from China last year, and he have one fine boy. Lee Chu, he Chinaman, but he all same Canadian man. He wear fur coat and fur hat and he drink plenty beer. He interpreter in Montreal court. Sometime he talk English, sometime he talk Chinese and sometime he talk the French talk. When I go to bid him good-bye, he say "Au Revoir." I say to my cousin, "What he mean?" and my cousin he say, "I think he mean to tell you he know something you not know."

After I see Lee Chu I see Wong Chow. Wong Chow he look serious and he not drink no samshu. My cousin he tell me that Wong Chow, he brought his wife from China, five, six, seven years ago, and the American lady come see and talk much foolishness to her so that when Wong Chow tell his wife do this to do that, his wife, she ask question, "What for?" This make much trouble in Wong Chow's house, and one day, when Wong Chow away, his wife, she take the dog and the cat and she go live with the American lady, and she not come back to Wong Chow for a long time, and then she tell him she never not come back to him at all unless he make agreement that he not do one thing she not advise and he not want her to do one thing she not want to do. So Wong Chow make agreement; but that great shame to Chinaman.†

* Justus Doolittle describes this ritual in *Social Life of the Chinese* (New York: Harper Bros, 1865: 251–2). Guests bow before and present gifts to the gods and goddesses in the temple. Guests who have experienced particularly good fortune in the preceding year are expected to present additional gifts.
† Eaton revisits this scenario in "The Wife of Lee Chu."

I say to my cousin, "I not think I bring my wife to America. What you advise?" And my cousin say, "Oh, that all right, if you not too familiar with her. Wong Chow talk to his wife too much. If a man do that his woman lose her humility. There is one place for the husband and there is one place for the wife."

"That very good advice," I answer, "but if you are reserve toward the woman she become discontented. It is difficult to know how to behave toward a woman."

Tye Loy on Bleury street in Montreal, he have a very fine store. It have plenty decorations for the New Year, and he close up all his business. Plenty people came to see him, but he not can sell, he only can give. The Chinese lily, the Chinaman call the Sui Sin Far, it bloom in all the house of the Chinese at this time and its fragrance greet me like a friend.

Wednesday evening I go pay my respects to the Gambling Cash Tiger. Why not? There is a time for business and there is a time for pleasure.

Wing Sing. "Wing Sing in Montreal."
Los Angeles Express, 27 February 1904: 6.

MONTREAL, P. Q., Feb. 22. – I never see no city more better than Montreal. It is as big as San Francisco, but though it much more quiet it make much more money and do much more business. The people they give plenty time to play. The cold, it is very cold, but the Canadian man and the Canadian woman they not like stay in the house too much. They sport like little child that is strong like man.

My cousin he take me to place called "skating rink." All the people there they have piece of steel under their shoe and they move fast on a big piece of ice like the bird that skim close to the ground, and their eyes they be so bright and the good luck color is on their cheeks and their nose. Also my cousin take me up one very big hill of snow and he say "What you think this sport? The Canadian man calls it tobogganing."

I watch. I see the man and the woman and the boy and the girl come up the hill pull very flat piece of wood with the end curl round like the roof of a Chinese house. My cousin say that piece of wood travel faster than the railway car. I say no can believe, but he speak true. When the man and the woman and the boy and the girl come top of hill they all sit in one row on the piece of wood and it shoot down so that I shut my eyes. One second go by I open my eye, and the man and the woman and the boy and the girl, they are coming up the hill again. My cousin say the hill more than one mile of snow.

One day I go out in the carriage with the bells. Never no carriage go so quick and smooth as it go. All the ground we cover is white and clean. It is so all over the city of Montreal. When I go out of my cousin house I wipe my shoes on the mat, for I not like soil the pretty snow in the street. After we ride two, three hours, my cousin say, "How you like ride on river?" I say, "What you mean?" He say, "You ride over the river St. Lawrence. Every winter the cold make it so hard that the steamer not can run, but the man can walk on it, and the horse can run on it and five hundred carriages with bells not can break it."

It is the war which all the people in Montreal talk about* – the war, and how to get men to build the Grand Trunk Pacific railway that they have charter for to build in three year. It is not possible to build it without they get Chinamen, but what Chinaman come to this country if he have to pay $500 head tax to come in?

Chinese people, their heart is more with the Japanese than the Russians. It is too bad that the selfishness of the rulers of nations should bring so much trouble. It is so always. If the rulers are not benevolent, the people are involved in death and ruin.

I think I come back to Los Angeles next month. This is no time for the man of peace to go visit his home. I write my wife that I be very sorry but I go see her next year.

* Eaton refers to the Russo-Japanese war, which began in early February 1904.

Wing Sing. "Wing Sing in Montreal."
Los Angeles Express, 9 March 1904: 6.

MONTREAL, March 3. – [Special Correspondence of The Express.] – Two
moons now gone by since I left Los Angeles and the Canadian climate so
agree with me that I think I stay here one moon more. Then I go to New
York and after I see that most stupendous city and all my cousins there
I be plenty refreshed to come back to my business in Los Angeles.

Now I tell my countrymen in Los Angeles about my countrymen in
Canada. Canada, Montreal, but it more than Montreal. Canada mean
many cities and places, but the first of all the cities and places is Montreal.
There be many big banks here and plenty insurance company for the fire
and for the life business, but the people they live to very good age and not
too many house or business fire up. I think that very good sign.

I hear that in Canada from Vancouver to Montreal there be about
17,000 Chinese. The most part of them live in British Columbia. The part
of Canada that is called Eastern Canada, it has not many more than 2,000,
and in the city of Montreal I learn there be about 800. Most of the Chinese
engage in the laundry work. That is, because it is a business that requires
but little capital – beside it is a business that the Chinaman is allowed to go
into. The white man he keep the Chinaman out of the millionaire business.
There also good number Chinese merchants.

There is some gambling and some opium smoking in Chinatown, but
not very much. The Chinaman gets fun out of life in other ways, too. The
Canadian Chinaman he like very much to learn to speak the English and
the French language and to learn the English and the French religions.
Some Chinamen here they be Protestant and Catholic both. Song Long he
go to six Sunday schools – Episcopal, Presbyterian, Methodist, Baptist and
Reformed Episcopal.* He keep up the Chinese religion, too. I think he be
what American people call very liberal man.

---

* Perhaps Jos Song Long, who opened the first Chinese hand laundry in Montreal in 1877
(Kwok B. Chan, *Smoke and Fire: The Chinese in Montreal* [Hong Kong: Chinese University
Press, 1991], 156).

There is more of the tribe of Lee in Montreal than any other tribe, but there also Wus and Wongs and Sings and Tongs, and those of our country-men who have had wives sent to them here have taken them from villages not their own as is proper in China.

As in America there is great difficulty in bringing female relatives to this country and it is harder then ever for a Chinaman to have his wife with him. If this state of things be, how can a Chinaman make his home here? It is not for the Americans and the Canadians to blame him if he save his money to send back to China or to take with him there.

If the Chinese woman could come to this country without too much trouble the Chinaman would spend his money here. It is not sensible to want to give the Chinaman religion and not want to give him a home, for what does the good religion teach if it teach not the love of home?

Wing Sing. "Wing Sing in Montreal."
Los Angeles Express, 12 March 1904: 6.

MONTREAL, March 9. – [Special Correspondence of The Express.] – Now I tell you that the Chinese children of Montreal, their case is much more fortunate than is that of the Chinese children of Los Angeles, for here they come to the government schools dressed in the dress that is proper to the children of the Chinaman.

When I go see the school here I see the son and the daughter of my countrymen study with the sons and daughters of the Canadian man, and the son and daughter of my countryman they pleasure my eyes, for the male child he wear the blue silk blouse of the Chinaman padded and wadded to keep him warm and the loose trousers most comfortable gathered at the ankles and his queue braided so neat. The female child she wear the modest dress of the Chinese woman, and her hair arrange in a bunch on each side, and so shining and so smooth that I feel proud and the teacher say to me "The little Chinese girl, her head more tidy than the head of all the Canadian scholars."

Now I Los Angeles Chinaman and I always speak good word for the city that I do business in; but to be sincere is the way of the superior man, and I want tell the Los Angeles people that I think they disregard ordinance of heaven when they say the children of the Chinamen, they must not come to the American government schools if they not put on the American clothes. It is too hard for the poor Chinese mothers to make the American costume. They know not how. Moreover, it please not the eye of the Chinese woman, however beautiful it be to be the American. For that reason and because it cost too much to the poor Chinese parents who have the Chinese clothes all ready for the body, there are too many Chinese children in Los Angeles not attending the government schools.

What you think my cousin do? He not have one son. No, not even one daughter. His wife she cry much on that account, and my cousin he sometime very melancholy and sad. One day my cousin hear that in New York there be a poor little baby not have one mother or one father. No parent at all. So he tell the people write to him on that account to send the baby to the city of Montreal, address to Wing Sing. Wing Sing be my cousin's name and be my name also.

Well, the baby he come, he be white baby with eye the color of the blue China teacup, nose like a piece of jadestone that is carved, mouth same as the red vine leaf and hair all same silk worm make – the color all light and bright. The parent of the baby they not be proper parent and they be Irish. Some time I hear they be dead, but that not matter much to baby; only one thing sure, they love him.

Now, when my cousin and his wife see the white baby, and observe that its blood and bones and flesh are all right and that it make good loud noise when it cry, their hearts incline to the white baby and my cousin's wife she say:

"Oh, I do love that pretty baby, it is so plump and so sweet and it have no mother but me," and she take it in her arms and rock it and sing the Chinese lullaby.

Then my cousin, he say: "I will take that white baby and I will bring him up to be as a Chinaman. I will teach him the Chinese language and the Chinese ways and the Chinese principles. Then one day I take him with

me to China and find a little Chinese wife for him – and he will be to me
as a son."

One week after that I call see my cousin. I find him not in his store and
not in the back room playing cards. He be in the sitting room above his
store. I walk up there and what you think I see? My cousin and his wife
give bath to the white baby. It be in a big tub, and on one side my cousin
and on the other side his wife. The baby it be very happy, its hair twist all
over its head, and so also its legs and arms. It laugh much, and my cousin
and his wife they laugh too. Never have I seen them so forget the rules
of propriety.

"What do you think?" ask my cousin, and I reply, "I not say what
I think."

Wing Sing. "Wing Sing on His Travels."
Los Angeles Express, 25 May 1904: 6.

Los Angeles' Americanized Chinaman Tells of His Journey from
Montreal to New York and of His Impressions En Route – An
Intelligent Observer

MONTREAL, May 20. – [Special Correspondence of The Express.] – Time
come for me to go to New York, so one morning I go down to the Grand
Trunk station and buy ticket, as my cousin advise. That be by Delaware
and Hudson railway train to Albany, and from Albany to New York by the
New York Central road.

My cousin he go with me to station. He say pay little attention to those
who talk much and to have not much to do with gamesters and chess
players, also to keep myself from the seductions of beauty, music and
pleasant food.

I listen to all that I hear and I smile. I Chinaman that have travel much,
and the suggestions my cousin make seem to me to savor of a small
shrewdness. All the same I receive them with respect, for they come from
my elder cousin and betray for me a large kindness. Hard is the case of the
man who not know how to take advice from those who come before him.

I have seat in the coach they call the parlor car. I look around me and behold that all is most pleasant to the eyes and gratifying to the senses. I could not wish for a better situation for my body, and my mind it is also at ease. The complacent countenances of the people in the car also agree with me.

After the train leave the station my interest in the country I see from the car window develop much. The sun it is shining bright and the green blades of grass show everywhere.

Victoria Next to Chinese Empress

We pass over the bridge call Victoria bridge which is name for the woman who, after the empress of China, was the most high up woman in the world before she leaves it.

St. Lambert, Brosseau, Lacadio – these be French names of the places we pass by. I hear that from the seat in front where I sit. A man and a girl sit there. The man he a father and the girl she a daughter, and I hear the father tell friend with him that the girl is sixteen years old and that this her first trip on the train away from home, and that they go to New York. The girl's eyes look as if they could see both before and behind her. Every time the train stop she say, "Oh, what place is this?" and "Isn't it lovely!"

When we come to a place call St. John's,* she say to the friend, "This where my cousin stay when he was soldier." My curiosity is arouse and I look out of window and behold a building and grounds prepared for military and the practice of arms. I speak to the conductor and he tell me St. John's most interesting place and entertaining, with business doing all the time, and in summer much pleasure on the water and in the woods. Also that it is a station for the practice of arms for Canadian soldiers of Great Britain.

But the train fly fast and pass by more French name places, and I hear the French talk, and back of the villages I see now and then a cross raised. It is a sign there is a place of worship. The French Canadians like plenty religious ceremony all same Chinaman. The girl that is sixteen clap her

---

* Now called Saint-Jean-sur-Richelieu.

hands and say, "Oh, now I am in the United States first time in my life." I ask what she mean, and the man in the front inform me we reach Rouse's Point, where we cross the border from Canada into the United States. Two men with cap mark "U. S. Customs" come into the car and speak to us. One comes to me and inquire if my papers be all right and to bring them forth. I comply with what he ask me, but the indignation of the just man overcome me, and for a time I take no interest in what pass around me.

Feels Charm of Travel

All the same the charm of the travel soon make me forget all unpleasantness. It is a bright sky that we have and a clear air. I see it is a most beautiful and fertile country, and I hear it connect with much French and English history, which make it more interesting to me. The Chinaman like to hear all things that connect with the doings of ancestors. That is history.

At the place call Plattsburgh I behold a part of the Lake Champlain. "We are come now near to the Adirondack and other mountain range," say the father to the daughter. I hear the men in the next [sic] speak of the air – how clear and how sweet it is – of the forests, how grand and how beautiful of the rivers and streams, of the birds and the fish, big game and small game – of all the sport to be had in this region – and I think how excellently beneficial to the mind and the body must be the days that are passed by the shores of this lake.

Still we proceed. Lakes and mountains always in view – also fine hotels, which the man in front say have very fine accommodation for the people who think better to stop in them than to camp in the woods. One man say he go camp one summer in the Adirondack for six weeks. First day, he get there he weigh 125 pounds. Last day he leave he weighs 175 pounds! If my wife comes to America next year I bring her to put in some time in the mountains, so excellent it seem to be for the production of good flesh and blood.

We pass many towns, the names which I forget to remember, but the father of the girl sit before me he know history of all, and he speak what he know – all about Indian and French man, and English man, and American man – all his ancestors – and how they shed blood to make trail to lead to pleasure grounds for their children.

Impressions of the Saratoga

We come to big place call Saratoga. Here the conductor tell me can change cars for the connection railway of the Delaware and Hudson, which take me into the lake and wood region, to fish and to shoot. I say, "That all right next time, but this my first trip to New York." The man with his daughter say to her: "I think I take you to live in the mountains for one month. I quiet you down. The trees and the streams will talk with wise tongues and their effect will be better than two hundred sermons." The girl she reply, "A nice green reformatory you would put me in" – and then she laugh like a mocking bird and say like me: "That all right in the summer. This be spring and I go to New York."

I learn that Saratoga very rich place and beautiful and much popular, and because is so, the high up people of America all want visit there in summertime. The train makes good run from Saratoga to Albany and I see the round lakes, also many first-class towns. At Albany I get off train and walk into the station, which is imposing building and much impress me. I wait here 45 minutes for New York Central train and I improve my time by ask question which obtain for me the information that Albany is to the cities of the United States what China is to the countries of Asia – an exemplar.

I see for myself that it be a city of excellent appearance, and that it do the American people credit. Very good hotel there, and much pleasure for the man that know how to enjoy himself with his eyes and his ears.

Between Albany and New York the New York Central train travel very fast, and I feel safe and comfortable and disposed to slumber. But even with but half an eye, as the Americans say, I keep up the interest of my mind, and when we reach the place call Hudson I listen to the talk of the father and the daughter who are near me in the car. Hudson, I hear, is very old place, and name after fine man of the old time. Long time back it a port for whaling business. On one side of the city flow the Hudson River.

Mountains Recall California

I see more mountains with red sandstone like mountains in California. The father tell his daughter these mountains the Catskills.

I see rocks and rivers and little hills and big hills and places where

America's first man, name George Washington, made battles and bridges
and speeches. The Hudson river it always very beautiful sight and I hear
that there spring from the land surround it many stories for the American
books of poetry and history.

Coming into the city of New York is more than all the trip in interest,
but it is too confusing to a Chinaman's mind for him to make clean expression of all he behold. It is lights along the river with monuments to ancestors and descendants and buildings so high that the tops the eye cannot
reach, and much more.

My cousin come meet me at the station and with him I behold my
friends, Dr. J.C. Thoms, Ju Chu and Joe Singleton.* They all high up New
York Chinamen. Ju Chu, he president of the Chinese reform party of
America. Joe Singleton he vice-president, and Dr. Thoms he secretary. I
drive with them to Chinatown and have big Chinese dinner in the swell
Chinese restaurant on Pell street.

Last thing I hear as I leave the station is the voice of the girl of sixteen.
She skip by her father's side and say, "I'm in New York; I'm in New York,"
and the pretty dimples of her artful smile seem to have much effect upon
her father, for he not once tell her once she talks too much. That the way
with her father and daughter in this country. It is not so in China, but
perhaps I better say no more for I not in China, I in New York.

* Dr. J.C. Thoms was a Chinese doctor and founder of the Brooklyn Hospital for the
Chinese. Ju Chu (Chu Su Gunn) was an importer as well as president and director of the
Chinese Mission of the United Congregational Church. Joe Singleton (Chew Mon Sing)
was an interpreter for the New York Court and for US Customs. All three were involved
in the Chinese Reform movement.

Wing Sing. "Wing Sing in New York City."
Los Angeles Express, 9 June 1904: 6.

Los Angeles American Chinaman, Away on His Travels, Tells
of His Experiences in Gotham and of Big Men of the Chinese
Reform Party He Meets

NEW YORK, June 4. – [Special Correspondence of The Express.] – Though
poor he keep possession of himself by walking straight. I speak of my
cousin, who is one of the head men of the Reform party of China in America. If my cousin remain in China and be content with rule not benevolent
to all, he have plenty riches and honors bestowed upon him; but my cousin
he have the sense of shame and the sense of propriety, and he not can put
up with some things and maintain a serene mind, so he prefer to live away
from his own country. He do pretty good business in America and the climate much agree with him, and he write to his friend "Here I stay till there
be more benevolent rule in China. To rule well, one must love well, and the
Empress of China and her advisers, they love not the people under them."

Ju Chu is the president of the Reform party of China in New York. The
vice president is Joe Singleton, and the secretary be Dr. J. C. Thoms. They
all very good friend of my cousin. Ju Chu is faithful man in business.
He have son seventeen years old in the American college call Yale. Joe
Singleton is interpreter in the New York court and he have American
woman for his wife. Dr. Thoms is Chinese scholar and American scholar
also. He know all the white man and all the Chinese man know. He go to
Chinese school to learn and he also study at the American university. He
American doctor with American certificate and he be also Chinese doctor.
His wife she American and they have two girls and one boy, very fine
children. Dr. Thoms is brother in name, but not in blood, to Dr. Thoms*
of Los Angeles.

Chinese Reform society head office at No. 5 Mott street, where also be
the sumptuous apartment of the Chinese Oriental club, also the room for
the composition and printing of the Chinese Reform News. My cousin

---

* Los Angeles herbal doctor and reformer Dr Tom Leung.

introduce me to the editor, who most excellent scholar, though his years be
not many and he come from China but three moons gone by. All the type
in the cases are Chinese type with Chinese characters – all but one case
and that be same type as in the American printing office. The Chinese case
for type and the press much like American case and press, but not quite
same. I not can all explain. I see American man and woman come to visit
the place and they exclaim, "How most amazing that the Chinese should
learn print all same Americans do," and my cousin make answer, "It is
from our people that people of other countries learn how to print." I send
to *The Express* a copy of the *Chinese Reform News*.

Chinatown of New York impress me much. The first morning after I
come to New York I wake up early, look out of window, and behold the sun
of the morning making beautiful the tops of many houses. My cousin's
apartments are high up in the biggest building in Chinatown. He landlord
of that building and have 200 of his countrymen for tenants. My cousin
have first-class cook and after good breakfast my cousin take me to see
Chinatown. New York Chinatown for most part in three streets – Mott,
Pell and Doyer. It much superior to Los Angeles Chinatown, both in size
and appearance, but it inferior to Chinatown of San Francisco. The reason
for this, perhaps, it is so much more far from China.

My cousin say that four years before New York's Chinatown very dirty
place, and the city bosses declare they pull down all the buildings in that
part of Bowery and make one big park for people; but when they come
count the expense to make the park they find it cost too much money,
so they clean the whole place and well repair it. That much improve New
York's Chinatown. There is one Chinese theater which I visit in company
with my cousin. It very much the same as in San Francisco. I make the
acquaintance of one Chinese actor. He bright fellow. I inquire if he be the
good princess in the play and he reply, "I the villain." All the actors in
Chinese theater of male persuasion. I see plenty white men and two white
women in the Chinese theatre. Also in the joss house I see plenty white
people. They much curious about things Chinese and sometimes their
behaviour be not proper.

I think the Chinese restaurants in New York much better than any Chinese restaurant in San Francisco. There is one call the Chinese Delmonico.

We take dinner there and I see plenty swell white people come in to eat chop suey. The American people think chop suey the best Chinese dish, but the Chinese, they know plenty better. I dine with Mr. Ju Chu and Dr. Thom[s] and Mrs. Thom[s] and Joe Singleton, and we talk much. I also meet Mr. [Lock] Wing, the Chinese vice consul. His conversation be much agreeable and he seem to be man of good understanding and polite manners. When I hear the vice consul and Dr. Thom[s] converse in the American language I say within: "Oh, that I were as accomplished as these my countrymen! How much I have yet to attain to."

Vice Consul Wing, he not hold same opinions as my reform party friends. He think China all right and there be no need to murmur against the government. He have American woman for his wife. With regard to the Chinese first consul, Mr. [K.F.] Shah, he also take dinner at the Chinese Delmonico, and I see that his costume is Chinese as also his manners. He is man that possess the respect and esteem of all the Chinamen and all the white men in New York. Never no Chinese consul so liked as he.

But this letter too long. I tell you more about New York Chinese at one other time.

Wing Sing. "Wing Sing in New York City."
Los Angeles Express, 14 June 1904: 6.

Los Angeles Chinaman Gives More of His Impressions of the Country's
Metropolis – Japanese, Chinese and Jews Affiliate in Common Cause

NEW YORK, June 9. – [Special Correspondence of The Express.] – Today I go again to Mott street to study my countrymen in this big city. At one table near where I sit there is a Chinaman and white man Jew. The white Jew talk much about the war between Russia and Japan and he say he think the Japanese spring from the Jews, and are the avengers of the wrongs the Jews suffer at the hands of the Russians. He say, Japanese all Jews. The Chinaman say, "How do you account for their changed features?"

I find Jew people like Chinese food, and many go to the Chinese restaurants, which seems strange, as the Chinese prefer the flavor of pork and ham in their dishes to that of any other flavor and the taste of the young pig is delightful to them.

New York Chinese sympathize much with the Japanese in the war between Japan and Russia, and they have entertainment in the Chinese theater for the benefit of the Japanese Red Cross society. The Chinese give most generously to the aid of the Japanese in their war, feeling as if it were that the Japanese also fight for the Chinese. For myself, I express no opinion. I am acquainted with many Japanese and know them to have better heads than hearts, and as the individual is, so the nation. The Japanese in New York much encourage the Chinese to help with funds their cause in the war.

All the Jews speak fine words to the Chinese and the Chinese merchants also contribute much to the aid of the poor Jews persecuted, as they say, by Russia. Therefore, some of the Jew people of New York, they buy medal for five leading Chinese merchants in New York, and I think the medals cost them much money for each one. The Chinese merchants feel flattered and give dinner to the Jews on the occasion of the presentation of the medal, and the Jews, they bring plenty friend to the dinner.

There is quite a number of Chinese women in New York, also children. The Chinese woman, she live in upstairs apartment of her husband's and keep to herself but many fine Chinese lady be quite Americanized and all same American woman. The Christian people of New York have many missions in Chinatown and school for children. The Chinese parents they wish their children to learn all same American children.

As to the business men. There are many more Chinese merchants in New York than there are in Los Angeles or San Francisco and they are much more like Americans in manners and customs than are my countrymen in California. Many are fine scholars and make much money. I go with my cousin to see General Grant's tomb. I bow my head with reverence before it, so great a man as he was with so much respect for the Chinese people deserves the esteem of all Chinamen. Behind the tomb I behold a tablet erected by my countryman, Li Hung Chang, the great Chinaman's tribute to the great American.

New York same as all other cities, only much bigger; it not pleasant in appearance. There is much noise and many high buildings and many poor people. Always, wherever I be, many poor people and many tough people and many unclean people. I feel sorry all the time. I not can feel happy. My cousin take me to walk where the rich people be, but there is something always to remind that there be much disagreeableness in the big city call New York.

Many wonderful things I see, but not one thing so wonderful or so beautiful as the Golden Gate park in San Francisco. No flowers here and no beautiful trees and even the sky I cannot see, for they build the railway in the air above our heads. The cars they travel so low and the people are slow, too, and have no life, but the life eating and drinking and making money. The sea is around, behind the tall brick buildings, but the New Yorker see it not and enjoy it not, and the sky seem so far away that their thoughts they never ascend, but dwell forever in the dust. I speak of the crowd. Of course, come not into the crowd.

Wing Sing. "Wing Sing on His Travels."
Los Angeles Express, 5 July 1904: 6.

Los Angeles Chinese-American, After "Doing" New York, Returns to Montreal and Then Journeys to Chicago, En Route Home to His Beloved California

ON THE RAIL, July 1. – [Special Correspondence of The Express.] – Mencius* has said, "I have an infirmity – I am fond of wealth," "I have an infirmity – I am fond of valour," "I have an infirmity – I am fond of beauty," but he has not said, "I have an infirmity – I am fond of travel." Therefore I can say without reproach that I derive much pleasure from travel in pleasant company, amidst refreshing scenes, all stations reached at their

* King Hsüan of Ch'î says this in chapter 4 of *The Works of Mencius, Book 1, Part 2*, by Chinese Confucian philosopher Mencius (372–289 BCE).

appointed time, and meals and accommodations for repose most excellent; all which fall to my lot when I come from Montreal to Chicago.

I leave the Grand Trunk station on the Express No. 3, at half past ten of the clock in the night. The big dark porter inform me that my bunk is already to receive me, so I retire for the night, and the next thing I know it is the morning and through the window the sun is shining— – shining also on Lake Ontario which we ride by. That the water I see is Lake Ontario I have knowledge of from the map of the road I keep by me. I refer also to my watch and this make the conclusion for me that we are near the place call Port Hope. I lie in my most comfortable bunk with the blind of my widow raised so that I can delight my eyes with a most beautiful water color. The Lake Ontario is as big sea and it seem to me as I behold the big ships and the small ships on the surface thereof that magnificent pleasure trips may be made upon its waters.

My appetite is keen when in the city of Toronto I arrive and there I take breakfast. If I have time I think I like to stay in Toronto for more than the railway time to wait. It is large city wherein there be many imposing buildings for business, for learning and for pleasure, and it is on the shore of Lake Ontario and near to one wonder of this world, Niagara Falls, of which my cousin in Montreal talk much, for he go visit them one time.

Again in my seat I become the acquaintance of a man of benevolent countenance and fluent speech. To me he address remarks on the country go by in the night. He say many time he journey by day over the same road and that the situation of the towns we pass by afford the best of scenery on the St. Lawrence river. He name Lachine, Pointe Claire, Vaudreuil and other names I not remember. In summer time he say the man that has money in Montreal comes out to these places to rest for one week, two week, three week, as he desire. The man also say to me that in the region of the Province of Ontario it is a farming country more fertile than the land of California and that the berries and fruit and vegetables that flourish there excel those that grow elsewhere. He speak of the City of Kingston, how one time it be most important town, both military and political and of the old fort built by a man with a Frontenac name that I escape see when we pass, which make me have much regret.

He say long time gone by, the King of England, but then the Prince of Wales, take trip from Kingston through the Thousand Islands and down the St. Lawrence river and that he ask the captain of the steamer to stop near one of the islands and when the captain obey him he take jewel from his pocket and throw it on the island. Then he tell the captain to proceed to all the other islands and to them he also throw jewels. For evermore after that many people go search the islands to find the prince's jewels, but all endeavors have been disappointed.

"Between Toronto and Sarnia you see one of the finest sections of the Dominion of Canada," say my friend, and with him my eyes advise me to agree. Sarnia particularly admirable place on Lake Huron. My acquaintance say one time he go see ship he build launch at Sarnia.

After Sarnia it is Port Huron, and now I learn that which fill me with admiring amazement. What I learn is this: Port Huron, Michigan is connected with Sarnia, Ontario by a tunnel which runs between the two places beneath the river St. Clair, which I behold. The tunnel is the work of the most clever engineers and it cost millions of dollars to build it; but the Grand Trunk Railway consider not the cost, so much benefit it is to the people of the Dominion of Canada and of the United States. The shipping of the great lakes all pass though this channel.

I express my admiration for the engineering work and my acquaintance remark, "So you appreciate enterprise and modern inventions, even though you are a Chinaman."

His remark displease me – it been made too often, and prove very plain to my mind that the white man he more bigoted to the Chinaman than the Chinaman be to the white man. Therefore I answer stern:

"No man who take little trouble to know the Chinaman speak as you. I be no scholar, but when a boy I learn, 'Let a man who is ignorant be fond of using his own judgement; let a man without rank be fond of assuming a directing power to himself; let a man who is living in the present age go back to the ways of antiquity – on the persons of all who act thus calamities will be sure to come.'

"If the schoolboy in China is taught this," I continue, "how then can it be said that he has no regard for the spirit of progress?"

Flint, Durand, Lansing, Cassopolis, these are the names of the interesting cities I hear of as we pass them in the state of Michigan, and after that South Bend, one hundred miles west of which I find Chicago.

"Great place, Chicago," say my acquaintance. "Noted for its big buildings, its stock yards, its parks, its wickedness and its goodness."

"Benevolence is the greatest characteristic of Chicago," I remark, and my acquaintance smile and answer me, "I did not say so, but if you choose to hear only what is good of the metropolis of the middle west the happier you will be while you are within it."

He shake hands with me in American fashion. And we part congratulating one another that we never have more enjoyable and interesting trip that that we had together from Montreal to Chicago.

Wing Sing. "Wing Sing on His Travels."
Los Angeles Express, 8 July 1904: 6.

CHICAGO, July 5. – [Special Correspondence of The Express.] – At the station there is a great crowd of people passing in and out; many are on their way to the St. Louis exposition and others are on the return. So also were there numbers of intending visitors to the St. Louis city on the train I take. I think the exposition very good plan to mingle the people of United States and of Canada and educate them with one another.*

My cousin with his one fine boy greet me with glad face, and the next day I stay with him in this city of Chicago. There not many of my countrymen to be seen in this city, but the Chinese restaurant business much succeed with the white people of Chicago, because I observe there be many

* The gap of almost two weeks between instalments for July 8th and July 20th invites speculation about whether or not Eaton visited the Louisiana Purchase Exposition, informally known as the St Louis World's Fair. Perhaps she filed anonymous stories about it to the *Express* or another publication. Several women reporters from Montreal – members of what became the Canadian Women's Press Club – covered the Fair (Linda Kay, *The Sweet Sixteen: The Journey That Inspired the Canadian Women's Press Club* [Montreal: McGill-Queen's University Press, 2012], 59); they visited earlier in the season and received a lot of media attention which Eaton, while in Montreal, may have read.

Chinese restaurant, and my countryman, the proprietor, say he make much money. Perhaps that because the Chicago people relish the flesh of the pork as do the Chinese. Chicago much famous for pork packing, The man Philip Armour, chief man in that business one time, but not now living of much consequence to his descendants and his descendants' friends, but my cousin tell me one story about him that make me smile.

One time my cousin have charge of plantation in Jamaica of West Indies. One year when he was there, the man, Philip Armour, and the ex-Governor [Roswell Pettibone] Flower of New York, also now depart to the land of the spirits, pay a visit to the island.* They very good friend, but one day at 8 o'clock in the morning Governor Flower not agree with his friend, Armour, concerning the quality of the air of Kingston, and so he depart for one week to the town of Port Antonio. Mr. Armour now left alone in a cottage by the sea, which is part of a hotel call the Marine Garden hotel.

One night a noise wake him from his sleep. He not know what the noise is, but it much like the sound of the blow of big club on the roof and door of his cottage. He listen for some time, but the noise it not cease, and Mr. Armour much alarmed, so he roll himself under his bed and call in loud voice, "I got one big pistol to shoot." But the big pistol not much effective, for the music still continue, and it come to pass that the great and the magnificent pork packer, Phil Armour, run to the window and shout, "Murder! Murder!"

They run to him in haste, the manager and the clerk of the hotel, and inquire of Mr. Armour wherefore he cry so loud. He explain unto them and they seek, but not one murderer can they find. So they report to Mr. Armour, but he say, "Sure, there be murderers. I hear them make noise most violent," and he demonstrate with his hand to the wall what manner of noise reach his ear. At that the clerk rub his head and cry, "Oh, I know now what your murderers are; they are cocoanuts," and he explain to Mr. Armour how the tall palm which stand beside the cottage bend its head above it and its ripe fruit fall upon the roof and make the noise Mr. Armour so much fear to be the voice of murderers.

* See also Eaton's "Our Visitors: Myrtle Bank" (131–4).

One man I meet with inquire what I think of Chicago women. I answer "I not think much." He seem very angry at that and say, "What you mean by speak so disrespectfully of the women of my city?" I very much impress and tell him that it not my intention to be disrespectful, and that in China it was more respectful to the woman to keep her out of the thought of the man. He say, "Oh, I see. It is Chinese custom to pretend not to notice the woman." "Not quite," I respond. "For example, I observe that the woman of Chicago is like the woman of other American cities in that she have many fashion of dress and there is not one dress like her cousin's. Moreover, the fashion of the dress change with the season, whereas, my countrywomen wear the same dress that they wear many centuries gone by, and all are in same style, the dress of the empress and the dress of the peasant."

In Chicago I go see the Pullman town, which much resemble a place in China where the high up Chinese mandarin with large retinue of servants build house for them so that all his servants live according to his desire.*

It is in Lincoln Park that I take the most of my pleasure, for there I behold at ease the lake call Michigan. Also with the boy of my cousin I pass many hours watching the wild animals within their cages appear as if tame, and the green lawns and the flowers and the signs, "Keep off the grass." The boy of my cousin say unto me, "All the people obey the sign, but not so the little bird. Behold the little bird hop on the grass before the sign and the policeman see him and reprove him not. It is well to be a little bird."

---

* Pullman was a town built in the 1880s by George Pullman to provide housing for employees of his Pullman Palace Car Company.

Wing Sing. "Wing Sing on His Travels."
Los Angeles Express, 20 July 1904: 6.

Los Angeles Chinese-American Returning from His Long Visit East – He
Tells of St. Paul and Minneapolis and of his Westward Ride to Seattle

SEATTLE, July 18. – [Special Correspondence of The Express.] – I proceed
by the Chicago Great Western train to St. Paul. It is half past six when I
leave in the most magnificent of cars. The ceiling is gold and green with
decorations, and there is a dome in the middle and most handsome lamps,
which make the effect on me of being in a Chinese temple. When the car
begin to move, though it very warm night, a refreshing breeze stir up
and I observe how enchanting is the landscape we follow from Chicago
and what a fruitful and happy state is Illinois.

Much historic ground we cover in the night, and in the morning behold the great river Mississippi, which name even in the Chinese school-
books refresh my eyes. The climate is most lovely and I rejoice as we move
along and enter the city of St. Paul. Now, of all the cities that I see I think I
prefer the one call by the name of the man in the Christian Bible. I also am
well pleased with the city of Minneapolis, which so near to St. Paul that the
electric car take me over in half an hour, for I stay from morning till night
at St. Paul and take the car for many rides, there be so many park and lake
for to enjoy.

I am inform the lake park region so near to St. Paul and Minneapolis it
includes hundreds of clear water lakes surrounded by shores most beautiful. I see also a fort of history and I have bath at the very fine baths of St.
Paul. The most part of the afternoon I pass at Indian Mound park.* That is
the name I discover because of the mounds I see wherein stand the dead of
the Indians who keep them. So are the mounds of the dead Chinese people
in the country that heaven loves. Indian Mound park is on high bluffs and
I see that for miles below the Mississippi river wind its way between green

* Indian Mounds Regional Park in what is now St Paul contains six two-millennial
old Native American burial mounds.

meadows and pastures in which the cattle graze and make pictures which speak of peace. The big railway office, the fine buildings, the most comfortable residences and the busy stores and manufactories proclaim to me that St. Paul and Minneapolis most fortunately established cities.

Bridal Tour to Avoid Death

From St. Paul to Seattle I am carried by the car of the Northern Pacific railway. So many lines stretch their arms wide across the great country to reach the four seas, yet I rejoice that I took the line I did that run me into Seattle, so great my appreciation of what I obtain by that journey, first knowledge, second pleasure, third amusement. To begin, three bridal parties accompany me, and as is the American custom the friends of the new married man and woman throw rice after them. The rice it seem go into the eyes, the nose, the mouth and down the back of the man and woman that marry, and some grain sting me also.

I suggest to the porter that the reason why the bride and bridegroom in America always fly from the city of their friends is because otherwise they might be killed, so manifest the intention of their friends who shoot the rice at all their vital organs. There is so much travel I am obliged to take upper bunk instead of lower, as is my custom; but as night is warm I congratulate myself on my situation high up above the heads of two women occupying the berth beneath me. The windows in the ceiling of the car allow for plenty of moving air, which blow upon my limbs and produce most happy summer.

Now in the morning when I descend one woman she say unto me, "Was it you who roll so much in the night and creak the bunk so that I could not rest?" And I assure her that she in nowise disturb me by her not rest and that I have no objection whatever to her occupy the berth below me for one night, two night or more night as she please.

On the map of the Northern Pacific railway system you can see all the fine state I pass through and the fine city I see, for to describe all that I enjoy is beyond me. I have good appetite for the good meals supply me. I tell the dining car conductor that I think his cook a Chinaman, and he laugh much and say I know a joke when I see him. When a man speak according to his thoughts in America – that is called a joke. That is a joke, is it not?

I have the pleasure to pass Medora in the state of North Dakota. This I mention because the conductor tell me that here Mr. [Theodore] Roosevelt lived for five years. He have the situation of sheriff of Medora and he also do work as cowboy. I very glad to hear that Mr. Roosevelt so well attend to his business that the best situation in the United States be give to him by the people he work for – that is the situation of president of the United States.*

When in Montana I see many places I read about in the books of America, but the memory of the Chinaman not been trained to recall history that is foreign to him. Nevertheless, Fort Keogh, Myers, Big Horn, Custer, Billings and other places speak to me of events which mean much more to you who are Americans.† Billings recall to my mind "The Virginian." Young woman read that story to me one time. She say the man who wrote is named Owen Wister, and he make very good tale. Very big tunnel at Billings.

I travel on a straight road, but it have many branches to the road leading to beauty spots, one being the Yellowstone National park. It is to see the Yellowstone and its attractions so many that the bridal couples leave our car at the place call Livingstone [*sic*], and as they depart I drop from my sleeve on their behalf three slips of Chinese good luck paper. The night we come into the Rocky mountains it is quite cold and there is snow on the ground. The Rocky mountains rise to view in solitude and quiet, all shapes and colors, some dressed with grass and trees, some patched up with moss, some hard and bare, and most all capped with snow rising and rounding into the most excellent beauty of nature.

Why American Soldier Is Nurtured

Much exhilarated am I by the pure, rare atmosphere. Helena, the capital of Montana, is most interesting. It seem so light and bright. There is also a

---

* Theodore Roosevelt was President of the United States from 1901 to 1909.
† Battle sites of the Great Sioux War of 1876–77.

fort call Fort Harrison now occupied by United States colored troops. Hot water springs for the good of the people that cold water spring not suit are situate in convenient position and I am inform that the American government think to buy them out for a soldiers' sanitarium, for the American government want try hard to keep soldiers alive for the foreign governments to kill.

After Montana come Idaho, and then the state of Washington. It is night when we enter therein and the next day excels all other days of the trip in scenery. Bridges and tunnels, mountains and valleys and rivers – so many changes all in one day. To reach Seattle we go over to the Cascade range of mountains, east of which we pass an arid country which resemble California and which when irrigated produce good vegetables and fruit and make the best of farm lands, and west of the Cascade, lo, I behold in but a few hours that it is all woods and forests most moist and green where everything produces itself without persuasion, the fish swarming in the waters, the birds on the trees and vegetables and fruit multiply most exceedingly.

Two hours before I reach Seattle the conductor have me change into another Pullman which he say join the car at Spokane. The Pullman I ride in from St. Paul proceed to Portland in the state of Oregon. In the new Pullman I perceive to my surprise the Irishman who take trip east with me. He greet me with loud voice and big smile. He ask me where I am bound. I answer, "Just now I go to Seattle." He say, "Ah, that great little city. No city in America so fascinating. It have a salt water bay and three fresh water lakes, handsome residence, beautiful parks, plenty shipping, mining and manufacturing business; headquarters for Alaska business, most healthful and pleasant climate, good restaurants and hotels and living very cheap." I say, "How you know?" He say, "Oh, I member of the board of trade." I say, "Ah, you member of the board of trade. Now I see the mud-flats and smell the sea." The conductor call, "Seattle!"*

* No explanation is offered in the text for why Wing Sing does not continue his journey in order return to his hometown of Los Angeles; Eaton, for her part, began working in Seattle after the last installment of "Wing Sing on His Travels."

Appendices

Appendix A

Unsigned. "A Visit to Chinatown." *New York Recorder*, 19 April 1896.

Edith Eaton, Known as Sue Seen Far (Chinese Lily),
Here from Montreal

———

She Realizes an Ambition

———

And Spends a Week with the Women in Mott Street – There Are
38 Chinese Wives from China

———

The most interesting little woman just now in the city is Miss Edith Eaton, known by Chinamen as Sue Seen Far (Chinese Lily), and when interviewed by a *Recorder* reporter told more bright things in a minute about Chinatown than a New Yorker would be able to discover in weeks.

Miss Eaton is a tiny, brown-eyed body, with a very gentle voice, laughing eyes and coy manners. She talks very, very fast, punctuating her sentences with ripples of laughter that make her indeed fascinating. Her father is an Englishman who went out early in life to China as a merchant: there he met her mother, a Chinese woman who was then in China doing missionary work. Edith is one of twelve living children. One of her sisters married Walter Blackburne Harte, the late editor of the *Arena*, and who now edits the *Philistine*. The family is a remarkable one, almost every member being skillful in some branch of science or art.

Miss Edith bears the Chinese stamp more plainly than any of the others, and it does not seem out of place that her interest in the Chinese people should be very great. It was with seeming great pleasure she told the following story of her visit:

"When I left Montreal for New York, I carried with me letters of introduction from Chinese merchants in the former city to their Chinese brethren in the latter, and it was my intention to live for a week or more in Chinatown, and then give to others the benefit of my experience.

"I was well aware that Chinatown was regarded as a dangerously wicked and unfragrant place. I had been warned that if I ventured there alone I would never come out alive, and even my Montreal Chinese friends had shaken their heads dubiously when apprised of my scheme. But this knowledge neither clouded nor burdened my mind. Indeed, as the train rolled out of the station I felt so elated that I could scarcely refrain from asking the man in the next seat if he didn't wish he were me and on the way to Chinatown.

"Through association with Chinese men in Montreal I had come to know that while I mingled among them without betraying either fear or prejudice no offense would be given me, no harm befall me. It had been my ambition for many a long year to see Chinatown – New York's China-town – where the women wear trousers and the men long blue blouses, where surnames come after the ones we call Christian, and men change their names on the day of their marriage; where the roast is carved fine ere it reaches the table, and humans eat food prepared for spirits; where a woman is married before she is seen and life's fortune is told at the hour of birth; where a man cures his headache by knocking his forehead, and incense is burned for 'the Gambling Cash Tiger.'

"I arrived at the Grand Central Station at 10 o'clock, and a conductor on the lightning express, of whom I inquired the easiest way to reach Pell street, advised me, with almost brotherly kindness, not to venture there at that time of the night. 'I'd be afraid to go myself,' said he. 'You'd better put up at the Grand Union.'

"A little later, when I stood on the station platform, my valise by my side and the clatter of a big city's life in my ears, it was a toss up in my mind whether it should be the hotel or Pell street and the former was uppermost when I heard a voice – the voice of a hack driver – Did you wish for a cab, lady?"

"'I don't think so,' I replied hesitatingly. 'I think I'll go to the hotel across the way, if you will please find a boy to carry my valise there?'

"'All right, ma'am; just wait a minute,' he answered and darted across the street returning at the appointed time, not with the boy I asked for, but with a cab.

"That settled the question of where I should lodge for the night, and, upon being ordered by the arbiter of my fate to enter the cab, I humbly obeyed, and meekly requested to be driven to No. 10 Pell street.

"As I neared my destination, I became slightly nervous. I was not afraid of what lay before me, but a woman passing through the lowest part of a strange city cannot feel quite comfortable. I gazed out upon the undisciplined crowd and listened; it was all so lonesome, and when we turned the corner of the Bowery and Pell street and I caught a glimpse in the dark of some of the haunts of unprosperous vice, my ambition for a moment seemed worthless – the spirit was willing, but the flesh was weak.

"'Ten Pell street!' called out my driver, coming to a standstill. I alighted, and, as a number of unconventional folk gathered around, scanned the red signs and Chinese names hanging before me. Several Chinamen stood near.

"'Does Mr. Ju Chu live here?' I inquired of them. Mr. Ju Chu was one of the merchants to whom I had been given my letter of introduction.*

"'No, he's three doors past – No. 16,' was the answer.

"Followed by my cab driver leading his horse, and a growing crowd, I proceeded a little further up the street. Then, perceiving the sign of the Quang Wang Wo Company, I pushed open the door and intruded myself into the midst of a group of Chinamen, whose astonishment at my sudden appearance was expressed by dumb silence.

"The cabman deposited my valise on a counter, received from me the sum of $1.50, grinned and left me alone in my glory.

"I summoned my wits together and presented my letter of introduction to an imposing Chinaman, who had a red button on his cap. He nodded glumly, and the others gathered around him while he read. The effect of the reading was magical, smiles appeared on all faces and every Chinaman seemed to have something to say to all the others, though not a word for me.

* Ju Chu is one of the Chinese men Wing Sing mentions in the 25 May 1904 instalment of "Wing Sing on His Travels."

"A forlorn-looking object, I stood in the middle of that Chinese store, with its rows of Chinese shoes and bundles of teas. I looked at the strange company, wondering what they would do with me.

"At last the red-buttoned one retreated into the inner room, from where he soon returned, accompanied by a pleasant-faced Chinese gentleman, who advanced and shook hands cordially, introducing himself as Mr. Ju Chu.

"'You have come from Montreal?' he asked.

"'Yes,' I replied, 'I have come from Montreal to see the New York Chinese people. It is too late now for me to go to a hotel. Will you please find me some place in Chinatown where I can stay for a few days?'

"Thus I put myself under the protection of a Chinaman in Chinatown, and though no doubt he was more than surprised at such an unusual occurrence, he did not appear at all bewildered, but calmly and kindly bade me be seated while he retired for a short confab with his partners, the result of which was that after a friendly chat I was escorted by him to a tenement house on Doyers street, near the corner of Pell, where he left me in the hands of a motherly colored woman, who rose from her bed – it was then near midnight – and made me as comfortable as she could.

"Ah! that night! Shall I ever forget it! There were two hundred Chinamen lodging in the same house, and the Chinese voices above, below and around me, the sound of footsteps ascending and descending, the knowledge that I was practically alone in the heart of Chinatown drove sleep away and taught me what it was to realize an ambition.

"When the morning came I looked out of my attic window. I could see very little but the tops of squalid houses, glorified by the beautiful morning sunlight; but the colored woman, housekeeper for the two hundred Chinamen above mentioned, informed me that those roofs sheltered some of the noblest souls in the world, which intelligence, though cheering, I was cynic enough to consider somewhat doubtful.

"After breakfasting on a mutton chop and potatoes I trotted down five flights of stairs and found myself on Doyers street, and a target for the eyes of representatives of many different nationalities. The sign of the Quong [*sic*] Wang Wo Company on Pell street looked like the consoling face of a friend standing by, so I ran across into the store, and received a hearty welcome from the Chinamen there, who all rose to say 'Ha la'* (good morning).

"Mr. Ju Chu inquired as to whether I had slept well, and expressed his regret at being unable to make me comfortable in his own place on account of his not having a woman housekeeper. He was just as nice and gentlemanly as he could be, and offered to take me around to see the Joss houses† and Chinese theatres. I thanked him, and said I would not trouble him more than I could help, but if he would lend me one of his young Chinese clerks to point out the different places I would spend the morning in visiting the other Chinamen to whom I had letters of introduction. He complied with my request, and I started on a tour through Chinatown, which means Mott, Pell and Doyers streets.

"We visited the Chinese stores, the theatre and the Joss house.

"I'm afraid one of the high priests was in bad company the night before we visited there. I don't like to tell, but I've got to. I saw the bowl of a wicked opium pipe lying on an altar. That reminds me that I was not invited to try any opium or gambling dens while in Chinatown.

"Upon the second day of my stay in Chinatown I had the rare fortune to see about twenty real Chinese women in their American homes. I had had some difficulty in gaining access to them, for the Chinese men, into whose good graces I had insinuated myself, were all either bachelors or grass widowers, and as it is not considered proper by the Chinese for a woman to be on terms of acquaintanceship with any man but her husband, not even with her husband's friends, they were unable to help me.

"To leave Chinatown without seeing the Chinese women, after having learned there were thirty-eight boxed up in this city, I would not, and just as I was desperately contemplating braving all dangers and stealing about through some of the dark alleys on Mott street, in the hope of finding a "lo pore" (the Chinese name for wife). I came across a girl, the wife of

---

* "Have you got up yet?" or "Get up."
† Traditional Chinese temples.

a Chinaman and daughter of a Chinaman, yet not in the true sense a Chinese woman, for her mother was Spanish, and the girl herself had been born and bred in New York's Chinatown.

"This interesting little person could speak both the English and Chinese languages. Though the mother of two children, she appeared to be still in her teens, fair complexioned, with wide open, brown eyes and soft brown hair. Mrs. Toy, she told me, was her name. Being half Chinese, she is known by all Chinatown.

"The English-speaking people, even the dissolute women and fast men, like and respect her, and she is the trusted friend and confidant of all the Chinese women who live in New York. She calls herself Chinese, and says she is proud to be the wife and daughter of honest Chinese men.

"Besides having the cares of her young children, she helps her husband, who is a chore man to make a living. Her life is hard, but her gentle, girlish face wears a contended expression, and she laughs blithely. I suppose, never having known a brighter lot, she has grown to love the shade.

"There are I know and believe many wicked places and people in Chinatown, but it is a part of God's Earth, and so some flowers bloom among the weeds even there.

"With the daughter of Chinatown as my guide, I threaded my way through the dirty passages and unventilated rooms of the Mott street tenements. Women with histories, some woefully beautiful, others wicked, depraved-looking old hags, gazed with curious eyes at me as we flitted by. I heard a drunkard singing, and saw groups of half negro, half Chinese; half Chinese, half white; and half white, half negro children playing together, making pandemonium. Chinatown does not mean a colony of pure Chinese people; there is a plentiful sprinkling of whites and blacks.

"The true Chinese women seem to have congregated in Mott street. They each have their own apartments, and within those four walls they spend their lives. Mrs. Toy, or 'Josie,' as she is called, ran before me with her baby in her arms, and whenever we came to one of the apartments she would loudly call the name of the occupant. The door would be opened, we would be invited to enter and presented with a cup of tea. I drank twenty cupfuls in all that afternoon, and do not regret it, for I saw three women with little feet.

"Some of the ladies who had families brought their little round-headed babies to me, and I took the poor little worms up one by one, and looked at their bright eyes and the tufts of hair in the middle of their little heads, and thought: 'Deary me; what a queer world this is!'

"When Mrs. Toy explained that I was the daughter of a Chinese lady, my hostesses looked very pleased and interested, and some of them, after inspecting me from head to toe, declared that I had eyes and hair just like a Chinese girl. They were very surprised and sympathetic upon hearing that I had no 'lo goon' – husband – and some were most anxious to know if I would marry a Chinaman.

"I enjoyed a 5 o'clock lunch with a Mrs. Tom, who lives at 4 Mott street. It was a Chinese lunch, prepared in a Chinese restaurant. We had duck, pork, chicken and rice served in Chinese fashion and eaten with chopsticks. I also drank a tiny bowlful of Chinese whisky. Oh! Oh! Oh!

"The Chinese woman in America, with her quaint manners and old-fashioned mode of life, carries our minds back to times almost as ancient as the earth we live on. She is a bit of olden Eastern coloring amid our modern Western lights and shades, and though her years be few, she is yet a relic of antiquity. Even the dress which she wears is cut in a fashion which was designed many centuries ago, and it is the same to-day as it was when the first non-fabulous empress of China begged her husband to buy her a new dress, which dress was to consist of a tunic, a pair of trousers and a divided skirt, all made of the finest silk and embroidered in many colors. A Chinese woman in a remote age invented the divided skirt and the same should therefore not be decried as a "new woman" invention.

"More constant than sentimental is the Chinese woman. Her love may not be of the quality to swing her to the tip-top branch of the tree of happiness, but it keeps her safely on the centre boughs. She has a true affection for her husband; no other man has any of her personal thoughts; she is exclusively his. She loves him because she has been given to him to be his wife. No question of 'woman's rights' perplexes her little brains. She takes no responsibility upon herself and wishes for none. She has perfect confidence in her man.

"The Chinese bride seldom goes out, and she does not receive visitors until she has been a wife for at least two years, and even then, if she has no child, she is supposed to hide herself from the gaze of her countrymen. After a child has been born to her, her wall of reserve is lowered a little, and it is considered quite proper for cousins and friends of her husband to drop in occasionally and have a chat with 'the family.'

"Not all the Chinese women in America are brides. There are some who have been born here, others are merely secondary wives, the first wives of their husbands being left in China, and then there are a few elderly women who were married long before leaving home. The majority, however, are brides, or, as the Chinese call young married females, 'new women.'

"In some households I found a little slave girl or hand woman. The word 'slave' does not convey the same meaning to an Oriental that it does to a Westerner, and the little girls are treated more as daughters of the family or sisters of the wife than as servants.

"On the whole the Chinese people of Chinatown are a more moral and a much happier lot than I had expected to find them. The odor of opium permeates many of the homes, but all nations have their vices, and I do not deem it my duty to exaggerate the Chinese man's, especially as there are many persons who are only too willing to look after that matter for me.

"Poor old Chinatown! The unsavory smells, the rows of funny signs, and the sadness, madness, badness of a life which cannot rest will ever have a place in my memory!"

Appendix B

Biographical Timeline
for Edith Maude Eaton

1839 Eaton's father, Edward Eaton, born in Macclesfield, Cheshire, England.

c. 1846 Eaton's mother, Achuen Amoy, born somewhere in China.

1863 Edward Eaton marries Achuen "Grace" Amoy.

1864 Brother Edward Charles born in China. Family returns to England soon afterward.

1865 Edith Maude Eaton born on 15 March in Macclesfield, Cheshire. Family moves to New York soon afterward, Edward arriving in May 1865 and Grace and two children following in June 1865. Family settles in Jersey City, New Jersey, and Edward opens a drug and dye wholesale outfit in New York.

1868 Eaton family sails to Liverpool, England February 22 on board the *Denmark*.

1871 Eaton family, including children Edith Maude, Edward Charles, Grace Helen, Sara, and Ernest, resident in London, in the Bow/Poplar sub-registration area.

1872 Eaton family sails from England to New York.* Family settled in Montreal by October 1873. Edward listed in City Directory as a commission merchant.

1875 Sister Winnifred born, the sixth of fourteen children. Edith's formal education ends. Mrs William Darling tutors Edith in music and French.

1879 Edith succumbs to recurring attacks of rheumatic fever.

* The family came to the US on the *Egypt* and arrived at Castle Garden, New York, 5 August 1872.

1881 Census lists Edward as a "clerk."

1882 US Chinese Exclusion Act passed.

1883 Edith working in composing room of the *Montreal Star*, teaches herself shorthand while there. Edward listed as "artist" in *Lovell's Montreal Directory*.

1885 Canada passes the Chinese Immigration Act, levying a $50 head tax on each Chinese labourer entering the country.

1887 Edith works as a stenographer for John Sprott Archibald, lawyer, at 1724 Notre Dame in Montreal. While working for him, she publishes humour in *Peck's Sun*, *Texas Siftings*, and *Detroit Free Press*.

1888 First of Edith's stories appears in the *Dominion Illustrated*. She publishes nine stories and poems in *Dominion Illustrated* in total.

1890 Edith begins to write Chinese-themed journalism for the *Montreal Witness*. Her sister Grace takes stenography exam that

qualifies her to practice as an official stenographer in the courts in Montreal.

1891 Edith's sister Grace marries writer-editor Walter Blackburn Harte and moves to Boston, where Harte starts *Fly Leaf*, and then to New York, where he edits *Lotus*. Edith visits Boston.

1892–93 Edith works for about a year as stenographer and journalist in Thunder Bay District, Northern Ontario. Publishes articles about smallpox, fires, and murder in an unidentified "big paper down East."

1894 Edith has her own office at 157 St. James Street, Montreal, and signs fashion reporting in the *Montreal Witness* E.E..

1895 Begins to publish anonymous journalism about Chinatown in the *Montreal Daily Star* and begins to advocate on behalf of Chinese through letters to the editor of the *Star*.

1896 In April, Winnifred returns to Montreal via Boston from Jamaica, where she has worked as a reporter for *Gall's Daily News*

Letter. Edith publishes first Chinese-themed short fiction and inaugurates her pseudonym, initially spelled Sui Seen Far, when she publishes "The Gamblers" in *Fly Leaf* in February. Edith visits New York's Chinatown for two weeks in April. In June, her father is arrested for smuggling Chinese into the US and she publishes "Ku Yum," her first story in *Land of Sunshine.* Edward escapes from Plattsburgh jail in August. In December, Edith goes to Jamaica to work as a reporter for *Gall's Daily News Letter,* writing under pseudonyms Fire Fly, Canadian Fire Fly, Girl of the Period, and The Woman About Town.

1897 In May, Edith, ill from malarial fever, returns home to Montreal from Jamaica via Boston on Boston Fruit Company's steamer *Barnstable.** Winnifred begins to publish under the Japanese pseudonym Onoto Watanna.

1898 Edith publishes story focusing on a mixed-race love quadrangle in a Jamaican setting. Works as stenographer for Sir Hugh Graham of the Montreal *Star,* and later for G.T. Bell of the Grand Trunk Railway. In June, moves to San Francisco, where her sister May lives, and finds typing work at the Canadian Pacific Railway offices; also canvasses for the *San Francisco Bulletin* in Chinatown. By December, she is working in Los Angeles' Canadian Pacific Railway offices.

1899 Moves to Seattle; works as a stenographer for lawyer W.F. Hays; occasionally teaches at a Chinese mission school.

1900 Says in a letter to *Land of Sunshine* editor Charles Lummis "I have not written anything for months." Spends a few months in Montreal with family before returning to Seattle. Canada raises Chinese Head Tax to $100.

1901 Works as a secretary for Seattle lawyers Samuel H. Piles and James B. Howe. In letter to Lummis, says she is disappointed in her "literary ventures" because

* "Miss Edith Eaton" in "Shipping and Maritime News," *Boston Daily Advertiser,* 18 May 1897: 7.

manuscripts sent to *McClure's*,
Youth's Companion, and *Ainslees'*
have been rejected.

1902 Works as a secretary for C.F.
Munday in Seattle.

1903 Relocates to Los Angeles.
Works as a stenographer and journalist for the *Los Angeles Express*,
edited by Samuel T. Clover, who
had published her fiction in
Chicago Evening Post when he was
editor there in 1900. Canada raises
Chinese Head Tax to $500.

1904 Travels from Los Angeles to
Seattle and then across continent
by rail to Montreal, New York, and
back to Seattle, writing a travel
narrative as "Wing Sing, Chinese
merchant" for the *Los Angeles Express*. Begins to publish syndicated
sensation fiction in regional newspapers through the Daily Story
Publishing Company.

1905 Begins long-standing relationship with Seattle's *Westerner*
magazine.

1907 Works in City of Seattle Legal
Department as a stenographer.

1908 Listed as "journalist" in Seattle's city directory. Begins to publish stories in children's magazines.

1909 Moves to Boston to write
full-time; occasionally teaches in
a Chinese Mission school.

1911 Writes Lummis that she is
writing a novel.

1912 Publishes *Mrs. Spring Fragrance*. When she sends Lummis
a copy, says she has completed
a draft of another book which
McClurg publishers have asked her
to shorten. This manuscript has
not been found.

1914 Dies in Montreal on 7 April
of heart disease.

Appendix C

Chronological Bibliography of Works
by Edith Eaton

Edith Eaton. "A Trip in a Horse Car." *Dominion Illustrated* 1.15 (13 October 1888): 235.

Edith Eaton. "Misunderstood: The Story of a Young Man." *Dominion Illustrated* 1.20 (17 November 1888): 314.

Edith Eaton. "A Fatal Tug of War." *Dominion Illustrated* 1.23 (8 December 1888): 362–3.

Edith Eaton. "The Origin of a Broken Nose." *Dominion Illustrated* 2.45 (11 May 1889): 302.

Edith Eaton. "Robin." *Dominion Illustrated* 2.51 (22 June 1889): 394–5.

Edith Eaton. "Albemarle's Secret." *Dominion Illustrated* 3.68 (19 October 1889): 254.

Unsigned. "The Land of the Free." *Montreal Daily Witness*, 15 March 1890: 8.

Edith Eaton. "Lines." *Dominion Illustrated* 4.92 (5 April 1890): 223.

Unsigned. "The Ching Song Episode." *Montreal Daily Witness*, 17 April 1890: 6.

Edith Eaton. "Spring Impressions: A Medley of Poetry and Prose." *Dominion Illustrated* 4 (7 June 1890): 358–9.

Edith Eaton. "In Fairyland." *Dominion Illustrated* 5.120 (18 October 1890): 270.

Unsigned. "A Chinese Party." *Montreal Daily Witness*, 7 November 1890: 7.

Edith Eaton. "The Typewriter." *National Stenographer* 2.1 (January 1891): 215.

Edith Eaton. "A Plea for Sad Songs." *Dominion Illustrated* 7.170 (3 October 1891): 334.

Unsigned. "Girl Slave in Montreal. Our Chinese Colony Cleverly Described. Only Two Women from the Flowery Land in Town." *Montreal Daily Witness*, 4 May 1894: 10.

E.E. "Hat and Bonnet Philosophy." *Montreal Daily Witness*, 12 May 1894: 12.

Unsigned. "Seventeen Arrests." *Montreal Daily Witness*, 10 July 1894: 1.

Unsigned. "Our Local Chinatown. Little Mystery of a St. Denis Street Laundry." *Montreal Daily Witness*, 19 July 1894: 10.

Unsigned. "'No Tickee, No Washee.'" *Montreal Daily Witness*, 25 July 1894: 10.

E.E. "A Chat on Dress." *Montreal Daily Witness*, 29 September 1894: 10.

Unsigned. "In the Chinese Colony." *Montreal Daily Witness*, 6 February 1895: 10.

Unsigned. "Dined by Hom Chong Long." *Montreal Daily Witness*, 12 February 1895: 1.

Unsigned. "The Lady and the Tiger." *Montreal Daily Star*, 23 March 1895: 1.

Unsigned. "Half-Chinese Children." *Montreal Daily Star*, 20 April 1895: 3.

Unsigned. "A Chinaman and His Bride." *Montreal Daily Witness*, 17 May 1895: 1.

Unsigned. "The Gambling Chinee." *Montreal Daily Witness*, 20 May 1895: 3.

Unsigned. "Abusing the Chinee: How Some White Christians Treat Them, Rotten Eggs and Stones." *Montreal Daily Star*, 5 July 1895: 8.

Unsigned. "Smuggled Chinese: The Last Batch Was Concealed in a Lumber Barge." *Montreal Daily Star*, 5 July 1895: 8.

Unsigned. "Chinese Visitors." *Montreal Daily Star*, 6 July 1895: 4.

Unsigned. "Thrilling Experience of a Band of Smugglers in the Lachine Rapids." *Montreal Daily Star*, 9 July 1895: 1.

Unsigned. "Smuggled Chinamen: Arrested and Sentenced to Terms of Imprisonment." *Montreal Daily Star*, 10 July 1895: 8.

Unsigned. "Beaten to Death." *Montreal Daily Witness*, 22 July 1895: 6.

Unsigned. "The Dead Chinaman." *Montreal Daily Witness*, 24 July 1895: 8.

Unsigned. "A Chino-Irish Family: The Father a Chinaman and the Mother an Irishwoman." *Montreal Daily Star*, 8 August 1895.

Unsigned. "They Are Going Back to China: Hundreds of Chinese at the CPR Station." *Montreal Daily Star*, 21 August 1895: 2.

Unsigned. "The Smuggling of Chinamen." *Montreal Daily Star*, 22 August 1895: 6.

E.E. "Letter to the Editor: Wong Hor Ching." *Montreal Daily Star*, 31 August 1895: 3.

Unsigned. "A Chinese Baby. Accompanies a Party Now on Their Way to Boston." *Montreal Daily Star*, 11 September 1895: 6.

Unsigned. "Chinese Religion. Information Given a Lady by Montreal Chinamen." *Montreal Daily Star*, 21 September 1895: 5.

Unsigned. "A Chinese Child Born. At the Hotel on Lagauchetiere Street." *Montreal Daily Star*, 30 September 1895: 1.

Unsigned. "Chinese Entertainment." *Montreal Daily Star*, 11 October 1895: 4.

Unsigned. "Another Chinese Baby. The Juvenile Mongolian Colony in Montreal Receives Another Addition – It Is a Girl and There Are Schemes for Her Marriage." *Montreal Daily Star*, 12 October 1895: 6.

Unsigned. "Trouble Over an Opium Deal." *Montreal Daily Star*, 12 October 1895: 9.

Unsigned. "Completion of the Moon." *Montreal Daily Star*, 23 October 1895: 6.

Unsigned. "Chinese Changes." *Montreal Daily Star*, 9 November 1895: 9.

Unsigned. "Chinese Food." *Montreal Daily Star*, 25 November 1895: 4.

Unsigned. "The Baby Photographed." *Montreal Daily Star*, 28 November 1895: 8.

Unsigned. "The Ancestral Tablet: A Curious Feature of a Chinese Home." *Montreal Daily Star*, 3 December 1895: 5.

Unsigned. "Chinamen with German Wives." *Montreal Daily Star*, 13 December 1895: 5.

Unsigned. "Will Montreal Have a Chinatown?" *Montreal Daily Star*, 14 December 1895: 7.

E.E. "The Chinese Question." Letter to the Editor. *Montreal Daily Star*, 16 December 1895: 4.

Unsigned. "Chinese Gambling." *Montreal Daily Star*, 17 December 1895: 6.

Unsigned. "One Chinaman Arrested." *Montreal Daily Star*, 18 December 1895: 6.

Unsigned. "The Chinese and Christmas." *Montreal Daily Star*, 21 December 1895: 2.

Unsigned. "Chinese Entertainment, at which the Chinamen Did Their Share of the Entertaining." *Montreal Daily Star*, 31 December 1895: 2.

Sui Seen Far. "The Gamblers." *Fly Leaf* 1 (February 1896): 14–18.

Unsigned. "The Chinese New Year." *Montreal Daily Star*, 11 February 1896: 4.

Unsigned. "A Chinese Entertainment." *Montreal Daily Star*, 18 February 1896: 7.

Unsigned. "John Chinaman Entertains." *Montreal Daily Witness*, 18 February 1896: 6.

Sui Seen Far. "Ku Yum." *Land of Sunshine* 5.1 (June 1896): 29–31.

Sui Seen Far. "The Story of Iso." *Lotus* 2 (August 1896): 117–19.

E.E. [your correspondent]. "A Plea for the Chinaman. A Correspondent's Argument in His Favour." *Montreal Daily Star*, 21 September 1896: 5.

Edith Eaton. "The Chinese Defended. 'E.E.' Replies to Her Critics of Saturday and Is Supported by a Brooklyn Doctor." *Montreal Daily Star*, 29 September 1896: 5.

Unsigned. *Bubble and Squeak. Lotus* 2 (October 1896): 216–17.

Sui Seen Far. "A Love Story of the Orient." *Lotus* 2 (October 1896): 203–7.

Unsigned. "Born a Britisher. But Fifty Dollars Is the Tax on Him as a Chinaman" *Montreal Daily Witness*, 27 October 1896.

Sui Seen Far. "A Chinese Feud." *Land of Sunshine* 5.6 (November 1896): 236–7.

Fire Fly. "The Woman about Town." *Gall's Daily News Letter*, 14 December 1896: 2.

Fire Fly. "As Others See Us." *Gall's Daily News Letter*, 16 December 1896: 2.

Fire Fly. "Good Cheer for Christmas." *Gall's Daily News Letter*, 16 December 1896: 2.

Fire Fly. "The Kingston Races. First Day. Descriptive Sketch." *Gall's Daily News Letter*, 16 December 1896: 6.

Fire Fly. "The Kingston Races. Second Day. Descriptive Sketch." *Gall's Daily News Letter*, 17 December 1896: 6.

Fire Fly. "Among the Stores." *Gall's Weekly News Letter*, 19 December 1896: 6.

Fire Fly. "The Kingston Races." *Gall's Weekly News Letter*, 19 December 1896: 15.

Fire Fly. "The Baby Show." *Gall's Daily News Letter*, 23 December 1896: 2.

Fire Fly. "The Firefly and Rum." *Gall's Daily News Letter*, 23 December 1896: 2.

Fire Fly. "Fire Fly's Christmas Budget." *Gall's Daily News Letter*, 24 December 1896: 7.

Fire Fly. "The Woman about Town." *Gall's Weekly News Letter*, 26 December 1896: 6.

Fire Fly. "Christmas Eve at the Post Office." *Gall's Daily News Letter*, 28 December 1896: 2.

Fire Fly. "The Woman About Town." *Gall's Daily News Letter*, 28 December 1896: 2.

Fire Fly. "The Woman about Town." *Gall's Daily News Letter*, 29 December 1896: 2.

Fire Fly. "The Woman about Town: The Horse Car, Sarah Bernhardt." *Gall's Daily News Letter*, 30 December 1896: 6.

Sui Seen Far. "The Daughter of a Slave." *Short Stories* 25 (January–March 1897): 218–23.

Sui Seen Far. "The Chinese Woman in America." *Land of Sunshine* 6 (January 1897): 59–64.

Fire Fly. "The Woman about Town." *Gall's Daily News Letter*, 2 January 1897: 6.

Fire Fly. "The Woman about Town." *Gall's Daily News Letter*, 4 January 1897: 2.

Fire Fly. "Fire Fly's Wanderings Up and Down." *Gall's Daily News Letter*, 11 January 1897: 2.

Fire Fly. "The Girl of the Period: The Projectographe, Jamaica Lawyers." *Gall's Daily News Letter*, 13 January 1897: 3.

Fire Fly. "The Girl of the Period." *Gall's Daily News Letter*, 19 January 1897: 6.

Fire Fly. "The Departure of the Royal Mail." *Gall's Daily News Letter*, 21 January 1897: 3.

Fire Fly. "The Girl of the Period: The Theatre." *Gall's Daily News Letter*, 28 January 1897: 1.

Fire Fly. "The Week's Story: How He Broke His Nose." *Gall's Daily News Letter*, 30 January 1897: 6.

Fire Fly. "The Girl of the Period: At Alpha Cottage." *Gall's Daily News Letter*, 2 February 1897: 7.

Fire Fly. "Reviews: The Month's Magazines." *Gall's Daily News Letter*, 3 February 1897: 4.

Fire Fly. "Colonel Plant at Myrtle Bank Hotel." *Gall's Daily News Letter*, 5 February 1897: 2.

Fire Fly. "The Girl of the Period: A Talk with Tommy Talker." *Gall's Daily News Letter*, 5 February 1897: 1.

A Canadian Fire Fly. "The Girl of the Period: A Veracious Chronicle of Opinion." *Gall's Daily News Letter*, 8 February 1897: 3.

Fire Fly. "Reviews: 'Marm Lisa.'" *Gall's Daily News Letter*, 9 February 1897: 3.

Fire Fly. "The Girl of the Period: Tommy Tattler [sic] Again." *Gall's Daily News Letter*, 10 February 1897: 4.

Fire Fly. "The Girl of the Period: At Church." *Gall's Daily News Letter*, 16 February 1897: 5.

Fire Fly. "Just What Jamaica Wants: An Industrial Farm School." *Gall's Daily News Letter*, 16 February 1897: 1.

Fire Fly. "The Union Poor House." *Gall's Daily News Letter*, 26 February 1897: 3.

Fire Fly. "Our Visitors: Myrtle Bank." *Gall's Daily News Letter*, 5 March 1897: 1.

Fire Fly. "Woman's Gossip: Victoria Order of Home Helpers." *Gall's Daily News Letter*, 6 March 1897: 2.

Fire Fly. "Woman's Gossip: The Best Memorial of the Diamond Jubilee." *Gall's Daily News Letter*, 8 March 1897: 2.

Fire Fly. "Woman's Gossip: Don't Tax Bicycles; Civil Service Examination." *Gall's Daily News Letter*, 17 March 1897: 6.

Sui Seen Far. "Sweet Sin: A Chinese-American Story." *Land of Sunshine* 8.5 (April 1897): 223–6.

Fire Fly. "Notes About Town." *Gall's Daily News Letter*, 1 April 1897: 2.

Fire Fly. "Another Pleasure Party. Mr. John Jacob Astor." *Gall's Daily News Letter*, 5 April 1897: 1.

Unsigned. "The Busy Bee." *Gall's Daily News Letter*, 9 April 1897: 8.

Fire Fly. "Easter Hats and Bonnets" *Gall's Daily News Letter*, 13 April 1897: 2.

F. F. "Senor Blitz's Entertainment" *Gall's Daily News Letter*, 13 April 1897: 2.

Fire Fly. "An Easter Story." *Gall's Daily News Letter*, 24 April 1897: 1.

Edith Eaton. "Away Down in Jamaica." *The Metropolitan* 7.12 (19 March 1898): 4, 13.

Sui Seen Far. "The Sing-Song Woman." *Land of Sunshine* 9.5 (October 1898): 225–8.

Sui Sin Fah. "Lin John." *Land of Sunshine* 10.2 (January 1899): 76–7.

Sui Sin Fah. "Gambling Cash Tiger." *Traveler* 13.2 (2 February 1899): 21.

Sui Sin Fah. "A Chinese Ishmael." *Overland Monthly* 34 (July 1899): 43–9.

Sui Sin Far. "The Three Souls of Ho Kiang: A Story of the Pacific Coast." *Traveler* 14.4 (October 1899): 52–3. Reprinted in *Mrs. Spring Fragrance* as "Three Souls of Ah So Nan."

Sui Sin Fah. "The Story of Tin-A." *Land of Sunshine* 12.1 (December 1899): 101–3.

Sui Sin Fah. "The Smuggling of Tie Co." *Land of Sunshine* 13.2 (July 1900): 100–4.

Edith Eaton (Sui Sin Far). "A Chinese Tom-Boy; The Perverseness of A-Toy." *Montreal Daily Witness*, 6 October 1900: 16.

Sui Sin Far. "Ku Yum's Little Sister." *Chicago Evening Post*, 13 October 1900: 4.

Sui Sin Fah. "O Yam – A Sketch." *Land of Sunshine* 13.6 (November 1900): 341–3.

Sui Sin Far. "The Engaged Girl in China." *Ladies' Home Journal* 29.2 (January 1902): 14. Reprinted as "Marriage Is a Lottery" in *The Elkhart Daily Truth*, 30 June 1902: 3; and *St. Alban's Daily Messenger*, 7 February 1902: 4.

Edith Eaton (Sui Sin Far). "The Coat of Many Colors." *Youth's Companion* 76 (24 April 1902): 208–9.

Sui Sin Far. "In Los Angeles' Chinatown." *Los Angeles Express*, 2 October 1903.

Sui Sin Far. "Betrothals in Chinatown." *Los Angeles Express*, 8 October 1903.

Sui Sin Far. "Chinatown Needs A School." *Los Angeles Express*, 14 October 1903.

Sui Sin Far. "Chinatown Boys and Girls." *Los Angeles Express*, 15 October 1903.

Sui Sin Far. "Leung Ki Chu and His Wife." *Los Angeles Express*, 22 October 1903.

Sui Sin Far. "Chinese In Business Here." *Los Angeles Express*, 23 October 1903.

Sui Sin Far. "The Horoscope." *Out West* 19.5 (November 1903): 521–4.

Sui Sin Far. "Chinese Laundry Checking." *Los Angeles Express*, 3 November 1903: 6.

Wing Sing. "Wing Sing of Los Angeles on His Travels." *Los Angeles Express*. 3 February 1904: 6.

Wing Sing. "Wing Sing of Los Angeles on His Travels." *Los Angeles Express*, 4 February 1904: 6.

Wing Sing. "Wing Sing of Los Angeles on His Travels." *Los Angeles Express*, 5 February 1904: 6.

Wing Sing. "Wing Sing on His Travels." *Los Angeles Express*, 6 February 1904: 6.

Wing Sing. "Wing Sing of Los Angeles on His Travels: Part 5." *Los Angeles Express*, 10 February 1904: 6.

Wing Sing. "Wing Sing of Los Angeles on His Travels." *Los Angeles Express*, 24 February 1904: 6.

Wing Sing. "Wing Sing in Montreal." *Los Angeles Express*, 27 February 1904: 6.

Wing Sing. "Wing Sing in Montreal." *Los Angeles Express*, 9 March 1904: 6.

Wing Sing. "Wing Sing in Montreal." *Los Angeles Express*, 12 March 1904: 6.

Sui Sin Far. "A Chinese Boy-Girl." *Century* 67 (April 1904): 828–31.

Wing Sing. "Wing Sing on His Travels." *Los Angeles Express*, 25 May 1904: 6.

Wing Sing. "Wing Sing in New York City." *Los Angeles Express*, 9 June 1904: 6.

Wing Sing. "Wing Sing in New York City." *Los Angeles Express*, 14 June 1904: 6.

Wing Sing. "Wing Sing on His Travels." *Los Angeles Express*, 5 July 1904: 6.

Wing Sing. "Wing Sing on His Travels." *Los Angeles Express*, 8 July 1904: 6.

Wing Sing. "Wing Sing on His Travels." *Los Angeles Express*, 20 July 1904: 6.

Edith Eaton. "Taken by Storm." *Montgomery* [Alabama] *Advertiser*, 20 July 1904: 8. Reprinted: *The* [San Diego] *Evening Tribune*, 21 July 1904: 3.

Edith Eaton. "The Woman's Part." *Montgomery* [Alabama] *Advertiser*, 3 September 1904: 2.

Sui Sin Far. "The Transformation of Wong-Toy." *Sunset* 15 (1905): 427–9.

Edith Eaton. "A Shoot of Goodness." *The Interior* 36 (2 March 1905): 263.

Edith Eaton. "A Shoot of Goodness." *Christian Evangelist* (11 May 1905): 619–20 and (18 May 1905): 652–4. Reprinted [in part] in "Little Stories Around Chinatown" *Seattle Post-Intelligencer* 12 September 1909: 1; and *Unitarian Register* 87 (1905): 187.

Sui Sin Far-Edith Eaton. "The Prize China Baby." *Westerner* 3.4 (August 1905): 32.

Edith Eaton (Sui Sin Far). "Yuko Katzima." *Westerner* 4.1 (November 1905): 25–7.

Sui Sin Far (Edith Eaton). "Aluteh." *Chautauquan* 42.4 (December 1905): 338–42.

Sui Sin Far. "Woo-Ma and I." *The Bohemian* 10 (January 1906): 66–75.

Sui Sin Far (Edith Eaton). "The Wife of Lee Chu." *Westerner* 4.6 (May 1906): 12–13.

Sui Sin Far (Edith Eaton). "The Best of the East." *Westerner* 4.6 (May 1906): 19–20.

Sui Sin Far (Edith Eaton). "Gambling Cash Tiger: A Chinese Story." *Westerner* 5.6 (November 1906): 37–8.

Sui Sin Far (Edith Eaton). "Chinese Children on the Pacific Coast." *Westerner* 7.4 (September 1907): 22–4.

Sui Sin Far. "The Jessamine Flower: A Chinese Christmas Story." *Westerner* 8.1 (December 1907): 6, 21.

Sui Sin Far. "Chinese Lily." *Out West* 28 (1908): 508–10.

Sui Sin Far (trans.). "The Puppet Show: Chinese Folk Lore." *Good House-keeping* 46.1 (January 1908). Reprinted: Sui Sin Far (trans.). "The Puppet Show: From Chinese Folklore." *Fort Worth Star-Telegram*, 4 December 1910: 6.

Sui Sin Far. "Two Little Pairs of Shoes." *Children's Magazine* 9.6 (January 1908): 178–9. Reprinted: *The Children's Book*, Frances Hodgson Burnett, ed. New York: Cupples and Leon Company, 1915. n.p.

Sui Sin Far. "The Crocodile Pagoda." *Children's Magazine* 10.1 (February 1908): 12–13. Reprinted: Frances Hodgson Burnett, ed., *The Children's Book*, New York: Cupples and Leon Company, 1915. n.p.; Bessie Blackstone Coleman, ed., *The Pathway to Reading*, Third Reader. New York: Silver, Burdett and Company, 1925: 128–31.

Sui Sin Far (Edith Eaton). "The Success of a Mistake." *Westerner* 8.3 (February 1908): 18–22.

Sui Sin Far (transcribed by). "The Wild Man and the Gentle Boy: Chinese Folk Lore." *Good Housekeeping* 46.2 (February 1908): 179–80.

Sui Sin Far (transcribed by). "What About the Cat?" *Good Housekeeping* 46.3 (March 1908): 290–1. Reprinted: *Colorado Springs Gazette*, 22 January 1911: 31.

Sui Sin Far. "The Heart's Desire." *Good Housekeeping* 46.5 (May 1908): 514–15. Reprinted: Kate Louise Brown, ed., *The Third Reader*. 128–31. Boston & New York: Thompson Brown and Co, 1911:; *Chester Times*, 4 November 1910: 9; *Greensboro Daily News*, 6 November 1910: 4; *Columbus Daily Enquirer*, 6 November 1910: 7; *Fort Wayne Journal Gazette*, 6 November 1910: 33; *Colorado Springs Gazette*, 5 February 1911: 30.

Sui Sin Far (Interpreted from the Chinese by). "The Rebel Silkworm" *The Housekeeper* (May 1908): 38.

Sui Sin Far (Edith Eaton). "The Spirit's Betrothal: A Romance of Seattle's Chinatown." *Westerner* 9.1 (June 1908): 14–15.

Sui Sin Far. "The Tangled Kites." *Good Housekeeping* 47.1 (July 1908): 52–3. Reprinted: *The Third Reader*. Kate Louise Brown. ed., Boston & New York: Thompson Brown and Co, 1911: 23, 62; *Chester Times*, 11 November 1910: 9; *Fort Wayne Journal Gazette*, 13 November 1910: 11; *Colorado Springs Gazette*, 16 April 1911: 31.

Edith Eaton. "Monte Cristo's Baby." *Beaver* [Oklahoma] *Herald*, 6 August 1908: 3. Reprinted: *Atlantic Evening*, 22 May 1908; *Stevens Point Daily Journal*, 5 June 1908.

Sui Sin Far. "The Little Silk Girl." *Good Housekeeping* 47.3 (September 1908): 287–8. Reprinted: *Colorado Springs Gazette*, 15 January 1911: 31.

Sui Sin Far. "In the House of Song: A Chinese Tale." *Housekeeper* 3.12 (October 1908): 11.

Edith Eaton (Sui Sin Far). "As a Kitten." *People's Magazine* 5.5 (November 1908): 929–36.

Sui Sin Far. "The Good and the Kind: (A Chinese Story)." *Holland's* 28.2 (1909): 29.

Sui Sin Far. "A Tale of the River: A Story for Children." *New Idea Woman's Magazine* 19.1 (January 1909): 32.

Sui Sin Far. "Leaves from the Mental Portfolio of an Eurasian." *Independent* 66 (21 January 1909): 125–32.

Sui Sin Far. "Ku Yum and the Butterflies: An Anecdote of Oriental Obedience, Written by a Chinese Woman." *Good Housekeeping* 48.3 (March 1909): 299.

Sui Sin Far. "The Little Embroidery Girls and Whose Father?: Japanese Stories Written for the *Gentlewoman*." *Gentlewoman* 16.3 (March 1909): 16.

Edith Eaton. "The Alaska Widow." *Bohemian Magazine* (April 1909): 491–6.

Hip Wo. "Hip Wo's Trip, As Told by Himself." *Westerner* 10.4 (April 1909): 34–5.

Sui Sin Far (Edith Eaton). "The Chinese in America: Part I." *Westerner* 10.5 (May 1909): 24–6.

Sui Sin Far. "The Half-Moon Cakes." *Good Housekeeping* 48.5 (May 1909): 584–5. Reprinted: *Greensboro Daily News*, 27 November 1910: 11.

Sui Sin Far. "The Little Wood-Carver." *Gentlewoman* 16.5 (May 1909): 8.

Sui Sin Far (Edith Eaton). "The Chinese in America: Part II." *Westerner* 10.6 (June 1909): 36–8.

Sui Sin Far (Edith Eaton). "The Chinese in America: Part III." *Westerner* 11.1 (July 1909): 18–19, 38.

Sui Sin Far. "Amoy and Her Dolls: Story of a Little Chinese Girl." *American Motherhood* 29.1 (July 1909): 36–7.

Sui Sin Far (Edith Eaton). "The Chinese in America: Part IV." *Westerner* 11.2 (August 1909): 24–6.

Sui Sin Far. "Ko Ku and the Cat." *American Mother/American Motherhood/The New Crusade* 29.2 (August 1909): 102–3.

Sui Sin Far. "The Little Duck." *Woman's Home Companion* 36.8 (August 1909): 26.

Sui Sin Far. "The Sister Flower: A Chinese Story." *American Mother/American Motherhood/The New Crusade* 29.3 (September 1909): 175–7.

Sui Sin Far. "In the Land of the Free." *Independent* 67 (2 September 1909): 504–8.

Sui Sin Far. "Little Stories of Chinese Life in and around Seattle." *Seattle Post-Intelligencer*, 12 September 1909: 1.

Sui Sin Far. "Glad Yen." *Ladies' Home Journal* 26 (October 1909): 40.
Reprinted as "Joyous Little Yen." *Muskegon News Chronicle*, 28 October 1909: 2.

Sui Sin Far. "The Little Fat One." *New Idea Woman's Magazine* 20.4 (October 1909): 79.

Sui Sin Far. "The Silver Leaves." *The Designer and the Woman's Magazine* 6 (October 1909): 362.

Edith Eaton (Sui Sin Far). "A Word from Miss Eaton." *Westerner* 11.5 (November 1909): 1.

Sui Sin Far. "A Word from 'Sui Sin Far.'" *Westerner* 11.5 (November 1909): 34–5.

Sui Sin Far. "The Gift of Little Me: How a Quaint Little Chinese Almost Turned the Christmastide into a Tragedy." *Housekeeper* (December 1909): 9, 20.

Sui Sin Far. "The Inferior Man." *New Idea Woman's Magazine* 21.1 (January 1910): 46.

Sui Sin Far. "Mrs. Spring Fragrance." *Hampton's* 24 (January 1910): 137–41.
Reprinted in *Washington Post*, 21 September 1919: SM1, 2, 3, 11, 12; *Ainslee's* 58.2 (October 1926): 149–55; *Toronto Star Weekly*, 23 November 1910: 13.

Sui Sin Far. "The Peacock Lantern." *The Designer and the Woman's Magazine*. 3 (January 1910): 206.

Sui Sin Far. "The Kitten-Headed Shoes." *Delineator* 75 (February 1910): 165.

Sui Sin Far. "The Orchid's Lesson." *American Motherhood* 30.2 (February 1910): 123–4.

Sui Sin Far. "The Peanut Sifter." *American Motherhood* 30.3 (March 1910): 187–8.

Sui Sin Far. "A White Woman Who Married A Chinaman." *Independent* 68 (10 March 1910): 518–23.

Sui Sin Far. "Sunny Side of Boston's Chinatown." *Boston Globe*, 3 April 1910: SM4.

Edith Eaton. "Real Chinese and Japanese." *New York Evening Post*, 15 April 1910: 8.

Sui Sin Far. "The Inferior Woman." *Hampton's* 24 (May 1910): 727–31.

Sui Sin Far. "The Palm Leaf Fan." *American Motherhood* 30.5 (May 1910): 327–8.

Sui Sin Far. "The Sugar Cane Baby." *Good Housekeeping* 50.6 (May 1910): 570–2.

Sui Sin Far. "The Son of Chung Wo." *Leslie's Weekly*, 16 June 1910: 592, 601, 602, 604.

Sui Sin Far. "Candy That Was Not Sweet." *Delineator* 76 (July 1910): 76.

Sui Sin Far. "The Dream of Little Yen." *American Motherhood* 31 (July 1910): 36–7.

Sui Sin Far. "The Little Brass Trumpet." *Fort Wayne News*, 6 July 1910: 12. Reprinted: *Muskogee Times Democrat*, 9 July 1910: 3; in "Playtime Stories" *Cincinnati Post*, 9 July 1910: 5; *Wilkes-Barre Times-Leader*, 11 July 1910: 5; *Winnipeg Tribune*, 11 July 1910: 3; *Ottawa Journal*, 11 July 1910: 10; and in "Three Stories from Faroff China." *Pittsburgh Press*, 10 July 1910: 42-3.

Sui Sin Far. "A-Toy's Tea Party." *Muskogee Times Democrat*, 8 July 1910: 3; Reprinted: *Wilkes-Barre Times-Leader*, 9 July 1910: 7; *Winnipeg Tribune*, 9 July 1910: 3; *Ottawa Journal*, 9 July 1910: 10; and in "Three Stories from Faroff China." *Pittsburgh Press*, 10 July 1910: 42-3.

Sui Sin Far. "The Merry Blindman." *Wilkes-Barre Times-Leader*, 12 July 1910: 8. Reprinted: *Winnipeg Tribune*, 12 July 1910: 7; *Ottawa Journal*, 12 July 1910: 10; and in "Three Stories from Faroff China." *Pittsburgh Press*, 10 July 1910: 42–3.

Sui Sin Far. "An Autumn Fan." *New England Magazine* 42 (August 1910): 700–2.

Sui Sin Far. "Ever Constant: An Ancient Chinese Poem." *Housekeeper* (August 1910): 11.

Sui Sin Far. "In the Bamboo Grove." *Housekeeper* (August 1910): 11.

Sui Sin Far. "Her Chinese Husband." *Independent* 69 (18 August 1910): 358–61.

Sui Sin Far. "The Banishment of Ming and Mai." *Housekeeper* (September 1910): 9, 20.

Sui Sin Far. "The Bird of Love." *New England Magazine* 43 (September 1910): 25–7.

Sui Sin Far. "Asof and His Pony: An Arabian Tale for American Children." *Des Moines Daily News*, 17 October 1910: 5. Reprinted: *Wilkes-Barre Times-Leader*, 5 January 1911: 10; *Fort Wayne Daily News*, 22 October 1910: 10.

Sui Sin Far. "Your Sun and My Sun: An East Indian Story for American Children." *Des Moines Daily News*, 19 October 1910. Reprinted: *Fort Wayne Daily News*, 21 October 1910: 7.

Sui Sin Far. "The Hawk and the Chicken: A Japanese Tale for Children." *Des Moines Daily News*, 31 October 1910: 5. Reprinted: *Fort Wayne Daily News*, 2 November 1910: 5.

Sui Sin Far. "The Dreams that Cooled; (A Chinese Tale)." *Little Folks* 14.1 (November 1910): 52–4. Reprinted: *Sabbath Recorder* 71.4 (24 July 1911): 122–3.

Sui Sin Far. "The Laughing Fountain: A Persian Story for American Children." *Logansport Reporter*, 8 November 1910: 3. Reprinted: *Milwaukee Journal*, 2 February 1911: 15.

Sui Sin Far. "When Hong Sing Carolled." *New York Evening Post*, 10 December 1910: 9.

Sui Sin Far. "The Homely Doggy." *Good Housekeeping* 52.1 (January 1911): 67.

Sui Sin Far. "The Folding Fans: A Japanese Tale for Children." *Wilkes-Barre Times-Leader,* 2 January 1911: 3.

Sui Sin Far. "The Stuffed Duck: A Japanese Tale for Children." *Wilkes-Barre Times-Leader*, 4 January 1911: 10.

Sui Sin Far. "'The Wild Man and the Gentle Boy' and 'The Story of Man-Yo-Yo' Transcribed from the Japanese by Sui Sin Far." *Chester Times*, 21 January 1911: 9.

A Half Chinese, "The Persecution and Oppression of Me." *Independent* 71 (24 August 1911): 421–6.

Sui Sin Far. "A Love Story from the Rice Fields of China." *New England Magazine* 45.4 (December 1911): 343–5.

Sui Sin Far. *Mrs. Spring Fragrance*. Chicago: A. C. McClurg, 1912. Includes the following stories whose original periodical publications have not been located: "Its Wavering Image," "Misunderstood," "Pat and Pan," "The Americanization of Pau Tsu," "The Deceptive Mat," "The Dreams That Failed," "The Garments of the Fairies," "The Story of a Little Chinese Seabird," "Tian Shan's Kindred Spirit," and "The Wisdom of the New."

Sui Sin Far. "Chan Hen Yen, Chinese Student." *New England Magazine* 45.5 (January 1912): 462–6.

Sui Sin Far. "Who's Game?" *New England Magazine* 45.6 (February 1912): 573–9.

Sui Sin Far. "Sui Sin Far, the Half Chinese Writer, Tells of Her Career." *Boston Globe*, 5 May 1912: 6.

Sui Sin Far. "The Moon Harp." *Independent* 72 (23 May 1912): 1106.

Sui Sin Far. "The Tired Teakettle: A Tale that Tells True Things" *Congregationalist and Christian World*, 5 September 1912: 315.

Sui Sin Far. "Not Little Too Good." *Little Folks* 17.4 (February 1913): 133–6.

Sui Sin Far. "The Harrison Street Confucius." *Boston Evening Transcript*, 13 June 1913: sec. iii, 1, 8.

Sui Sin Far. "Chinese Workmen in America." *Independent* 75 (3 July 1913): 56.

Pau Tsu. "The Colored Glasses." *Everyland* 5.2 (March 1914): 89. Reprinted: Sui Sin Far, "The Colored Glasses" in *Children's Anthology*.

Sui Sin Far, The Author of "Mrs. Spring Fragrance," "The Completion of the Moon." *Everyland* 5.2 (March 1914): 67.

Sui Sin Far. "The Fairy of the Rice Fields: She Makes an Attempt to Steal Pau Tsu's Little Brother." *Woman's Magazine* 29.4 (April 1914): 56.

Sui Sin Far. "The Chinese Spirit of Non-Resistance Will Disappear." *Boston Globe*, 7 February 1915: 46.

Sui Sin Far. "The Girl of the Duck Farm." *Everyland* 10 (1919): 235.

Index

Fu, Bennett, xv, xxiii

Traveler, The, xxi, xlvii, liv
travel writing, xlix, l
Tye Loy Company, 67, 213
typesetting, 20
typewriters, 115–16

Uncle Tom's Cabin, 179–80
Union Poor House, 130–1

Vancouver, BC, 202, 204
Vaudeville, 119
Vaudreuil, Quebec, 228
ventriloquism, xliii
Victoria Bridge, Quebec, 219
voyeurism, xlii, 6

Warman, Cy, 125*n*
wars, 220, 225
Washington, George, 222
Washington state, 204, 236
Watanna, Onoto. *See* Eaton, Winnifred
Watson, William, 118
Westerner, xxi, xxix, liv, lxivn34, lxivn35, 250
West Indies, xxiii, xxix, 171*n*, 231. *See also* Caribbean *and* Jamaica
Wharton, Edith, lxiiin27, lxn8
White-Parks, Annette, xviii, xix, xx, xvii, xxx, xxxi, xxxviii, xlvii, l, liii, lvii, lxn1

Willis, Sara Payson, xlvi. *See also* Fern, Fanny
Windsor Street Depot, 43
Wing, Lock. *See* Wing, Luk
Wing, Luk, 225.
Wing, Mahlon T., lv
Wing Sing (Montreal merchant), xxv, xxvi, xxxviii, liii, 44–7, 201, 217
Wing Sing (pseudonym), xxvii, xxxi, l, liii, lv, 250
Wing Wah, 50
Winn, Moy C., 65
Winnipeg, Manitoba, 209
Wister, Owen, 235
Woman's Home Companion, xxii, liv
women: Chinese, 188, 226, 232, 243; talkative, xlix, 148, 150, 170
women's clothing, 102, 103–4, 112, 120, 132, 133, 135
Wong Faw, 82, 83
Wong Hor Ching, xxxix, 63

Yale, BC, 205
Yellow Emperor, 52
Yellowstone National Park, 235
Yen Moy, 96–7
Youth's Companion, xxii, liv, lxivn34, 250
Yu, Ning, xlvi